# HOW TO GET
# A JOB
## *in the*
# San Francisco
# Bay Area

7/5/84

Dear Anne —

Thanks for joining
me and bringing the
super roses. to see.
Best wishes to your
you in all career endeavors

Jane Bead

# HOW TO GET
# A JOB
## *in the*
# San Francisco Bay Area

JANET L. BEACH

Contemporary Books, Inc.
chicago

**Library of Congress Cataloging in Publication Data**

Beach, Janet L.
    How to get a job in the San Francisco Bay Area.

    Includes index.
    1. Job hunting—California—San Francisco Bay Region.
2. Job vacancies—California—San Francisco Bay Region.
3. Vocational guidance—Information services—
California—San Francisco Bay Region.    I. Title.
HF5382.75.U6B4     1983       650.1′4′097946       83-5126
ISBN 0-8092-5692-4

Published by Contemporary Books, Inc.
180 North Michigan Avenue, Chicago, Illinois 60601
Manufactured in the United States of America
Library of Congress Catalog Card Number: 83-5126
International Standard Book Number: 0-8092-5692-4

Published simultaneously in Canada by
Beaverbooks, Ltd.
150 Lesmill Road
Don Mills, Ontario M3B 2T5
Canada

This book is dedicated to my parents, Joyce and Bill Lee, who have made it possible for me to try new things, and to Ralph Keeney, who reminds me that I can do them.

# Contents

# Foreword

Welcome to San Francisco. As a newcomer or a new job hunter here, you will find our city and region to be a vital, thriving business headquarters.

There are a lot of reasons why we are confident about San Francisco's business future. During the last decade we've seen an impressive increase in the demand for office space which reflects San Francisco's attractiveness to a broad range of businesses. San Francisco is a major "headquarters" city and is the economic hub of the thriving Bay Area metropolitan region.

The employment picture here is bright. The California Employment Development Department estimates that our new office space will generate 80,000 new jobs for personnel in retail stores, restaurants, and service companies. Corresponding increases in job opportunities are foreseen throughout the Bay Area.

The future prospects for our tourism industry—a billion dollar industry right now—are promising, too. The new $100 million George R. Moscone Convention Center holds 25,000 people and vastly increases the area's convention capacity.

Our Bay Area cities need the active involvement of business, industry *and* private individuals to shape our common future. This book makes an important contribution and will be an excellent resource for employers and job seekers alike. In reading it I hope you will decide to take advantage of the wide-ranging career opportunities available here and will decide to become part of the dynamic growth we expect in the future. San Francisco is called "everyone's favorite city." I hope it will be yours, too.

Dianne Feinstein
Mayor of San Francisco

# Acknowledgments

This book exists because so many Bay Area managers took the time to offer advice and information on how to find jobs in their fields. Of course, not every individual and company in the Bay Area could be listed. However, most major employers are included here, and I thank them for the information they contributed.

The researchers who worked on this book are Christina Frost, Stacey Bovero, Laura Pierce, Jean Isobe, Sharon Garret, and Martha Landy. Their contributions of time, intellect, and cheerful spirit are sincerely appreciated.

# HOW TO GET
# A JOB
## in the
# San Francisco
# Bay Area

# Introduction

The gold rush is over, the frontier has been settled and the population civilized; yet everybody still seems to want to live in the San Francisco Bay Area.

Since for most people living in the Bay Area means working here as well, you need to figure out how to find a satisfying job that pays well. This book will give you a real head start by eliminating hours of research you would otherwise have to do in order to even get started.

The San Francisco Bay Area job market is unique. It's not organized like most other cities, and, as a result, many people spend a great deal of time going about job hunting in the Bay Area the wrong way. This book was compiled from over 1,000 personal and telephone interviews with Bay Area managers in 65 fields. It will shorten the time you have to spend in figuring out the Bay Area employment picture. It's intended primarily for people who are looking for white-collar career opportunities. Whether you are a newcomer to the Bay Area or a career switcher who has lived here and wants to stay, the book is designed to make your job search easier, through recommending job-hunting ideas and resources it could take you months to find on your own.

- If you are changing jobs or careers and you don't want to leave the Bay Area, this book can help you review the career options available to make sure you aren't overlooking any.
- If you are just finishing your education and considering where to

1

begin your career, you can use this book to get a feel for the area and the kinds of jobs and lifestyles you can attain.

• If your spouse has an opportunity to come here and you are trying to figure out what kind of work you'll be able to do, the book's descriptions of the available fields may help you both decide on whether to move here.

• If you have already started looking, but are not having much success or encouragement, this book can help you refocus and decide what it is you are looking for.

• If you've raised a family and are ready to reenter the job market and wonder where to begin, you'll find the book a helpful guide to what fields to consider. Be sure to read the section called "Special Advice for Special Problems."

In this book, you will also find:

• A "Simple Job Search Method"
• Practical, behind-the-scenes advice from "Insiders" employed in Bay Area companies and in local Employment/Recruitment agencies
• Industry profiles
• Insiders advice
• Job titles and salary ranges
• Company listings
• Company address and telephone number
• Contact person
• Description of each firm
• Local clubs and associations for making job contacts

Conducting a thorough job search is rarely easy. Reading unemployment statistics or predictions of next year's difficulties can be discouraging, and can lead you to focus on your own perceived inadequacies. Keep in mind that even in difficult economic times there are job openings. The key to finding and winning your job is careful planning and focused hunting based upon good information and good contacts.

The Bay Area companies who provided advice and information for this book hope it will help *you*. I do too.

# Part I: The Job Search

# 1

# How to Use This Book

## First Half

The first half of the book has two purposes:

1. To provide an overview of what the Bay Area has to offer in employment and lifestyle opportunities;
2. To recommend a simple job search method to get you organized and keep you focused until you get the job you want.

## Second Half

The second half of the book gives you more specifics on Bay Area employment than you can find in any other single source. This section is broken down into individual industries. Related industries are grouped together under the assumption that you may wish to consider employment possibilities in several related fields. Most of the leading Bay Area companies, including the Bay Area's Top 100, are described, and the name of a contact person, potential positions, and training opportunities are listed, among other information.

You can start by reading the more general first half or the more specific second half of this book. But, keep in mind that successful job hunting is really a chronological process which starts with an assessment of your goals. For those people who feel they need to familiarize them-

5

selves with examples of jobs or fields before they can begin to think about their goals, a quick review of some job fields you think you'd like may help. In this case, start reading the second half of this book and then go back and read the first half later. It works fine either way.

To get the greatest benefit from the book, active rather than passive reading is recommended. That means you'll need some quiet time and a pad of paper beside you to write down hints and reminders on what to consider in your job search. And you'll need to set aside the time to participate actively in the self-assessment exercise of Chapter 4. In short, to get the most out of this book you'll have to invest a bit of effort. Of course, even if you just scan the book, you will get a quick overview of the Bay Area market so that you can identify which companies to contact first.

# 2

# Living and Working in the Bay Area: An Overview of the Nine-County Bay Area

If you are a newcomer to San Francisco, you probably don't know exactly what the Bay Area encompasses. The Bay Area, as the maps illustrate, is that nine-county northern California region that features the city of San Francisco as its crown jewel.

San Francisco, "the city by the bay," is just about everybody's favorite city. It is situated on a hilly peninsula separating the Pacific Ocean from the San Francisco Bay. Its special geography provides the city with stunning water views and some unique weather. But a lot more than the weather, the geography, and the city of San Francisco make the Bay Area a fascinating place to live and work.

To help you decide whether the Bay Area is for you, this chapter gives some basic facts as well as a feeling for the northern California lifestyle.

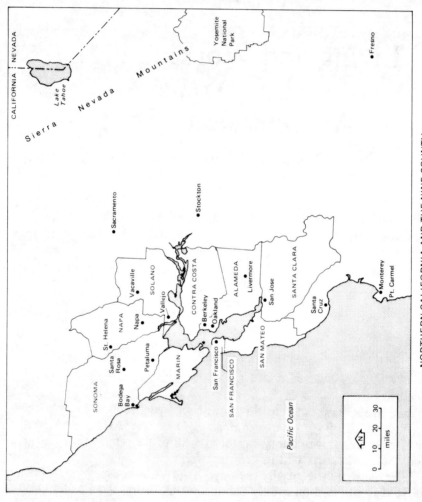

NORTHERN CALIFORNIA AND THE NINE COUNTY
SAN FRANCISCO BAY AREA

## Bay Area

The San Francisco Bay Area includes nine counties: San Francisco, Alameda, Contra Costa, Solano, Marin, Napa, Sonoma, Santa Clara, and San Mateo. The Bay Area population is about 5 million. Another 1 million are expected by the year 2000.

During the next five years the fastest growing counties are expected to be Santa Clara and Contra Costa, while Napa and Marin will have the most moderate growth. San Francisco is expected to remain fairly stable.

## SAN FRANCISCO COUNTY

San Francisco is perhaps the most like a European city of any city in the United States. It is known for its beauty and style. It is a city of history, sophistication, culture, and class, yet it also has earned a reputation for kookiness and alternate lifestyles.

Through the years San Francisco has been noted for the flower children of Haight Ashbury, Bohemian poets like Allen Ginsberg, rock groups like the Jefferson Airplane (now Starship), and comedians like Robin Williams. And existing side by side with these experimental types is the Bohemian Club, San Francisco's famous club of rich, powerful white men; and the sophisticated Commonwealth Club, featuring current events lectures for well-educated proper San Franciscans; and conservative Paul Gann who, along with Howard Jarvis, started the grassroots personal income tax revolt in the United States. And, of course, there are the Maiden Lane, Union Square, and Embarcadero Center retail centers, which offer elegant shopping and services to our very cosmopolitan city.

All these somewhat conflicting images developed because San Francisco offers an environment of personal freedom for its residents, most of whom are relative newcomers who have been attracted by the opportunities and lifestyles the Bay Area offers.

### Size

San Francisco is a relatively small city and county of 47 square miles of land, surrounded on three sides by water. Approximately 650,000 people live here. Another 200,000 commute to San Francisco for their work.

### Diversity

The population is quite diverse. It is estimated that one out of every

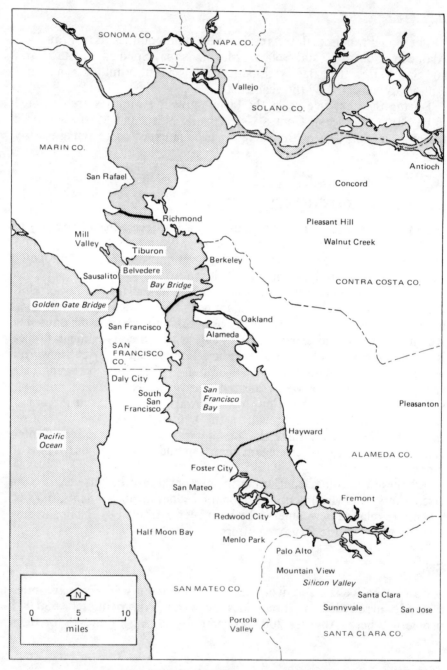

SAN FRANCISCO AND THE BAY AREA

seven residents was born outside the United States or to foreign-born parents. San Francisco has the largest Chinese community (approximately 65,000) outside of Asia. Other large Oriental communities include Japanese, Filipinos, Koreans, Tibetans, and, more recently, Vietnamese and Cambodian peoples. Other predominant ethnic groups are Italian, black, Irish, Hispanic, and Russian.

## Geography and Climate

The weather and the city's natural beauty are a major part of the attraction for many newcomers to San Francisco. All year long the temperature in San Francisco is a springlike, exhilarating 50–75° F., and the sky is usually clear. In fact, San Francisco has more sunny days per year than most other U.S. cities. (Only about 20 inches of rain fall between November and April.) You may have heard of San Francisco's famous fog. It is caused by the warmer inland temperatures of California attracting the cool, damp ocean breezes. In San Francisco a day may start out foggy, with foghorns blasting eerily in the bay, and then clear by noon to gloriously bright sunshine. However, some sections of the city are more prone to fog than others. San Francisco weather is very localized and may vary from sunshine to fog within a two-block area. This may be a factor to consider when you start looking for work or housing in San Francisco.

It doesn't snow in San Francisco. To find snow and winter sports one travels northeast (about a three– to four–hour drive) to Lake Tahoe and the Sierra Nevada Mountains and some of the best skiing in the country.

There is also little hot summertime weather in San Francisco. September and October are the warmest months, with average temperature highs of 70° F. If you must have hot *summer* weather, you should consider living outside San Francisco proper (Marin or Contra Costa County, where it is significantly warmer) and commuting into San Francisco to work.

San Francisco is, of course, famous for its 40 hills. This geography has contributed to the development of distinct neighborhoods such as Telegraph Hill, Russian Hill, Nob Hill, Twin Peaks, etc. Many of these hills offer residents very dramatic water views, making San Francisco one of the prettiest U.S. cities to live in.

## Housing

Obviously, not everyone can have a commanding view of the bay or the ocean. However, San Francisco offers a wide variety of pleasant residences. Since San Francisco is a densely populated and small city, two out of every three living units are multifamily units. These include old Victorian homes that have been converted to rental apartments as well as more modern high-rise apartment buildings. Monthly rents range from about $400 to $800 for one- and two-bedroom apartments.

In all of California private homes and condominiums are expensive relative to those in other areas of the country. San Francisco is no exception. In fact, the Bay Area is the most expensive housing market in the nation. In the city's prime residential areas homes start at $150,000, but most are considerably higher in price.

There is an acute shortage of housing in San Francisco because most new development has gone to office space, so finding the apartment or home of your choice will require some persistent searching.

### Overall Cost of Living

San Francisco ranks fourth in cost of living in U.S. cities behind Boston, Los Angeles, and Washington, DC. Its cost of living is about the same as that of New York and Chicago. The 1982 consumer price index (CPI) for San Francisco is 304.6 versus the U.S. city average of 290.6. (The CPI is based on prices of food, clothing, shelter, transportation, health and other day-to-day goods and services.) This means that San Francisco has a slightly higher than average cost of living compared to most other U.S. cities and that our cost of living has risen at a slightly faster than average rate since 1967, the CPI base year.

Bay Area cost of living is higher due to our housing costs. However, some other expenses are lower than they are in other cities. For example, here in San Francisco you will need only one wardrobe for all seasons, and foods such as fresh vegetables and fruits are lower in cost since they are grown nearby.

### Salaries

Salaries in the Bay Area are very competitive with other major U.S. cities. In fact, a recent salary survey of U.S. cities indicates that the San Francisco Bay Area ranks third in middle management salaries and second for clerical and support staff salaries. Therefore, you can be assured that you are being compensated for the higher cost of living.

### Tax Rates

Sales tax is 6.5 percent and includes city, state, and a public transportation tax. The property tax is 1.19 percent of new sales price. California state income tax increases from 0 to 11 percent on a graduated scale.

**Transportation**

San Francisco has excellent, inexpensive public transportation including streetcars, buses, trolleys, and cable cars. (This most famous San Francisco form of transportation is currently shut down for repairs and will reopen in 1984.) A single fare with transfer privileges allows you to travel throughout the city for a relatively low cost. Call "673-Muni" for information on how to get anywhere in the city using public transportation.

The Bay Area Rapid Transit (BART) system, the ferry boat service, buses, and the railroad provide pleasant, easy transport to other communities outside of San Francisco proper.

San Francisco is connected to Marin County by the famous Golden Gate Bridge and to Alameda County and the East Bay by the Bay Bridge. The San Francisco International Airport is located 12 miles from downtown.

**Education**

Few cities can compete with the wide variety of educational opportunities available in San Francisco, and for California residents, much of it is extremely inexpensive. San Francisco has the San Francisco State University, City College of San Francisco, University of San Francisco, and Golden Gate University. The University of California also has several branches in San Francisco. Most of the schools offer career-oriented courses. For information or catalogs detailing regular or adult education courses, call:

> San Francisco State University—(415) 469-2141
> City College of San Francisco—(415) 239-3000
> University of San Francisco—(415) 666-6563
> Golden Gate University—(415) 442-7000

The San Francisco public school system has had a remarkable renaissance. Only 10 years ago San Francisco schools, like those in many U.S. cities, were a disaster of classroom violence, busing protests, and declining student test scores. Now they are a model for other big cities to follow, featuring tough academic standards, sharply rising test results, and stricter classroom discipline. Most of the San Francisco public school population now performs above the California average on state achievement tests.

Among the many obstacles faced—e.g., tax cuts, teachers' strikes, etc.—the schools have had to deal with the fact that more than half of their students come from homes in which a language other than English is spoken. In fact, the school system has to deal with about 27 different foreign languages. In spite of these problems, the schools are now able to woo back many of the city's white middle class families, who had previously sent their children to private schools. For more details on San Francisco schools, write to or call the San Francisco Board of Education, 135 Van Ness Ave., San Francisco, CA 94102; (415) 595-9000.

## Recreation and Cultural Activities

San Francisco has more than 150 parks and public recreation facilities. The parks offer swimming, tennis, baseball, golf, bowling, and hiking and bike trails. Golden Gate Park is the largest San Francisco park (more than 1,000 acres). It features a Japanese tea garden, the San Francisco Planetarium, arts museums, the arboretum, the aquarium, and a small herd of American buffalo.

Water sports are easy to pursue, including swimming on city beaches (on the ocean or the bay), sailing, boating, wind-surfing, etc.

The city has always been sports oriented, and residents actively support their professional teams—49ers football, Giants baseball, and in Oakland the A's baseball and the Warriors basketball teams.

There are lots of sporting events for nonprofessionals, too. For example, San Francisco boasts more than 200 running races a year. Perhaps there are so many because the mild climate makes it comfortable for year-round running, or perhaps it is because jogging in San Francisco is less boring than in other cities. After all, you can run beside beautiful San Francisco Bay along the Marina Green running path. The "Bay to Breakers," a 7.6-mile event that begins downtown and culminates at the Pacific Ocean, is San Francisco's most famous running race. About 40,000 people annually test their stamina and enjoy themselves in this crazy, costumed foot race.

The same vitality is also apparent in the many musical, theatrical, and dance activities held in the city. San Francisco has an abundance of the traditional and the experimental. For traditionalists there's the San Francisco Symphony, the opera, the San Francisco Ballet, and the American Conservatory Theatre (ACT).

The symphony is directed by Edo de Waart and is flourishing in San Francisco's beautiful new Louise M. Davies Symphony Hall. The San Francisco Opera is considered the best opera company in the United States and regularly draws major international talent and performs to SRO crowds. The San Francisco Ballet Company is the oldest classical ballet company in the United States, and the ACT is one of the best-known repertory theater companies in the country.

In addition to these major cultural traditions, San Francisco offers a rich variety of music—including jazz, bluegrass, folk, rock, new wave, big band, and classical—that can be heard on college campuses and in bars, nightclubs, coffeehouses, and parks. There are also plenty of small theater and dance groups that will welcome your support, as will the various sidewalk entertainers who enliven the city's street corners and tourist centers.

San Francisco is full of museums as well. Just to name a few of the more unusual ones, there's the Cable Car Museum, where you can see how the cable cars work. The Exploratorium allows you to participate actively in scientific exhibits designed to give you a better understanding of the world. And there's the National Maritime Museum and its deep-water cargo sailing ship, the Balclutha, where you learn a bit of San Francisco seafaring history.

The diversity of the population contributes to the wide range of recreational, dining, and shopping facilities in this city. To help you really imagine living in (or near) San Francisco, consider the opportunities for dining at restaurants serving Italian, Basque, Chinese, German, Japanese, Moroccan, Vietnamese, French, Mexican, Greek, Indian, and Hungarian dishes, as well as that famous San Franciscan specialty, fresh seafood. Of course, this is only a *partial* list.

Also imagine that on any given day or evening you can visit Chinatown and browse through its import shops and food markets, visit The Japan Center to sample sushi, or relax in Little Italy at one of North Beach's sidewalk espresso cafes for dessert, good coffee, and conversation.

San Francisco is also a city of many festivals, including Chinese New Year with a lavish parade, the Columbus Day Parade and blessing of the fleet, Cinco de Mayo, Mexican Independence Day, Japanese Cherry Blossom Festival, and St. Patrick's Day.


## BUT WHAT'S SAN FRANCISCO REALLY LIKE? ANSWERS TO SOME FREQUENTLY ASKED QUESTIONS


### Meeting People

It's true that San Francisco is a city in love with its own beauty, its weather, and its past, so you'll often find its residents quite smug and perhaps provincial about it (especially if you try to compare it to New York City). Yet San Francisco is a very friendly city, quite open to newcomers because most San Franciscans were once newcomers themselves.

A few statistics: Sixty-five percent of Bay Area households are family households. The remainder are singles (divorced, widowed, or never married). San Francisco ranks first among single parent and "unrelated" households.

### Working Women

Attitudes toward career women seem generally very positive and relatively open-minded. And Bay Area women have experienced some modest professional success. (About 20 percent of Bay Area working women have an annual salary of more than $20,000.)

Many San Francisco groups and organizations provide moral support and professional contacts for these women (see Chapter 23 for descriptions of these). Service-oriented businesses represent the largest segment of the San Francisco business community and will provide the most growth in the next 10 years, and these are the kinds of businesses in which women seem to have made most progress.

### Gay Population

San Francisco is well known for its gay community. Population estimates range from roughly 15–25 percent of the total San Francisco city population. Many thousands of gay men and women visit San Francisco on vacation as tourists as well.

Being gay is acceptable in San Francisco, and gay men and women are very much a part of everyday working life. To gay residents, being gay seems to be just one part of otherwise busy lives and not the main focus. This may contrast sharply with what newcomers are used to in other cities, where homosexuality is less open or prevalent and thus perhaps is more of a big deal. For information on gay businesses in the area, write or call to order the *Gay Area's Private Telephone Directory*, PO Box 14752, 4111 18th St., No. 4, San Francisco, CA 94114; (415) 861-3905.

### Earthquakes

As you probably know, both major California cities, San Francisco and Los Angeles, are situated along the San Andreas fault, and as such, both cities experience earthquakes from time to time. Most of these are relatively slight, and sometimes go unnoticed.

San Francisco residents seem to have a rather matter-of-fact attitude toward the prospect of serious earthquakes. Indeed, it seems somewhat similar to the attitude of Americans living in tornado or hurricane country. People know this is a threat, and many companies provide earthquake preparedness packages to educate their employees. In addition, all of the newly constructed office buildings are built to shift with the quakes and thus (it is hoped) withstand the earth's vibrations. Actually, the statistical risk of being killed in an earthquake is significantly lower than that of dying in a car accident in any major U.S. city.

## Crime and Urban Decay

Both the overall housing shortage and the restoration of old Victorian homes have contributed to urban renewal in many city neighborhoods. A recent census bureau study found that 92 percent of San Francisco residents considered their neighborhood very safe by day. However, uniform crime statistics indicate that San Francisco, like most other U.S. cities, has a relatively high crime rate.

## Ambition

Easterners have sometimes accused Californians of extending their laid-back attitude to the business area and thus not working as hard or being as ambitious as those back East. This judgment may strike you as accurate if you listen to San Franciscans describe their priorities. Number one is usually to remain in the Bay Area. But, ironically, this creates quite a lot of ambition and work-oriented energy. People want to make a career for themselves here. Sometimes this means starting their own business or being willing to change careers in midstream. In any case, the Bay Area has quite an entrepreneurial, hardworking spirit.

## *The Bay Area Counties*

## THE PENINSULA

"The Peninsula" includes San Mateo County and the northern part of Santa Clara County.

## San Mateo County

San Mateo developed as a bedroom community for the city of San Francisco and as a handy location for the San Francisco International Airport.

Recently, a growing number of corporate headquarters, industrial parks, services, businesses, and wholesale and retail operations have increased the number of jobs in the county. Now many people both live and work in the county; others reverse the traditional commute and travel from San Francisco to San Mateo for their jobs.

San Mateo County is 530 square miles and mostly suburban and rural. It includes cities like South San Francisco, San Mateo, Redwood City, Menlo Park, Portola Valley, Half Moon Bay, and Daly City. The population is approximately 600,000.

San Mateo has a temperature range of 40–82° F., with about 235 clear sunny days a year. The topography is generally hilly and runs the gamut from redwood groves to agricultural fields of artichokes.

Approximately half the county is employed in white-collar jobs. The San Francisco Airport is the biggest employment center (approximately 30 thousand workers), and United Airlines is the county's largest employer. The unemployment rate here is lower than in the state of California or the Bay Area as a whole. Business services lead the race in the number of new job opportunities.

### "Silicon Valley"—Santa Clara County

Don't try to find "Silicon Valley" on a map. It's not there, but Santa Clara County, its real name, is. Santa Clara is the largest of the nine Bay Area counties, with 1.2 million people spread out over 1,300 square miles. "Silicon Valley" is a narrow 25-mile stretch of industrial parks stretching from Palo Alto to San Jose, named for the silicon chip that has made the growth in computers, electronics, and video games possible. (For the technologically uneducated, it is those little wafers of silicon that host the transistors, diodes, and capacitors that have allowed the high-tech boom to happen.)

The county is best known as the high-technology capital of our country, with the densest concentration of high-tech electronics firms than anywhere else in California or the nation.

It all started when a Stanford University professor, deploring the brain drain of his graduating students to the East Coast, began to encourage them to start their entrepreneurial electronic ventures in the Stanford Industrial Park. Now the area is known for firms like Apple, IBM, Memorex, Varian, Hewlett-Packard, Syntex, National Semiconductor, General Electric, Lockheed, and Intel, to name just a few.

Santa Clara County is actually rather diverse. The southern portion of the county is agricultural, while the north is urban/suburban. The Santa Cruz Mountains are on the west, the Diablo range on the east. Two valleys are formed by the mountains. The climate is Mediterranean, sunny, and mild all year long, with average temperatures ranging from 48 to 71° F.

The county has shifted away from its former agriculture-based economy, but it is still a food-processing center. It is well located for seasonal workers and agricultural produce from the south.

San Jose is Santa Clara's county seat and the fourth-largest city in California.

Santa Clara County is first in median household income in the state and has one of every three workers employed in manufacturing. As you know, U.S. durable goods manufacturing (except some electronics) has been trending down. The Ford plants in Santa Clara have had shutdowns, but these employment losses have been partially offset by gains in missile and spacecraft manufacturing. Recently the semiconductor industry has been down due to price competition, aggressive Japanese marketing, and some overproduction.

Since the county's population has been growing steadily, the services, retail trades (especially food and apparel), and public utilities are all up.

An imbalance between job growth and housing has caused housing prices to rise sharply. And the population increases have created some short-term growth problems, such as traffic congestion. This means that some high-tech companies have begun to look elsewhere, to Contra Costa or Sonoma, for expansion.

In spite of this, the job outlook for Santa Clara is good, especially for people with high-tech or specialized skills in marketing electronics. The area is projected to have one of the highest rates of new job opportunities in the future.


## THE EAST BAY

"The East Bay" includes Alameda County and parts of Contra Costa County.


### Alameda County

Alameda County includes the cities of Oakland, Berkeley, Alameda, Fremont, Pleasanton, Livermore, and Hayward, among others. It's located a few miles across the Bay Bridge from San Francisco and is urban/suburban in character.

The county has a population of 1.2 million, making it the second-largest county (after Santa Clara) in northern California. The climate in cities like Oakland and Berkeley is similar to, though a bit warmer than, San Francisco's, with mild year-round temperatures and some early morning fog in summer, which usually clears by noon. The more southern cities, such as Livermore and Fremont, are considerably warmer.

The East Bay has most of the Bay Area's heavy industry, including car and truck assembly plants, metal and glass container manufacturers, government nuclear labs, and makers of fabricated metal products, chemicals, and electrical components. Other major employers are food processors, household products manufacturers, and the health care, universities, and data processing businesses. A major naval air station; the University of California, Berkeley, campus; and World Airways are located here. The Port of Oakland is thriving, due to its modern container-cargo facilities, which have made it number two in container tonnage in the United States. The county seat of Oakland, long plagued by inner-city problems of decay and neglect, is going through a bit of revitalization, with the addition of new office buildings, a convention center, and more housing.

Much of the future growth is expected to be in the southern part of the county around Fremont and Hayward.

### Contra Costa County

Contra Costa County is flourishing and is expected to continue to be among the fastest growing counties in the state. The county offers pleasant suburban living and working conditions and housing and business rentals that are lower than is typical for the Bay Area.

Currently the county has a population of 660,000 and is expected to grow to 730,000 in the next few years.

The area includes the communities of Walnut Creek, Concord, and Pleasant Hill, which are connected to San Francisco by BART (Bay Area Rapid Transit).

The county offers a balanced mix of employment opportunities. Agriculture is still important, especially in the eastern "Delta Area." But retail trade, services, government, and manufacturing account for three-fourths of the employment. Most of the industry in the county is located near the cities of Richmond and Antioch.

Living in Contra Costa is especially pleasant for those who prefer to be away from the fog and like a hot, dry summer (often 90–100° F.).

Employment prospects for Contra Costa are good because some of the high-tech firms are planning to expand here rather than in Santa Clara, where local zoning makes expansion difficult. Additionally, some San Francisco firms are migrating to this county for cheaper office space and a shorter commute for their personnel.

### MARIN COUNTY

Already known for its picturesque charm and its views of the bay and San Francisco, Marin County has recently earned a reputation as the home of the "me generation." The media image is one of endless (and mindless) purchasing, Perrier quaffing, and jogging, of hot tub orgies and a Mercedes or BMW in every driveway.

It is true that Marin County has one of the highest per capita incomes in the United States and is one of the most gorgeous spots to live in. But the popular image doesn't do Marin justice, and it doesn't provide a sense of the other Marin, including the western part of the county, which is rural and agricultural and includes the beautiful, rugged Pt. Reyes and The Golden Gate National Recreational Area, Muir Woods, and Mount Tamalpais.

Marin County is 607 square miles and includes towns such as Sausalito, Belvedere, Tiburon, and Mill Valley. The county has about 225,000 people and 115 miles of coastline. The climate is reputed to be the best in the United States. It features a mild winter and a dry summer.

Marin is primarily a bedroom suburban county for San Francisco. Most of its major employment is related to tourism and agriculture. Recently, business services, office building rentals, retailing, and light industry have grown and large firms such as Fireman's Fund Insurance have relocated from San Francisco to Marin. However, most local residents are opposed to growth in office buildings or apartment complexes. Apparently most residents prefer to live in Marin but commute via ferry boat or over the Golden Gate Bridge to work in San Francisco.

## THE WINE COUNTRY—NAPA, SONOMA, AND SOLANO COUNTIES

North of San Francisco lies the romantic Bay Area wine country. The three wine counties are principally known for their vineyards and pleasant rural surroundings.

### Napa County

Napa was named for the Nappas Indians; now the name is practically synonymous with California wine. Farming and wine still dominate the economy in Napa County, but the wineries also bring the tourists, principally to the picturesque town of St. Helena.

Napa County is 794 square miles, with a population of about 100,000. The average annual temperature is a sunny 60° F. Generally the weather is warmer than in San Francisco proper. For example, Napa in the summer has high temperatures in the high 80s while in San Francisco, it is in the low 70s. But it is the cool, damp winters that make it ideal for wine. You have probably heard of Inglenook, Christian Brothers, Charles Krug, Beringer, and Mondavi, to name just a few vintners that are located in Napa.

Wineries and the resulting tourism lead the employment picture. But Napa also has Mare Island Naval Shipyard, a Kaiser steel plant, some apparel factories, and a couple of large hospitals.

## Sonoma County

Historically, Sonoma is quite interesting. Wine growing north of San Francisco started here. *Call of the Wild* author Jack London lived here. It's the site of the last of the 21 California missions founded by the Franciscan monk followers of Father Junipero Serra.

Currently the county has about 300,000 residents in an area of 1,604 square miles and is growing fastest of the three wine counties. As in Napa, its climate is sunny and warmer than San Francisco.

Sonoma is gradually changing from its rural roots to a more urban industrial center. But the agriculture-based industries are still the principal employers.

There are 14 wineries—including Italian Swiss Colony, Sebastiani, and Korbel—and about 27,000 acres of vineyards, as well as apple and pear orchards, dairy farms, sheep ranches and turkey breeding farms.

The area between the cities of Santa Rosa and Petaluma shows the best prospects for growth. Various industries, including pump manufacturers, diesel power plants, and machine part plants, are located in the Sonoma Valley area. From May to October Sonoma County also has the second-busiest Pacific salmon port, located at Bodega Bay.

Sonoma County is a real mix of urban/suburban communities (Petaluma and Santa Rosa) with more rural agricultural areas.

Sonoma also boasts the famed Bohemian Grove, located on the banks of Sonoma's Russian River, the summer campsite for the Bay Area's exclusive Bohemian Club men's club.

Sonoma also offers some vacation outposts for gays in and near Sonomatown, the Russian River recreation area.

The employment outlook is excellent for Sonoma in that some of the Bay Area's high-tech companies are considering expansion to the county because of its available land and lower relative costs.

## Solano County

Solano, like Sonoma, is a growth county. Its population is growing twice as fast as the rest of California and three times as fast as the nine-county Bay Area. Current population is about 240,000 in a county of 827 square miles.

Farming and food processing are the principal employers. Also notable is Travis Air Force Base, Mare Island Shipyards, and the California medical facility in Vacaville. Because of Solano's affordable housing, many people live in Solano but commute to work in Contra Costa, Alameda, or San Francisco Counties.

A large new retail shopping center is being built with major department store openings scheduled for 1983.

# 3

# An Overview of Business and Industry

You *can* find a job in the San Francisco Bay Area. Economically, the Bay Area market is still in a moderate growth phase of development. It isn't burdened with the aging manufacturing plants of the Northeast, the declining automobile production of the Midwest, or the ailing lumber industry of the Northwest.

It is a rather unique business center with a diverse character that has helped it maintain relatively stable economic growth in spite of the nation's difficult economic trends.

The Bay Area is known primarily as the West Coast's financial capital and the spawning ground for computer semiconductor technology. The area's major areas of employment are business services, finance and government, and tourism. Farming and durable goods manufacturing (except electronic) are declining industries.

San Francisco is called the "Wall Street of the West," with many of the country's largest banks and insurance companies represented here and the Pacific Stock Exchange located in the city. And, San Francisco has the nation's largest bank corporation, Bank of America. San Francisco proper is also headquarters city for a diverse range of companies, including the following, to name just a few.

## San Francisco Firms

- Bechtel—engineering development
- Crown Zellerbach—paper
- Dean Witter Reynolds—financial services
- Del Monte—food
- Di Giorgio—consumer products
- Foremost McKesson—distribution services, chemicals
- Levi Strauss—apparel
- Natoma's—oil, gas, energy
- Shaklee—personal care and household products
- Standard Oil—petroleum
- Transamerica—diversified services (insurance, transportation, finance)

## Bay Area Firms

- Apple Computer—home computers
- Atari—video games
- Clorox—household products
- The GAP—apparel chain
- Heublein—wine and liquor
- Hewlett-Packard—computers
- Kaiser Aluminum—aluminum and industrial
- Paul Masson—wine
- Safeway—retail grocery chain
- Syntex—pharmaceuticals
- World Airways—transportation

In total the Bay Area is home to 43 of the Fortune 500 companies, with 21 of them in San Francisco.

Part of the reason the Bay Area is unique as a marketplace is its tourism. The city attracts an abundance of American and international visitors, who spend about $1 billion a year. The result is that there are employment opportunities in entertainment, leisure/tourism, and retailing businesses.

The area's trade with the Far East is also significant. The economies of Singapore, Indonesia, Malaysia, Thailand, and the Philippines all need more of what the Bay Area produces, especially agricultural and electronic products. The city's recently revitalized port is helping to make these trade opportunities a reality.

San Francisco has prepared for continuing growth by investing in more downtown office space than most other U.S. cities and by building the new multimillion-dollar Moscone Convention Center to attract trade shows and conventions.

Income levels in the Bay Area are among the highest in the state and the nation. And the diversified economy helped make the impact of the nation's economic recession weaker and slower than in most other regions of the United States.

Not every type of employment projects a rosy image, however. For example, there seems to be an abundance of lawyers, social workers, and teachers who want to live and work in the Bay Area. This makes San Francisco one of the most competitive of U.S. cities for these jobs. It's not impossible to find a good opportunity, but it does take time and perseverance.

Though government is still a major Bay Area employer, the passage of the so-called "Proposition 13" tax law has resulted in a reduction in the state's tax surplus and cutbacks in government employment.

While the business services industry is a major employer, it is not very easy to land that super job in marketing, strategic planning, finance, public relations, advertising, and the like. MBAs frequently expect to move to San Francisco and go into product management, but there are just not that many traditional packaged goods or consumer goods companies with these kinds of brand management jobs. On the other hand, the newer Bay Area companies with new technologies, which have experienced rapid growth, are under a good deal of pressure to make a successful transition from unlimited initial opportunity to more moderate growth and competition. For this, they will need fast-paced, experienced managers with imagination, entrepreneurial spirit, and good communication skills. An estimated 60 percent of California's products are said to come from companies created or revamped during the last 35 years. This means that California and the Bay Area is still a land of opportunity, but there are different opportunities here than you are likely to find in New York or Chicago.

## Bay Area's Fastest Growing Firms*

The following fastest growing firms are good companies to consider for employment opportunities. These Bay Area firms have had a 30-percent annual growth rate in either income or sales between 1979 and 1981.

*Reprinted from *California Business,* September, 1982.

- Ada Corporation—Building Components, San Francisco
- Advanced Micro Devices—Utility Electronics, Sunnyvale
- Amdahl—Computers, Sunnyvale
- Anthem Electronics—Industrial Products, San Jose
- Apple Computer—Personal Computers, Cupertino
- Avantek—Communications Equipment, Santa Clara
- Brae—Railcar Leasing, San Francisco
- Cetus—Genetic Engineering, Berkeley
- Community Psychiatric Centers—Medical Care, San Francisco
- Consolidated Freightways—Motor Freight, Palo Alto
- Dean Witter Reynolds—Investment Securities, San Francisco
- Dreyer's Ice Cream—Ice Cream Production, Oakland
- Dysan—Computer Products, Santa Clara
- Genentech—Genetic Engineering, South San Francisco
- Harper Group—Freight Forwarder, San Francisco
- Impell—Energy Services, San Francisco
- KLA Instruments—Electro-Optical Systems, Santa Clara
- Magnuson Computer Systems—Computer Systems, San Jose
- Natoma's—Petroleum and Shipping, San Francisco
- NEA—Computer Products, Sunnyvale
- Pacific Gas Transmission—Public Utilities, San Francisco
- Pizza Time Theatre—Restaurants, Sunnyvale
- Ramtek—Computer Products, Santa Clara
- Rolm—Computer Products, Santa Clara
- SAGA—Food Services, Menlo Park
- System Industries—Computer Products, Milpitas
- Taco Charley—Restaurants, San Mateo
- Tandem Computers—Computer Products, Cupertino
- Technology for Communication International—Antenna Systems, Mountain View
- Triad Systems—Computer Systems, Sunnyvale
- Velo-Bind—Industrial Products, Sunnyvale
- Viking Freight Systems—Motor Freight Carrier, Santa Clara
- Western Pacific Railroad—Railroad, San Francisco

# 4

# How to Identify the Right Bay Area Job for You

You are lucky. You have a head start on the job search in that you have made one difficult decision—that of location. You have decided you want a job in the San Francisco Bay Area. Now it is vitally important that you take some time for additional self-assessment, to identify your other job goals. You need to do this *before* you get too involved in actually hunting for a job. The end result of the self-assessment procedure described in this chapter will be a more focused job search and a better program for marketing yourself to your target employers. It will be worth it.

The process of self-evaluation can be time-consuming and anxiety-provoking. It is often much easier to figure out how to help other people than to make choices for yourself. To make the task easier this chapter provides some easy-to-follow exercises to help you identify your work preferences and your marketable skills.

If, *after* you complete the exercises in this chapter on your own, you feel you need more help, several other resources are recommended that will provide additional help.

## First Look at Yourself

Most people tend to start an active job search before they are really ready. But when you rush into lots of activity, you tend to ignore the most valuable person you have on your team—yourself.

You know more than anyone else does what you enjoy, find satisfying, and do well. It is important that you take some time to review and inventory your preferences and strengths before going off to consider actual job options. This self-assessment process is perhaps even more important for job or career switchers than it is for the first-time career seekers. You need to take the time to examine what your life and work experiences have already shown you. You cannot do this simply by considering alternative ready-made career moves (e.g., becoming a lawyer, going back to school to get an MBA). Instead, you must identify where your skills, abilities, and interests lie. Later, once you have done this thoroughly, examine various career or job options to decide whether various job possibilities include the skills and interests that would make it a good choice for you. As you know, it is highly unlikely that you will just happen to stumble onto the perfect career or job for you. Instead of hoping that this will happen, you need to define what it is that would be perfect for you *if* you could find it. You do this by analyzing your life in terms of interests, knowledge, abilities, and transferable skills.

## INTERESTS, KNOWLEDGE, AND ABILITIES

Sit down with a large pad of paper and follow each of these exercises. Answer each question in writing so that you can review your answers and see any patterns that will lead you to insights about yourself.

1. *Make a list of your life skills and accomplishments.* Complete these sentences (or similar ones) to help you to be as specific as possible:

- Most of my experience is in _____.
- I have read a lot about _____.
- I like studying _____.
- The major contribution I made in my last job was _____.
- I am known as a person who is _____.
- I'm pretty good at _____.
- My family and friends think I'm a good _____.
- The best thing I ever accomplished was _____.
- The thing I am proudest of is my ability to _____.
- In my previous jobs I've been particularly good at _____.

2. *Examine what you have found satisfying in your life so far.* Answer the following questions.

- What do you like to think about? What topics or themes often come up in your conversations or thoughts?
- What would others say you are particularly interested in?

- Consider whether you prefer working closely with others or more on your own.
- What skills did you use in each job you've held in the past?
- Did your previous jobs have anything in common?
- List as many of your job activities as you can and divide them into those you like and those you dislike. Identify why.

3. *Talk with a couple of colleagues, friends, or family members and ask them to provide input.* Have a few people who know you well describe you in terms of the following.

- Your main interests
- Abilities you have that they particularly admire
- Skills they think you could develop further
- Things you could be very good at doing (in addition to what you do now)
- Things you would not be good at doing

Compare what these individuals said with what you already believe about yourself.

When you have completed all of these exercises, review your answers and look for common themes. *Without* considering whether it is possible to get such a job, simply fill in the blanks in this sentence:

"I would like to work in a job in which I can utilize my interests and abilities in _____ and _____."

## TRANSFERABLE SKILLS

Almost all jobs require skills that are transferable and which have to do with these two fundamental objectives:

1. increasing productivity or sales
2. cutting costs

If you can figure out what your experience has taught you about these two fundamental things, you will have begun to identify very relevant and saleable transferable skills. When you put your transferable skills together with what you like to do and find satisfying, you have a blueprint for the kind of job you should look for. Since the Bay Area job market is so competitive, it is imperative that you have a clear idea of your own strengths and that you can *communicate* them to your prospective employer.

Everyone has skills in the sense that skills are those things that you have some abilities and interest in. You do not have to be unique or perfect in a particular skill in order to rightfully claim it as one of your assets.

Beyond the fundamental tasks of increasing productivity or sales and cutting costs, most jobs include some form of at least 12 skills. As part of your self-assessment process you can determine which of these you find satisfying and in which of these you can demonstrate some past job or life achievement. These skills are:

1. Budget Control
2. Communicating Orally
3. Writing
4. Setting Priorities
5. Meeting Deadlines
6. Selling
7. Managing/Organizing/Supervising
8. Teaching/Training
9. Public Relations
10. Negotiating/Team Building
11. Researching/Analyzing
12. Decision Making

Many of these skills or abilities overlap. By breaking them out separately, you will be helping to sort out your preferences and articulate your strengths.

## How To Analyze Your Skills

Your answers to the following questions will tell you a lot about the content of the job you will want. Almost all jobs use similar skills, but the percentage of your time that is spent using each skill will help determine whether any particular job will be a good fit for you. To get the best value from this exercise, *write down* the answers to each question so you can refer to your answers later.

This self-assessment exercise will help you identify what kind of job you are looking for and prepare in advance the information you will use to communicate to prospective employers the benefits of hiring you. Plan to use the information to prepare for interviews later on in your job search.

### 1. BUDGET CONTROL

• Do you enjoy the responsibility for management of budgets or do you really wish someone else would/could handle it?
• What budgets have you managed?

## 2. Communicating Orally

- Do you enjoy articulating your thoughts orally in meetings, in interviews, in speeches, etc.?
- Do people usually seem to understand what you are saying to them?
- Do they grasp your ideas as you express them?
- Do you listen actively?
- Do you learn from what others say?
- Are conversations or meetings or lectures pleasant or satisfying to you?
- Can you think of any ways in which your skills in oral communication have helped you accomplish a difficult task?

## 3. Writing

- Do you write memos, letters, instructions, or papers easily?
- Can others follow your instructions or understand your viewpoint when you write to them?
- What have you written that demonstrates your writing skill particularly well?

## 4. Setting Priorities

- What experience have you had in determining appropriate priorities and being flexible enough to change them as the situation changes?
- Can you adjust your priorities easily?
- Can you give examples of situations in which you were able to accomplish a difficult task because you were adaptable and set appropriate priorities for various demands on your time?

## 5. Meeting Deadlines

- Can you do your best within the time that is available?
- In what ways have you demonstrated this ability?
- Are you motivated by pressure?
- Can you often do more when there is more to do? (Give examples of this from your past work experience.)

## 6. Selling

- What aspects of your past jobs involved selling something? (Selling, or motivating or convincing, is present in many jobs where no physical

product actually changes hands, but concepts, ideas, attitudes, or services are exchanged.)
- Do you enjoy selling?
- In what ways have you been successful at it?

### 7. MANAGING/ORGANIZING/SUPERVISING

- What have you had responsibility for organizing and accomplishing?
- What is the project or business for which you were responsible?
- Whom did you supervise or what did you coordinate?
- Would you say that you find the management of people or data or things most satisfying?
- Do you like supervising and delegating to others, or would you really prefer to do the job yourself?

### 8. TEACHING/TRAINING

- Do you enjoy instructing or helping people so that they may take on more responsibility themselves and do their jobs better?
- Are you comfortable giving others feedback on performance?
- Can you provide constructive criticism?
- Whom have you taught?
- What have you taught them?
- What were the results of your instruction or training?

### 9. PUBLIC RELATIONS

- Are you good at finding solutions to problems or complaints? (PR skills may or may not actually involve the public.)
- Do you enjoy troubleshooting or presenting yourself or your department or company in the best possible light?

### 10. NEGOTIATING/TEAM BUILDING

- Have you had experience in bringing opposing factions to a consensus?
- Have you developed a team spirit where there was once little or no communication or sharing of resources?

### 11. RESEARCHING/ANALYZING

- Do you enjoy searching for or developing information to be used in problem solving?

- Do you like identifying the right questions and then figuring out how to get information to answer them?
- Is the process of data analysis satisfying and helpful to problems you have solved?

## 12. DECISION MAKING

- Are you able to make an informed choice and provide necessary leadership even when all the information is not available and will not be forthcoming? (All the research analysis, communication, and fiscal management in the world cannot make up for the inability to *make a decision.*) In other words, can you make up your mind and take responsibility for a plan even though you do not know *for sure* it is right?
- How have you demonstrated this very sophisticated skill in your past work?
- Do you like taking risks (i.e., having to make decisions based on little available information)?

If you have completed the exercises described here, you have now *consciously* identified a lot about the kind of work you prefer to do. This knowledge should now become an important basis for checking out career options. You should use your inventory of interests and skills to evaluate Bay Area career or job opportunities you may have in mind. Take some time to review all your answers to the questions in this chapter and ask yourself which of the jobs you were considering earlier include the skills you like and are good at.

If you had no career options in mind, or you don't know what skills or interests a job involves, don't worry. This book will give you more information on how to research this. Many different fields are described in the second half of this book. These will give you some clues as to how you could fit your interests and skills to each job field.

Many people have trouble disciplining themselves to conduct a thorough self-examination. (It can be difficult and somewhat lonely work!) If you would like more help or access to more detailed or more formal programs, here are some additional Bay Area resources to try:

1. A formal career identification survey, including an interests/skills questionnaire and analysis, may help you. The program is free. Contact:

   Community College District Office
   31 Gough St.
   San Francisco, CA
   (415) 239-3039

The testing and counseling involves a two- or three-step process. It takes two to three weeks to receive the results of these tests.

2. More detailed self-examination procedures to follow are offered in these excellent books:

> *Discover What You Are Best At,* by Barry and Linda Gale.

> *Where Do I Go from Here with My Life?,* by John C. Crystal and Richard N. Bolles.

> *What Color Is Your Parachute?,* by Richard N. Bolles.

Well-known Bay Area author Dick Bolles is also the project director of the National Career Development Project (NCDP), which is a clearinghouse of job hunting information headquartered in the Bay Area. The NCDP has a newsletter ($10 to join the mailing list) and holds workshops. Write for information:

National Career Development Project
PO Box 379
Walnut Creek, CA 94597

## Practical Questions to Consider

Some practical aspects of your lifestyle/workstyle will certainly affect your daily life, so they may also merit careful consideration early in your Bay Area job search. Think about them in terms of your preferences and keep them in mind when you begin talking to people about career or company options. Here are a few examples of the kind of practical questions to answer in choosing a Bay Area job. Write down your answers to these questions along with your reasons for giving those answers.

*1. Do you think you would prefer to work for a small, medium-sized, or large organization?*
SMALL
*Positives:* Might provide a more casual, less bureaucratic, more family atmosphere. May offer broader work responsibilities and breadth of experience with fewer backup departments. There may be an opportunity to create custom-tailored jobs, entrepreneurial challenge, high visibility.
*Negatives:* There may be less opportunity for advancement. Is there a chance to switch from one assignment (or division) to another? The training may be less formal and provide less exposure to business sophistication or state-of-the-art techniques.

LARGE

*Positives:* Consider the opportunity to add a famous brand or company to your resume and learn from the best. You can specialize here. You may have the security of the big firm and its benefit package, more opportunity for a variety of job assignments, and perhaps more financial resources to manage.

*Negatives:* There may be more bureaucracy, with an emphasis on administrating rather than doing. Perhaps it is impersonal and offers low visibility. Does it reward entrepreneurial spirit or try to dampen it?

*2. What kind of work environment do you prefer?*

*Office Environment:* Separate offices, a large active work center, or open cubicles?

*Location:* Urban or suburban? A site with shops and cultural resources nearby or an industrial park?

*3. Where do you want to live?*

*Location:* City, suburb, country?

*Type of Residence:* House, apartment, condominium?

*4. What about the commute?*

- How far is it?
- What form will it take (drive or public transportation)?
- Do you think you need the separation time-period facilitated by a physical distance between work and home or would living closer to work be more ideal for you?
- Can you use commute time to catch up on reading, etc.?

*5. What about salary and benefits?*

What salary range would be satisfactory?

What company benefits would you prefer?

- dental as well as general medical insurance
- maternity/paternity leave?
- day care assistance?
- flexible hours?
- generous vacation time?
- profit sharing?
- annual bonus?
- educational reimbursement?

While these practical questions may not seem as important as the *kind* of work you do, they certainly will affect the quality of your life and contribute to your ability to do your job well.

In spite of difficult economic times and/or scarcity of opportunity in your preferred field, it is still worth your time to identify explicitly the job environment you prefer. You can't find the job that is perfect for you if you don't spend time defining what you want. If the job you want is not available in the environment you prefer, then (because you have defined all this) you can decide which of your priorities are more important to you. In other words, you can make choices later. So don't be afraid at least to write down what you would like. Consciously identifying what you want is the best way to improve your chances for achieving it.

# 5

# How to Get the Bay Area Job You Want

Getting a job in the Bay Area is similar to getting a job anywhere else—only it seems to be much harder! You will notice that everyone you talk to seems to have the basic experience required to be hired. Everyone seems to have the educational background and credentials the jobs call for. Many people in all the usual career fields want to live here, so available openings are snapped up quickly. New people with excellent educational and work backgrounds are moving to the San Francisco Bay Area in search of "the better life." And most difficult of all, San Francisco is a small town.

Given all these obstacles, what can you do to get the job you want? There are only two answers:

1. simply be better and more thorough in your job search than anyone else.
2. be persistent.

This chapter presents what I call the "simple job search method." This method will help you organize a thorough job search and stay at it until you succeed. There are lots of exciting jobs in the Bay Area, and with effort you can find the right one for you.

The top two complaints business managers and personnel directors have about job seekers are (1) their lack of preparation and knowledge about the business or field and (2) their inability to articulate what job they want and why they should get it. The job search method described in this chapter will help you get organized and will help you avoid these two pitfalls, positioning you to get the Bay Area job you want. The method is simple in that it is easy to follow, but keep in mind that job searching is really anything but simple. This simple job search method will work *only if you thoroughly follow all the steps and persevere.*

What follows are detailed suggestions on how to conduct your search, compiled from interviews with over 1,000 managers and employment specialists in the Bay Area.

## The Simple Job Search Method

1.  Self-Assessment
2.  Information Gathering
3.  Targeting
4.  Action Plan
5.  Cataloging
6.  Positioning and Selling Yourself
7.  Asking for Feedback
8.  Revising, Adding, Updating Your Action Plan
9.  Persevering

## 1. SELF-ASSESSMENT

You are about to begin searching for the job at which you will spend 250 days (and probably some nights, weekends, and holidays) working each year. How do you know that it is the job that's right for you? You can know this only if you have analyzed your own talents and preferences in order to recognize the right choices for you.

If you have read Chapter 4 and followed the exercises, you are probably the proud possessor of some increased self-knowledge. If you have not gone through this or a similar process, I strongly suggest that you do so.

The process of defining your job goals is not some self-indulgent luxury, reserved only for those who don't really *have* to worry about finding work. Actually, it is the most pragmatic place to start any job search because it will help you get the job you want. It is also the hardest step for most people to accomplish. Now that you know this, please get on with it!

## 2. INFORMATION GATHERING

A tremendous amount of information about job categories and job-finding methods is readily available to job seekers. The real challenge is to gather and organize it in a way that will make it helpful to you. The following are the resources, in addition to this book, that you should consider including in your Bay Area job search.

## The Library

New job seekers tend to target a career and look up that category in the library. This is very helpful, but keep in mind that specific career books are not the only helpful tools the library has to offer. Here are others:

- Use the librarian. Ask open-ended questions such as, "I am interested in the _____ field. What do you suggest I look at that might help me?"
- Ask for trade journals for each field (some suggestions are listed in the industry profile chapters in this book).
- Use industry association resource books (see industry chapters).
- Ask for any government publications that may be relevant (e.g., *Dictionary of Occupational Outlook* gives employment projections by field).
- If you need additional lists of Bay Area firms ask to review *Bay Area Employer Directory,* by James Albin, which lists 2,000 employers with addresses. This book can be purchased for $35 in local bookstores and used as a mailing list. Or write to James Albin, 431 Bridgeway, Sausalito, CA 94965.
- The Bay Area cities have excellent public libraries. Be sure to check out the San Francisco Business Library, 530 Kearny Street, (425) 458-3946. This branch specializes in business publications, resources, and trade journals. Head librarian Gil McNamee is especially helpful and a source of good information.

## Books and Bookstores

Visit local bookstores in the career, business, and self-help sections as well as in the sections pertinent to the fields you have an interest in. Bookstores tend to have new paperbacks that most libraries do not yet offer. The small investment you make in purchasing these helpful volumes will be well worth it because of the time you save and the mistakes you spare yourself in your search.

The job books most often recommended to me by Bay Area employment professionals include these:

*What Color Is Your Parachute?,* by Richard N. Bolles.

*Guerrilla Tactics in the Job Market,* by Tom Jackson.

*Who's Hiring Who,* by Richard Lathrop.


### Clubs and Organizations

Myriad professional clubs and job-hunting organizations are active in the Bay Area. These are excellent resources for expanding your knowledge about how a career field operates and for increasing your contacts with others who are already employed in your target field. You will find many helpful Bay Area organizations cataloged in Chapter 23 of this book. Also, selected resources and organizations are recommended in each chapter by field. In many cases you do not have to become a member to go to a club meeting.


### Free Resources

STATE EMPLOYMENT DEPARTMENT

745 Franklin St.
San Francisco, CA 94102
(415) 557-8651

A job resource library is available at the Employment Development Department. Many valuable books, articles, and annual reports are there for your use as well as a listing of job openings for which you can apply.

"Job Search Workshop" is a free three-day course that focuses on career research, resume preparation, interview techniques, salary negotiation, and much more. Call Chet Crawley, Director of "Job Search Workshop," to schedule a date. The course is offered on Tuesday, Wednesday, and Thursday mornings each week. Call ahead to reserve a spot since it is a very popular and very effective program to get you organized for your job search.

Individual counseling is also available at the Employment Development Department. Call (415) 557-8896 for information.

CHAMBER OF COMMERCE ("THE JOB FORUM")

465 California St.
San Francisco, CA 94104
(415) 392-4511

"The Job Forum" offers a free session on the Bay Area job search. Call for information or go to the board room of the San Francisco

Chamber of Commerce, ninth floor. The session is offered every Wednesday evening (except holidays) and starts promptly at 7:00 P.M. It features a panel of business executives from a variety of firms who advise job hunters on resumes, contacts, interviews, and job search ideas. William Cobaugh, who runs "The Job Forum," is extremely knowledgeable and generous with his time. You will find him to be a remarkable source of good advice.

## Want Ads

Looking through want ads can be part of a job search program, but it should never be the central focus. Most jobs are not advertised, so spend your valuable job-hunting time more productively in developing contacts in your target job fields.

## Family, Friends, and Acquaintances

Asking questions of people you know can provide a tremendous amount of information and help. Yet surprisingly, many job seekers are hesitant to take advantage of this valuable resource. Successful career people who have conducted extensive job searches know that family, friends, and acquaintances are usually happy to provide information and even suggest names of other people as contacts. After all, people enjoy talking about their own interests and accomplishments. And when you ask them about their career field and their experiences and contacts, you are expressing a genuine interest in them and learning valuable information about a subject they spend all year thinking about. Approach them as experts, and they will probably enjoy being asked about their area of expertise.

Newly graduated students and those people reentering the job market often feel awkward asking friends and family members career-related questions. Here are a few tips on making your conversations go smoothly.

- Read a few books on the careers you are interested in so you know the jargon used in the field. (Each industry chapter in this book recommends a book or a journal you can read for more information on that field.)
- Practice asking people what they do day to day in their work. If you feel silly, then try it first with strangers, in cases in which it doesn't matter to you what they think. For example, try asking department store salespeople, computer store salespeople, the librarian. This practice will help your questions about job hunting flow more easily.
- Start asking everyone you know general work-related questions. For instance, say "I've never known as much as I'd like to about your job.

What are your responsibilities? What's your typical day like? How many divisions or employers does your company have?"
* Take a work/career inventory of your family's friends and business contacts. (You may be surprised to learn that someone your family has known for years actually works in the field you are interested in.)
* Ask people who else you could/should talk to to learn more about a particular field or company.
* Specifically ask who you could approach for an informational interview (i.e., just to learn more about the field or company, not to seek an actual position).

All of these questions should yield some leads. Now your responsibility is to follow through and contact the people you said you'd contact and then thank them in writing later. (It's a nice gesture to send a copy of the thank-you letter to the person who suggested the contact, too. That way they know you have met their friend or associate and can thank them if they wish.)

You may be concerned about putting friends or acquaintances on the spot or bothering them with your job search troubles. One way to handle that is to try to present the facts of your job search in a positive manner, thereby gaining their respect and not scaring them away from helping you. (After all, you are not helpless!) A good way to phrase things positively is to say "I've decided to change my life a bit and am actively looking for a career/job in _____." If you appear eager to face the challenge, they can feel comfortable about offering help or suggestions.

### Colleges and Universities

You probably are familiar with college placement services from your days as a student. Placement offices have become more sophisticated as students have become more focused on career options in addition to a good education.

You don't necessarily have to be a current student to use many of the resources available in the placement offices.

These Bay Area schools have quite active placement offices.

* University of California, Berkeley
* California State University, Hayward
* California State University, San Francisco
* California State University, San Jose
* Stanford University, Palo Alto

### The Telephone Book

It may seem obvious, but this information source is often overlooked.

Don't forget the Yellow Pages. The Bay Area phone books hold valuable information that is well indexed for easy use. For example, the San Francisco Yellow Pages directory has a helpful index in the back of the book that is 30 pages long. Use it.

## 3. TARGETING

Finding the Bay Area job you want requires that you make some tough decisions. It is imperative that you *specifically choose* a target career and a set of firms to pursue. This is not a time to overdo the "keeping your options open" routine. That approach will merely spread your job search energy too thinly and will probably result in frustration.

So, target a career and a set of firms and force yourself to stay on course. If you have no clear idea of which career or list of firms to target, then go back to step 2 and do some more information gathering until you *can* make a clear choice or, at least, eliminate many of the less promising possibilities.

The industry profile chapters in this book can help you with the targeting process since they describe many of the various industries in the Bay Area and list some of the local firms in each field.

In selecting your list of firms you may wish to consider how the company rates in terms of the following.

- Financial Health
- Size
- Growth Phase
- Reputation for Innovation
- Advertising Image
- Market Position
- Office Facilities
- Integrity

Some of you may be saying to yourselves, "My target firm is any one that has a job opening for me. After all, I need a salary." I do not agree with this logic. If you spend all your time vaguely looking for "openings," you may miss an opportunity at the firm that would really be your first choice. A directed, knowledgeable job-searcher is always more attractive to those in the position to hire than the candidate who simply wants any job. For that reason it makes sense to approach the job search by targeting the firm you want rather than by limiting your search to publicized openings. You may want to read more about this approach in *The Hidden Job Market for the 80's,* by Tom Jackson.

Once you have developed your target list of firms, you need to prepare your strategy for getting that job.

## 4. ACTION PLAN

The strategy you will use to get the job is your action plan. You should include everything you plan to do in this plan. For example, your plan for making contacts at a target firm might include:

- attending professional organizational meetings,
- asking your friends who they know who works there, and
- going to the company offices to try to meet an employee or learn a contact name.

Your action plan should also include some attitudinal actions you plan to take. For example, you may wish to make job-finding resolutions similar to these:

- *I will not believe or automatically accept as gospel everything I am told.* (E.g., "We aren't hiring until 1990.") Instead, I will assume that no one at a firm is likely to know about *all* potential job openings. I will keep making contacts at that firm until I become convinced that there really is no hope.
- *I will plan to make at least one job search contact by phone or in person every day.* (Writing letters to personnel departments does not count.)
- *I will make job searching my first priority.* Therefore, I will try not to procrastinate by reading the newspapers, baking brownies, fixing the car, cleaning my closet, or sending out hundreds of useless job inquiry letters and resumes.

You can undoubtedly add some other job search resolutions of your own to your action plan.

No plan can be complete without a timetable. You know from your own life experiences that work tends to expand to fill the available time. This holds true for job searching as well. When making a timetable for your action plan, divide your job search tasks into small steps with many small deadlines. Then, strictly discipline yourself to stick to the timetable.

The action plan you create should include separate actions and time-tables for each target firm on your list. Here is an example of one job seeker's action plan.

### Sample Action Plan

Objective

A marketing manager job with a medium-sized to large firm in the Bay Area.

General Actions

1. Check college alumni office for any classmates who are here in the

Bay Area and might be in marketing. (Call the alumni office by Tuesday.)
2. Call Curtis Nabors (Dad's friend) at Brown Bean Coffee Company for his ideas. (Call by Wednesday.)
3. Check which San Francisco ad agencies have large marketing accounts and ask Cudge Ellingwood (friend from business school) who he knows at those agencies—need information interviews. (Go to library on Wednesday and look in ad agency directory. Call Cudge on Thursday.)
4. Go to an American Marketing Association meeting and try to make some contacts. (Call on Thursday to find out about meeting dates.)
5. Leave the house by 8:30 *every day* to be on my way to some job search–related activity, even if it's only to go back to the library.

SPECIFIC ACTIONS FOR FIRST-CHOICE TARGET FIRM

1. Get an annual report and company newsletter (call or write to the firm by Wednesday.)
2. Call the operator and ask the name of the manager in charge of marketing (call on Tuesday).
3. Check the "Reader's Guide to Periodicals" for any recent magazine or journal articles on the company (Wednesday at the library).
4. Look the company up in *Everybody's Business, An Almanac, The Irreverent Guide to Corporate America,* by Moskowitz, Katz and Levering, published by Harper & Row (Wednesday at the library.)
5. Go over to the company and see if I can meet anyone in an informal way to tell me about the firm's organizational structure, etc. (Thursday).

## 5. CATALOGING

Get some three-by-five cards and use them to catalog the information you have and your action plan for your target companies. On one side, list the useful facts about the firm, such as name, address, phones of contact people. Use the other side to keep track of your action plan ideas and your progress in making contacts at the firm:

- people to call
- letters you've written
- family/friends who may know someone there
- the specific benefits of hiring you for *this* firm.

Carry the cards with you everywhere and review them (like flash-cards) in free moments. Ruminate over them and try to add at least one new idea a day to your action plans.

Write down the smallest bits of information or leads (á la Sherlock Holmes). They may come in handy later.

## 6. POSITIONING AND SELLING YOURSELF: HINTS ON HOW TO HANDLE THE RESUME, COVER LETTER, INTERVIEW, AND THANK YOU.

What are your relatively unique or positive features, and what benefits will you provide the prospective employer? In short, why are you right for the job? That is what positioning yourself is all about.

In order to be effective you must address this kind of question specifically for each company about which you are serious.

The most important rule of thumb for positioning yourself to get the job you want is to force yourself into the habit of thinking of the other guy, not only of yourself and what you need. The other guy in this case is the hiring decision maker at the target firm, and what matters when you are positioning yourself to get the job is to have a clear understanding of what he or she needs.

Consider this example. Here are two descriptions of the same job from the point of view first of the job seeker and then of the hiring manager.

- You (the job seeker) want a job that offers an exciting challenge, in which you will grow, learn new skills, and advance in your career.
- He or she (the hiring manager) needs a hard worker who will take much of the burden of the heavy workload off his or her shoulders, can learn quickly, and will approach problems with confidence and enthusiasm.

It is important to think about this rule of thumb and get into the habit of focusing on the viewpoint of the other guy. Rigorously review every part of your Bay Area job search strategy to be sure you are communicating the benefits for the other guy of hiring you. Once you have really absorbed this concept you are ready to present yourself effectively to your target companies.

### Skills Inventory

Start by reviewing the inventory of your skills and experience (from step 1) and the information you have gathered on your target firms (from step 2). Try to find specific ways to make your skills relevant and beneficial to the target firm. This will really set you apart from other Bay Area job seekers. Here's an example. Your past experience as an assistant buyer at a retail store has at least three selling points for a target job at an ad agency with a large computer account:

- Retail selling has given you good experience selling to customers, identifying consumer needs, defining product benefits, and overcoming obstacles to make a sale.
- Your experience in retailing included use of sophisticated equipment and systems for budget and inventory control. You are very knowledgeable about recent technological breakthroughs in these areas.
- Your job in retailing frequently brought you into contact with the store's advertising department, and you have studied how effective various ad campaigns have been in bringing customers into your department to buy what was advertised.

## Name the Job You Want

Many job seekers at all professional levels go to interviews expecting someone at the prospective firm to tell them what job they can fill. Because of the competition for good jobs in the Bay Area, this approach will not work to your advantage. You must do your own homework and have an understanding of the organizational structure *and job titles* of the target company before you write to or meet the key hiring manager. Then you can name the job you want and explain why you are a good choice for it. Rely on your reading and talks with "gatekeepers," the firm's personnel department and your friends and family contacts. All of these will help you name the job you want, using the language of your target firm. (Remember, you are supposed to be thinking of the other guy's point of view.) Unless you are specifically in an information-only interview, then he or she is not interviewing you merely to educate you about the firm.

## Positioning Your Resume

There are lots of good books on how to write an effective resume. (I recommend *The Damn Good Resume Guide* by Yana Parker, PO Box 3044, Berkeley, CA 94703; $4.95, postage paid.) And there are many opinions about how resumes should be written. Here are some helpful tips from the collective experience of the San Francisco Chamber of Commerce Job Forum Panel:

- Do not send a resume that is not specifically targeted at the firm with a clear job objective. (Vague, general objectives like "management of aggressive marketing firm" seem more annoying than helpful.) Take the time to rewrite the objective and refocus the description of your work experience to make it relevant in terms of implied benefits to your target firm. If you can it is a good idea to name specifically the job title you are looking to fill.

- Descriptions of your height, weight, and health seem silly and irrelevant (interviewers will presumably meet you and can judge your appearance for themselves.)
- Do not try wild or outlandish styles of resumes. These make employers question your good judgment. Typing on good paper stock is fine.
- Have someone check your resume for grammatical errors and typos (you would be amazed at how many are submitted with these childish mistakes).
- Do not mass produce your resume with offset type or "trick folds." These communicate to the employer that you are not specifically interested in them and are blanketing the area with your resume. You want them to feel they are your first choice, so regular office quality typing is preferred.
- Do include honors and community organizations and *briefly* define them if necessary.
- Consider carefully what interests, if any, to include. If included, they should communicate your well-rounded and dynamic approach to life. If they don't, leave them out altogether.
- Word your resume for impact by focusing on action words such as *supervised, planned, initiated, guided, managed, designed, developed, led, coordinated, organized, implemented, advised, monitored,* etc. In other words, explain your last jobs in terms of accomplishments, which are implied benefits for a prospective employer.

**The Cover Letter**

Getting to the point quickly and as relevantly as possible is the key to good business writing. For a good overall guide to cover letters, read *Who's Hiring Who,* by Richard Lathrop, Ten Speed Press. Here is a checklist for cover letter content:

- Demonstrate your knowledge of the firm by naming your job goal by title and even, perhaps, division.
- *Briefly* (in one or two sentences) state why you are right for the job.
- Promise to follow up for an informational telephone call.
- Always address the person by name and title and always call up and check with the operator or personnel department first to be sure it is correct. (Is the manager still employed there? Is he or she still in the job you thought? Are spelling of the name and title correct?)

**Getting an Interview**

A lot has been written about how to act once you are in an interview, but not as much has been written on how to get one in the first place. Writing cover letters and sending your resume is a start, but usually not very effective in getting you in the door. Since the Bay Area job market is competitive, you risk getting the standard "We'll keep you on file" routine (many companies really will keep you on file, but you want a job now). Even if you get this kind of letter, do not assume that this is the end of your chances at that firm. You are still free to recontact the company and try to get an interview.

The Bay Area executives interviewed for this book concur; the best method of creating interview opportunities is this: *find ways to make contacts.*

- Check your family's and friends' contacts again and ask for names of people to call or write to in order to get the chance to spend 15–20 minutes in an informational interview on this firm or field.
- Go to professional club or organizational meetings and introduce yourself. Ask various people if you may call them in the future to arrange for just 15–20 minutes to talk about their job.
- Go over to the company location and try to meet people and ask them about their jobs and their firm. For example, follow someone to a lunch counter and sit next to him or her and introduce yourself. Or if possible, ride the elevators at the firm and introduce yourself cordially and openly to company employees (one on one is best.) Try standing at bus stops or cab stands at quitting time and talk to employees of the firm. Or call or visit the company and try to talk to those gatekeepers (secretaries, receptionists, etc.). Learn the name of the manager to call, then call and ask for an informational interview. If you call before or after work the manager may answer his or her own phone, so 7:30–9:00 A.M. or 5:00–6:30 P.M. are good times to try to reach hiring managers.

Remember that, nine times out of 10, people will admire your nice, friendly, gutsy manner and reward you with some bits of information and/or their time and help. This is especially true if you remember to spend more time asking about them than you spend telling them about you and your needs. There's that rule of thumb again: think of the other guy.

### A Word About Personnel

It is important to keep in mind what the job of the personnel manager is and what it is not. It is not the job (nor the goal) of the personnel department to find jobs for people, but rather to find the best person for a company manager to interview for an existing job opening.

Many job hunters believe that personnel managers cannot help them find a job and so they avoid them. A better strategy is to plan to contact *both* personnel and line managers at your target company. In this way you will be more certain you are being considered by both personnel and the hiring manager, and at most companies both will be involved in a hiring decision.

This book lists a contact person at most Bay Area firms. This person is a good place to start. But, before sending a letter and request for interview always call the company operator and confirm the name and title to be sure the individual is still there. If you see or talk to the personnel manager always try to learn the name, or even a title, of a hiring manager with whom you can follow-up.

Bay Area personnel managers advise you always to try to arrange for someone at the company you are interested in to request that you be interviewed by the department or division in which you want a job. This is apt to work well because it is part of the personnel manager's job to be responsive to requests from company line managers.

### How to Handle the Interview

Be prepared and be sincere.

For hints on interview questions and techniques, read *Sweaty Palms,* by Medley (Van Nostrand, $6.95).

Again, remember to focus on the other person, and keep these tips in mind:

*Don't assume the interviewer has actually read or will remember (or can even find) your resume.* He or she has a lot to think about besides you and the interview. Even though it was scheduled, he or she is probably busy and under pressure and may still be thinking of something else even while interviewing you. For this reason, bring additional copies of the resume with you and offer to take the manager through it and briefly review your past experience.

*An interview is a two-way conversation.* Always have multiple questions in mind and be prepared to take the initiative (especially if the interviewer seems to run out of discussion topics). Be sincerely interested in the answers to any questions you ask.

- Ask the manager about his or her job and typical workday and how it relates to the job to be filled. Ask how the person who is hired will help in accomplishing the day-to-day tasks.
- Ask questions about the interviewer's own career path and experience at the firm. Most people form a very good impression of those who are

interested in them, and you'll learn more about the field or the company from the answers they give.
- Ask to meet other members of the firm (future peers, coworkers, etc.).

*Emphasize your interest in the work, not the location.* Presumably, the hiring manager knows that living in the Bay Area is pleasant (that's probably why he or she is living here). However, if you convey the impression that you want the job mostly because it is in the Bay Area, you are expressing a need of yours rather than offering any benefit of hiring you. When I hear a job seeker say that above all else they want to live here, I immediately question not only their ambition but also the excellence of their credentials.

*Express your interest in the position.* At the end of the interview, always briefly state that you are very interested and explain why you believe you are right for the job and how you will be a benefit to the company and to this hiring manager. Relate your interest to statements made earlier in the interview by the manager. This will show you are genuinely interested in what was said and are basing your judgments about the job at least partially on what he or she told you about the position/company.

## The Thank You

It should be obvious that thinking about the other guy includes *always* writing a brief thank you letter for an interview (even a phone interview). Keep a copy of the letter for yourself.

A thank you letter has these advantages:

- It is common courtesy.
- It reinforces your interest in the job and reminds the recipient that he liked you.
- It distinguishes you from other interviewees, most of whom are too thoughtless to bother to thank a manager for his or her time.
- It gives you a record of when you interviewed.
- You can put your phone number in the letter and once again request a call if any leads or opportunities arise.
- You can succinctly restate the ways hiring you will be of benefit to the hiring manager and the company.

## 7. ASKING FOR FEEDBACK

Most people are tactful and polite and try to be considerate of others' feelings. Unfortunately, this is not very helpful to your job search, since it means they may not readily tell you when you are making incorrect assumptions or are approaching things in the wrong way. Given this social impediment to getting vital information, it is very important that you ask for feedback in the most direct ways possible.

### Example 1: To Hiring Manager

"Ms. Brite, would you mind spending a few extra minutes telling me why you decided to hire the other finalist candidate? I'd like to learn from this experience and improve my chances for the next job opening."

### Example 2: To Friend In The Business

"I'd like to tell you how I plan to begin my interview with Mr. Korab next week. Would you listen to how I plan to present my background and offer me any advice on how to change my emphasis?"

Feedback is the important information you need at every step of your job search process. For those of us who don't relish criticism (who does?), keep in mind that feedback usually includes information on what you are doing *right* as well as wrong. So asking for feedback can be a means to getting the encouragement and morale boost you'll need to keep going.

## 8. REVISING, ADDING, UPDATING YOUR ACTION PLAN

This step is simple: learn from experience. Ask yourself, "What did I learn today that could help me go about this search better or differently? What else could I try?"

The easiest way to add to your action plan is to find out from the people you meet what they suggest you try next. If you are successful in getting an information interview at a target firm, *always* ask who else you should meet or telephone to further the process. Always ask for suggestions. Always ask managers what they would do if they were in your position.

Often job seekers are not really very thorough about following the action strategies they lay out. You may get discouraged or get too scattered in your search activities. To prevent that syndrome, go back to your action plan and review it carefully to be sure you really have followed all the leads. Take the time to refocus, revise, and reconsider.

## 9. PERSEVERING

Blind perseverance probably won't work. Creative persistence probably will. Here's how you can do it:

Welcome negatives (turndowns, dead ends, etc.) as signs that positive things may start happening soon. And try to learn from your negative experiences.

When you reach a dead end, try to think of new ways to develop additional job search activities that may work better. For example, you may wish to gather a group of friends or business associates for a brainstorming session. The subject is your job search, and the group tries to develop additional options for you to try. Your role is to give out information from your research and to be open to any suggestions they make. (Note: You did not plan this meeting to prove that finding you a job is impossible, did you?)

If quite some time has passed since you approached your first target firms, go back and start again with new contacts and recontacts. Their employment situation could have changed, so call back and inquire. Above all, don't assume that, since they told you they'd keep you in mind or your resume on file, you are automatically first in line for any opening. Since you are not yet employed and you are still interested, call back and say so. They will probably not conclude that you are a pest. It's more likely that your interest in a job with them will seem more genuine. They will respect you for your perseverance.

Be courageous. Try new things. Ask yourself, "What's the worst thing that could happen to me if I try this and it doesn't work?" Also ask, "What's the best thing that could happen?"

Remember, in a very short while no one will recall how long and difficult your job search might have been. All they will remember is that you are the person who landed that great job in the San Francisco Bay Area.

# Part II: Industry Profiles

This section of the book contains industry profiles of all the major fields in the Bay Area. Approximately 65 different industries are listed, accompanied by information garnered from personal and telephone interviews with more than 1,000 insiders in Bay Area companies.

Each chapter provides some perspective about the field, the current trends in it, the challenges managers are facing, and the size and vitality of the field in the Bay Area. Also included in each chapter is a listing of the key Bay Area companies, with names of individuals to contact for employment at the firm. Where relevant, the number of employees, dollar sales or billings, and other descriptive information are also included.

Perhaps the most important, and often the most difficult, part of an effective job search is making contacts at target firms. This book makes it easy for you! This portion of the book lists many clubs, associations, organizations and publications recommended by executives in each field. You can use this insider advice to gain information and make contact with other managers in your field.

Because some of this information can get out of date quickly as managers or company offices move, be sure to call and check names and addresses before sending off your resume or visiting a company. Use the contact names in this book to lead you to the appropriate hiring manager.

# 6

# Finance

The field of finance is diverse and competitive, and Bay Area financial institutions are at the forefront of innovative changes in management and marketing.

Included in this chapter are discussions of accounting, banks and savings and loans, insurance, and brokerage.

Other financial businesses in the Bay Area include the smaller investment counselors and portfolio managers; they are not listed here but should be considered in your job search.

## *Accounting*

Career opportunities requiring an accounting background are found in all kinds of business and industry. And in relatively difficult economic times, accounting professionals tend to do even better than usual because more businesses turn to accounting professionals more frequently for auditing or management consultation.

Accounting jobs fall into three basic categories: public, private (business), and government accounting.

Due to cutbacks in government spending the opportunities in the private and public sectors are more numerous than through government accounting.

Public accountants are hired on a fee basis by outside businesses, whereas private accountants receive a salary and work on internal financial affairs for their employer companies.

The field of accounting is broad and covers maintenance of simple budget records to complex top management financial decisions. Some of the many functions may include those of auditor (testing company systems for accuracy), cost accountant (unit cost analysis and inventory), controller or comptroller (accounting director), forecast accountant (planner), and tax accountant (prepares tax returns and identifies tax advantages).

In this chapter the focus is on the big public accounting firms, in which it is estimated that more than half of the nation's accountants start their careers. However, all corporations have an accounting function, and large companies require the services of many different accounting specialists.

Public accounting firms usually have three different functional departments:

- tax
- auditing
- management consulting

Each year, entry level positions are available in the tax and auditing functions. In the Bay Area the big firms recruit 90 percent of their entry level employees from local colleges and universities. Most of this recruiting is completed in the spring of each year.

The management or investment consulting functions, on the other hand, require experienced personnel with three to 10 years' experience in business.

In the state of California you must have had two years' experience with an accounting firm and have passed the examination given by the American Institute of Certified Public Accountants before you can become a certified public accountant (CPA). The exam is considered quite difficult and covers four areas: accounting practices, theory, commercial law, and audits.

Your chances for advancement and salary increase significantly with attainment of CPA status.

Here are some of the Bay Area resources to contact for information or help in a job search in accounting:

California Society of Certified Public Accountants
  100 Pine St.
San Francisco, CA 94111
(415) 986-5254

*Contact:* Robert Knox; very knowledgeable and helpful to job seekers. Society keeps job file and resumes.

## ACCOUNTING JOB TITLES AND SALARY RANGES

In public accounting firms the career path begins with an entry-level job called *staff assistant* or *staff accountant.* In this job you perform routine work under close supervision. After about three to four years you can qualify as a *senior accountant.* At this level you are responsible for client contact and client projects (e.g., audits). With experience you may become a *manager* and then perhaps a *partner* in the firm.

It is quite common for senior accountants and managers to leave their public accounting firms to work for a former client company on a full-time basis.

- Staff Accountant: $18,000–$23,000
- Senior Accountant: $20,000–$30,000
- Manager: $40,000–$70,000
- Partner: $100,000 +

In government accounting positions the salaries and titles are essentially the same as in public accounting firms. In private industry, however, corporate accountants earn approximately 20–40% more.

In corporate accounting, entry level jobs are often *ledger accountant, junior internal auditor,* or *accountant trainee.* As you advance the jobs include *cost accountant, budget director, manager of audit, controller, treasurer, vice president finance,* or *president* of the corporation.

- Entry Level: $12,000–$17,000
- 1-3 years experience
  (Auditor, Accountant, etc.): $20,000–$30,000
- 3-5 years experience: $26,000–$40,000
- Chief Accountant, Manager, etc: $45,000–$60,000

## INSIDERS' ADVICE

Employers say they look for analytical people with good quantitative and organizational abilities. Graduates who have worked part-time in business while in school will have greater opportunities for full time jobs. Tact and discretion are sought because accountants are trusted with confidential information about the firms' financial decisions and status. To get to the top of the profession, accountants usually must continue their study. Accounting firms and accounting associations often offer seminars for continuing education.

## ACCOUNTING DIRECTORY

**Arthur Andersen & Company**    (415) 546-8200
1 Market Plaza
Spear Street Tower
Suite 3500
San Francisco, CA 94105
*Contact:* John Greene, Managing Partner
*Description:* Management consulting, tax, audit; headquarters in Chicago.

**Coopers & Lybrand**    (415) 957-3000
333 Market St.
San Francisco, CA 94104
*Contact:* Bob Harper, Personnel Director; James T. Clark, Managing Partner
*Description:* Primarily finance, 60 percent in auditing; also tax, benefits, and
    compensation consulting and computer auditing; headquarters in New York
    City.

**Deloite, Haskins & Sells**    (415) 393-4300
44 Montgomery St.
San Francisco, CA 94104
*Contact:* David Paulson, Recruiting Manager
*Description:* Full-service accounting firm including accounting, audit, and
    management services; headquarters in New York City.

**Ernst & Whinney**    (415) 981-8890
555 California St.
Ste. 3000
San Francisco, CA 94104
*Contact:* Marilyn Marx, Personnel
*Description:* Auditing, accounting, tax, and management information services;
    headquarters in Cleveland, Ohio.

**John F. Forbes & Company**    (415) 398-1212
4 Embarcadero Center
San Francisco, CA 94111
*Contact:* Bruce Yarian, Director, Professional Personnel
*Description:* Bay Area-based accounting firm with auditing and full
    accounting services.

**Peat Marwick Mitchell & Company**    (415) 981-8230
3 Embarcadero Center
San Francisco, CA 94111
*Contact:* Larry Cushing, Tax Partner; Dave Estabrook, Recruiting Manager,
    Audit; Don Castle, Consulting
*Description:* 50–60 percent finance, 3 divisions: audit, tax, and consulting.

**Price Waterhouse Company**    (415) 393-8500
555 California St.
36th Fl.
San Francisco, CA 94104
*Contact:* Gary Bellat, Recruiting Manager
*Description:* Finance, audit, tax, and management advice; headquarters in
  New York City.

**Touche Ross & Company**    (415) 781-9570
1 Maritime Plaza
San Francisco, CA 94111
*Contact:* Joe Palazzola, Director of Personnel; Mary Henshell, Recruiting
  Manager
*Description:* Finance and tax consulting services, mergers and acquisition
  consulting, legal consulting; headquarters in New York City.

**Arthur Young & Company**    (415) 393-2700
1 Post St.
San Francisco, CA 94104
*Contact:* John Crosby, Recruiting Manager
*Description:* Finance, operations, general management; audit and accounting
  are largest; headquarters in New York City.

## Banking

San Francisco is the finance capital of the western United States.
There are approximately 40 commercial banks and 25 savings and loan
associations in San Francisco, with many branches throughout the nine-
county Bay Area.

Recently the profit margins of the nation's banks and savings and
loans have been squeezed because of the low-interest, long-term real
estate loans in their portfolios. In addition, the fluctuating interest rates
have reduced the level of low cost demand and savings deposits, which
has cut further into profits.

Deregulation has blurred the distinctions between banks and savings
and loan associations, and they are competing fiercely to win the role of
primary financial institution for the consumer. Banks are also competing
with the money market funds offered by brokerage houses, and Sears,
the nation's largest retail chain, has gotten into the act by purchasing
Dean Witter and offering a "supermarket" of financial services. Competition has come to banking, and though the consumer may be the
short-term winner due to the new financial packages being offered, the
long-term implications are unclear for both consumers and the banks
and savings and loan institutions that we know today.

One result of all these events has been the creation of all kinds of new programs, promotions, and deals offered by financial institutions, especially by the major California institutions. There are the "asset management accounts" offered by Crocker and Wells Fargo to compete with the money market funds. There are all sorts of new mortgage arrangements (e.g., "flexible payments," "renegotiable rates," "graduated payments" and "balloon payments"). More recently the banks and savings and loans have been able to offer market rate savings and checking accounts that will bring deposits back from the money market funds with the lure of federal insurance and greater convenience. And there's the move by bank lobbyists for Congress to allow geographic expansion so that banks and savings and loans are better able to compete with less regulated financial institutions.

The implications of the climate facing banks and savings and loans include major bank reorganizations, cutbacks in bank expenses (mainly payroll), and a deluge of advertising offers to attract consumer dollars.

The implications for job hunters are clear. Banks will be more leanly staffed, so to get a job you will have to sell yourself even more effectively than in the past. There are, however, opportunities if you emphasize your experience or ability in communication, creative problem solving, and consumer marketing. Financial institutions are becoming more oriented to service, and they need new kinds of managers who will contribute to the fundamental changes in the ways banks manage their businesses.

Most of the large financial institutions are geared to regular recruiting of MBAs and college graduates, and they will send career pamphlets on request. Training programs, especially at the larger institutions, have traditionally been excellent and quite comprehensive. In spite of profit pressures, most Bay Area banks say they expect to continue these programs.

Banks make most hiring decisions based on experience, and college degrees are not necessary if the individual has some banking experience. Systems and·data processing professionals, along with marketing product managers with excellent financial skills, seem to be in great demand.

For more information on banking, you may wish to read these periodicals:

- *Banking Journal,* published by the American Bankers Association
- *Bankers Magazine*
- *Pacific Banker and Business*
- *Western Banker*
- *The American Banker* (the industry's daily newspaper)

Local clubs and organizations that may be of some help include:

American Institute of Banking
650 California St., Ste. 846
San Francisco, CA 94108
(415) 392-5286

California Bankers Association
650 California St.
San Francisco, CA 94104
(415) 433-1894

The services of these organizations are aimed at bank managers who are at the middle level and above.

For an expanded list of banks and contacts, write to *Western Banker* publishers at 49 Geary St., Ste. 210, San Francisco, CA 94104; (415) 362-5452. Request their *Directory of Western State Commercial Banks* ($21.50).

For savings and loan information, contact Federal Home Loan Bank of California, PO Box 7948, San Francisco, CA 94120; (415) 393-1000. Request the *Directory of Savings & Loans* ($7).

## BANKING JOB TITLES AND SALARY RANGES

There are usually four basic functions common to full-service banks:

- commercial banking
- trust
- investment
- operations and administration

Commercial banking may be divided into corporate, loan administration, credit card, and real estate functions.

The trust department may include personal and institutional services in legal as well as advisory functions such as pension policy, asset allocation, retirement planning, and investment research.

The investment (or funding) area oversees the bank's assets and liabilities and may include trading, money market management, and strategic funding. The operations and administration department may include support functions such as computer services, electronic banking, public relations, financial analysis, personnel, and property management. Functions such as marketing, if not centralized in a marketing department, are often part of the bank's commercial banking and consumer banking divisions.

Many Bay Area banks offer training programs. Credit training can lead to a career as a loan officer or branch manager. Lending experience is considered a good foundation for bank management. There are also training opportunities in operations, systems, trust, customer service, and marketing.

In general an advanced degree is necessary for a job in commercial or investment banking, whereas college or even high school may suffice for jobs in other departments at lower levels.

In the Bay Area banking salaries vary widely, depending on the size of the bank, your degree, and your experience.

MBAs are generally recruited from the top business schools and may start with salaries of approximately $27,000–$32,000.

A management trainee without the MBA degree may begin at $15,000–$19,000.

Here are approximate salary ranges for a variety of higher-level banking positions:

|  | Bank Assets Under $40 Million | Bank Assets $100–$250 Million | Bank Assets $1 Billion Plus |
|---|---|---|---|
| Junior Loan Officer | $18,000 | $21,000 | $26,000 |
| Mortgage Loan Dept. Manager | $33,000 | $38,000 | $42,000 |
| Operations Manager | $30,000 | $36,000 | $39,000 |
| Branch Manager | $23,000 | $27,000 | $35,000 |
| Investment Manager | $35,000 | $45,000 | $85,000 |
| Marketing Manager | $30,000 | $40,000 | $75,000 |
| Data Processing Manager | $35,000 | $40,000 | $80,000 |
| Chief Executive Officer | $70,000 | $150,000 | up to $700,000 |

## INSIDERS' ADVICE

Bay Area employers point out that the new emphasis in banking will be on a combination of quantitative and marketing/selling skills. People who can contribute this special combination will have a big advantage in the job search.

Another highly desirable background is an MBA with a systems analysis orientation.

A frequently voiced complaint of bankers was that job seekers seemed not to know the differences among the various banking functions and had not done their homework. If you are interested in a banking career, write for the career booklets the banks offer so that you can see what departments or functions are emphasized. Another helpful move may be to visit a small branch of the bank or savings and loan and interview the branch manager or local bank president for information.

Local bankers point out that job seekers often overlook the estimated 10 European and Asian banks that are located in the Bay Area. For those who have an interest in international banking these can offer good opportunities. Many American banks, of course, also have financial connections to foreign banks (e.g., Security Pacific, Bank of California).

Banks say they will be looking for entrepreneurial, analytical risk takers with good decision-making skills who can contribute to the new banking organizations that will be emerging over the next few years.

Finally, in your first assignment, unless you are involved in a formal training program, try to avoid a suburban branch, since in such a location it may take quite a while for management to identify you as a high-potential employee.

## BANKING DIRECTORY

**Bank of America**   (415) 622-3456
#3616
Personnel Administration
PO Box 37000
San Francisco, CA 94137
*Contact:* Michael Reid, Management Recruiting
*Description:* World's largest commercial bank. Operates in 90 nations. Entry
   level positions in credit, operations, or systems functions in one of four
   division: (1) California branch banking, (2) global wholesale banking, (3)
   administration, and (4) systems and data processing. Offers training
   programs. Write Bank of America for its job pamphlet called *A Place for
   You in the New World of Banking.*

**Bank of California**   (415) 765-0400
400 California St.
San Francisco, CA 94145
*Contact:* Peggy Taylor, Manager of Human Resources
*Description:* Oldest incorporated commercial bank in the West. Training
   programs for college graduates, MBAs, and bank employees who wish to
   advance.

**California First Bank**   (415) 445-0200
350 California St.
San Francisco, CA 94104
*Contact:* Debbie Andrews, Personnel, Steve Antwell, Personnel
*Description:* Headquarters of an international commercial bank which is a

subsidiary of the Bank of Tokyo Ltd. (which owns 78 percent of the shares). The bank has two subsidiaries: (1) Bankers Commercial Corporation, equipment leasing; and (2) Cal First Properties, property holdings, which offers a training program to BAs called Loan Associates Program.

**Central Bank**   (415) 676-3500
399 Taylor Blvd.
Pleasant Hill, CA 94523
*Contact:* Susan McCormick, Human Resources
*Description:* Commercial bank with 20 branches. Divisions include finance, branch administration, operations, real estate, and administrative services.

**Crocker National Corporation**   (415) 477-0456
1 Montgomery St.
San Francisco, CA 94104
*Contact:* Mavis Varien, VP, Personnel; Scott Lakis, Branch Employment— (213) 253-3591; Dave Norris, Branch Systems; Drew Langevin, Recruiting Manager; Dave Lewis, College Relations.
*Description:* Twelfth-largest bank in the United States. Divisions include commercial services, domestic branch, international branch, investment management, merchant banking, money market, real estate industries, and operations. Offers training program in several divisions. Write for a job pamphlet called *Find Your Place in the Future of Crocker Bank.*

**Fair Isaac & Companies**   (415) 472-2211
55 Mitchell Blvd.
San Rafael, CA 94903
*Contact:* Sue Kramer, Personnel
*Description:* Bank service company specializing in credit and approval system.

**Fidelity Financial Corporation**   (415) 465-0628
1430 Franklin St.
Oakland, CA 94612
*Contact:* Manager of Human Resources.
*Description:* Second-largest savings and loan in Bay Area; ranked 21st in the United States. Recently acquired by Citicorp of New York.

**First Interstate Bank of California**   (415) 544-5000
405 Montgomery St.
San Francisco, CA 94104
*Contact:* Manager of Employment Resources
*Description:* Commercial bank and holding company for First Interstate Bank Corporation, headquartered in Los Angeles; largest multistate banking corporation in the United States.

**Great Western Financial Corporation**   (415) 788-1036
401 California St.
San Francisco, CA 94104
*Contact:* Gladys Saunders, Personnel

*Description:* Savings and loan association headquartered in Los Angeles. Divisions include retail customer services, real estate services, administrative services, and property development.

**Golden West Financial Corp.**   (415) 645-9420
1970 Broadway
Oakland, CA 94612
*Contact:* Manager of Human Resources
*Description:* Eighth-largest savings and loan and largest in the Bay Area.

**Hibernia**   (415) 505-7388
201 California St.
San Francisco, CA 94111
*Contact:* Phillip Pellerita, Manager, Personnel
*Description:* Headquarters of commercial bank with 21 branch offices in Bay Area; entry positions in commercial lending and data processing.

**Northern California Savings & Loan**   (415) 326-2790
300 Hamilton Ave.
Palo Alto, CA 94301
*Contact:* Manager Human Resources

**Homestead Financial Corporation**   (415) 692-1432
1777 Murchison Dr.
Burlingame, CA 94010
*Contact:* Manager Human Resources
*Description:* Savings and loan with 28 California offices.

**San Francisco Federal Reserve Bank**   (415) 544-2000
101 Market St.
San Francisco, CA 94120
*Contact:* Susan Hoffman, Employment
*Description:* Part of the Federal Reserve System ("the bank's bank"). Established to serve and regulate nation's banks, always recruiting for computer systems and bank analysts. Write for pamphlet *Career Perspective with San Francisco Federal Reserve Bank.*

**San Francisco Federal Savings & Loan**   (415) 982-8100
85 Post St.
San Francisco, CA 94104
*Contact:* Norman Bowen, Personnel
*Description:* Savings and loan with 32 branches in the Bay Area.

**Security Pacific National Bank**   (415) 445-4298
1 Embarcadero Center
San Francisco, CA 94111
*Contact:* Catherine Bursey, Assistant Vice-President, Personnel
*Description:* Tenth-largest commercial bank in United States; headquartered in Los Angeles. Offers management associate training program of seven months (80 percent on the job and 20 percent classroom instruction); write

to *College Relations Coordinator,* Box 2097 Terminal Annex, Los Angeles, CA 90051 for training information.

**Transamerica Financial Services**    (415) 474-7200
1301 Post St.
San Francisco, CA 94115
*Contact:* Manager of Human Resources
*Description:* Subsidiary of TransAmerica Corporation; consumer lending service.

**Wells Fargo**    (415) 396-0123
420 Montgomery St.
San Francisco, CA 94101
*Contact:* Careers Information Coordinator, (415) 396-2765; Susan McGovern, Employment Manager
*Description:* Eleventh-largest commercial bank. Departments include retail banking, commercial banking, corporate banking, credit card, business services, escrow, marketing, customer relations, international banking, operations, trust, and funding. Offers traning programs. Write for the pamphlet *Career Information Planning System.*

**Citizen Savings & Loan Association**    (415) 772-1400
700 Market St.
San Francisco, CA 94102
*Contact:* Virginia Livingston, Personnel
*Description:* Major savings & loan

**Federal Home Loan Bank**    (415) 393-1000
600 California St.
San Francisco, CA 94108
*Contact:* Jody Altman, Human Resources
*Description:* Central bank for 200 California, Arizona, and Nevada savings and loans.

**Golden State Sanwa Bank**    (415) 772-8371
300 Montgomery St.
San Francisco, CA 94104
*Contact:* Personnel Department
*Description:* Headquarters for large international bank.

**Toronto Dominion Bank**    (415) 989-4900
114 Sansome St.
San Francisco, CA 94104
*Contact:* Thomas Bassett, Personnel
*Description:* U.S. headquarters for full-service bank.

**World Savings & Loan Association**    (415) 645-9250
1970 Broadway
Oakland, CA 94612
*Contact:* Stephen Voss, Employee Relations
*Description:* Nation's sixth largest savings and loan association.

## *Diversified Financial Investments and Leasing*

The Bay Area has a broad range of diversified companies whose operating income comes primarily from leasing, lending, investment syndication and other financial services. There are two basic kinds of leasing firms: 1) those that own the property and lease it to corporate users; 2) those who broker or package the transaction for investment by individuals or groups looking for investments and tax write-offs.

Generally, the bank companies represent the first group. Major bank corporations with large leasing divisions include Transamerica Corporation, Bank of America, Crocker Bank, Wells Fargo Bank, Security Pacific Bank, and First Interstate Bank just to name a few.

Bay Area leasing companies who broker investments divide broadly into those who specialize in: a) transportation and equipment, b) real estate, c) oil and gas natural resource exploration.

Job titles and functions in leasing companies usually include lease administration, investor services, marketing, accounting, data processing, public relations and legal. An entry level position may be junior financial analyst or administrative assistant. Business degrees with emphasis on bookkeeping and accounting are preferred.

For more information on leasing companies consider these sources:

Association of Equipment Leasors
1300 North 17th Street, Suite 1010
Arlington, VA 22209
(703) 527-8655
Association for member firms publishes a newsletter which discusses
  trends in investment leasing.

Real Estate Forum
12 West 37th Street
New York City, NY 10018
(212) 563-6460
Publication highlights real estate investment issues.

National Real Estate Investor
(404) 256-9800
Publication on trends in real estate investment.

## LEASING

### Bank Corporations

**Transamerica Corporation**   (415) 983-4000
600 Montgomery St.
San Francisco, CA 94111
*Contact:* Personnel Department

*Description:* A diversified company with 10 major companies and many
smaller ones. 70 percent of income comes from insurance and financial
services. Specializes in transportation and equipment leasing.

**Security Pacific Leasing Corporation**   (415) 445-4482
4 Embarcadero Center
San Francisco, CA 94111
*Contact:* Dorothy Brook, Personnel
*Description:* Subsidiary which specializes in leasing computers, industrial
equipment, planes, ships, etc.


## Transportation and Equipment Leasing

**Brae Corporation**   (415) 951-1500
4 Embarcadero Center
San Francisco, CA 94111
*Contact:* William Texido, President
*Employs:* 500
*Description:* Transportation leasing and management: rail cars, containers,
trucking, etc.

**GATX Leasing Corporation**   (415) 955-3200
4 Embarcadero Center
San Francisco, CA 94111
*Contact:* Personnel Department
*Employs:* 212
*Description:* One of the largest nonbank leasing companies in the world.
Departments include finance, marketing, personnel, controllers and financial
analysts. Hires MBAs.

**Itel Corporation**   (415) 955-0615
1 Embarcadero Center
San Francisco, CA 94111
*Contact:* Mary Llewellyn, Corporate Communications
*Employs:* 1,100
*Description:* Large transportation equipment and leasing company most well
known for its 1979 bankruptcy.

**United States Leasing International, Inc.**   (415) 323-8111
633 Battery St.
San Francisco, CA 94111
*Contact:* Anne Halsted, Personnel
*Employs:* 750
*Description:* Largest subsidiary U.S. leasing corporation: transportation,
communication, and high technology-computer leasing. It is the largest
independent leasing company in U.S.

**PLM, Inc.**   (415) 989-1860
50 California St.
San Francisco, CA 94111
*Contact:* Janett Spirer, Personnel
*Employs:* 50
*Description:* Specializes in brokerage leasing and maintaining of rail cars (coal cars).

**Phoenix Leasing, Inc.**   (415) 383-9700
495 Miller Ave.
Mill Valley, CA 94941
*Contact:* Rima Vogensen, Personnel
*Employs:* 100
*Description:* Specializes in brokerage leasing of computer equipment.


REAL ESTATE LEASING

**Fox & Carskadon Financial Corporation**   (415) 574-3333
2755 Campus Dr., #300
San Mateo, CA 94403
*Contact:* David Marzen, Personnel Director
*Employs:* 300
*Description:* Real estate investment syndication broker.

**Consolidated Capital Equities Corporation**   (415) 652-7171
1900 Powell St.
Emeryville, CA 94608
*Contact:* Elizabeth Schaeffer, Personnel Manager
*Employs:* 240
*Description:* Real estate investments and limited partnerships.

**Robert A. McNeill Corporation**   (415) 572-0600
2255 Campus Dr.
San Mateo, CA 94403
*Contact:* Mike Spencer, Personnel Director
*Employs:* 400
*Description:* Limited partnerships for real estate investment, primarily shopping centers and condominiums.

**Boothe Financial Corporation**   (415) 989-6580
100 Bush St.
San Francisco, CA 94104
*Contact:* Cynthia Vincent, Office Manager
*Employs:* 16
*Description:* Real estate investment brokerage and services.

**Oil and Gas**

**Mission Resources**    (415) 638-1800
PO Box 2300
800 Edgewater Dr.
Oakland, CA 94614
*Contact:* Tina Melton, Personnel Manager
*Employs:* 50
*Description:* Limited partnerships for exploration and development of oil/gas
   resources.

## Brokerage

There are four good reasons for considering the field of brokerage in
the Bay Area.

First, you work on your own, on commission, with no direct supervision and no boss to speak of. Second, you can make a lot of money.
During your first year as a broker you could make $30,000, the second
year $50,000 and after five years $100,000. Brokerage houses will even
pay you a stipend of $800–$2,000 a month while you are going through
the training and licensing process, which can take up to a year. Third,
the Bay Area continues to offer a lot of opportunities in brokerage since
it is the West Coast's financial center and because it continues to be better off economically than most other major urban areas. Fourth, no particular background or training is required to get hired. Brokerage firms
look for self-confident, assertive personalities, good general knowledge
(especially of current events and some business), self-discipline, and
strong motivation.

There are some popular misconceptions about this field. Many people
believe that brokers are a stodgy, gray-pin-striped lot. In California at
least, the dress mode is more casual, and brokers tend to be high-energy,
interesting people. Many people have the idea that brokers have easy
hours and earn easy money. This isn't true either. Brokers must work
hard and keep long hours. They may start work at 7:00 A.M. with the
opening of the New York Stock Exchange and usually leave at 3:00 or
4:00 P.M. There is weekend and evening work, and the work is difficult
in that you are selling and will usually receive 100 "nos" for every "yes"
you get.

The top three brokerage houses in the United States are Dean Witter,
Merrill Lynch, and E.F. Hutton. Their San Francisco Bay Area offices,
as well as those of many other brokerage houses, are listed in the Brokerage Directory in this chapter.

Dean Witter was founded here in San Francisco in 1926 and was recently acquired by Sears.

As background for a job in brokerage, start by regularly reading journals such as these:

- *Barron's*
- *Forbes*
- *Tax Shelter Digest*
- *Registered Representative*
- *Wall Street Journal*
- *Institutional Investing Magazine*
- *Robert Stanger Report*

General information on brokerage is available at the local office of the National Association of Security Dealers at (415) 781-3434.

Other sources of information include:

- *The Only Investment Guide You'll Ever Need* by Andrew Tobias.
- Investment seminars that are offered by local brokerage houses such as Dean Witter and Merrill Lynch.

## Brokerage Job Titles and Salary Ranges

Sales is the primary career area in brokerage. You begin as a *trainee*, usually at a branch office. Once you pass the registered representative exam, you are called a *broker* and must begin to develop your own client list and work on commission. Your progression depends on your winning new clients through referrals or in developing good clients who wish to invest heavily in your services. Some brokers become *sales managers* and then *branch office managers*. Some brokers establish their own firms and pay a commission to a member of an exchange. A few become members of the stock exchange themselves.

An alternate career path is through research, beginning as a *trainee* or *analyst* in the research department. You may become a *senior analyst* next, then a *portfolio manager* or an *investment counselor*.

As mentioned earlier, sales trainees may be paid $800–$2,000 a month during training. After they become brokers they can expect to earn at least $30,000 a year. Higher annual earnings will depend on their sales skills and the economy. In the Bay Area making $60,000 a year is not uncommon for a broker.

Analysts' salaries compare favorably with brokers' incomes. In the Bay Area research trainees with a bachelor's degree in economics, business, or liberal arts may start at $16,000, and by the time they reach senior analyst the salary is likely to be $30,000–$45,000.

## INSIDERS' ADVICE

Most Bay Area brokerage houses have several offices, and the branch manager makes the hiring decisions. The best way to proceed is to contact a couple of friendly brokers for informational interviews to learn their insights about their jobs and familiarize yourself with the lingo. A good time to contact brokers is after 1:00 and before 3:00 P.M. (In the mornings they are generally tied up with the stock exchange.) Keep in mind that you can approach them for information on investment options and ask them to tell you about their jobs while you are there.

Brokers advise that their personnel departments are not the best bet for career level job seekers. You stand a better chance of being hired when you select the brokerage office at which you'd like to work and then contact the branch manager with an impressive marketing pitch that tells why you'd make an excellent broker.

Brokerage houses will be looking for good sales skills, strong ambition, effective communications abilities, and grace under pressure.

## BROKERAGE DIRECTORY

**Bache, Halsey, Stuart, Shields**    (415) 981-0440
350 California St.
San Francisco, CA 94104
*Contact:* Branch Manager.
*Employs:* 3,000 nationwide; 72 in Bay Area.
*Training:* Three months at branch, one month in New York; must pass rigid
    requirements for licenses for commodities, insurance, state, etc.
*Description:* Full-service financial investment house offering 75 products,
    including stocks, commodities, securities, gold, silver, insurance, etc. One of
    the top 10 brokerage houses.

**Birr Wilson & Co. Inc.**    (415) 983-7700
155 Sansome St.
San Francisco, CA 94104
*Contact:* W.D. McGee, Marketing Manager for brokerage positions.
*Employs:* 168 in Bay Area.
*Description:* Headquarters of West Coast full service broker/dealer.

**Dean Witter Reynolds Inc.**    (415) 955-6000
101 California St.
San Francisco, CA 94111
*Contact:* Conrad Frankowski, Hiring Manager.
*Employs:* 550 in Bay Area.
*Description:* Largest Bay Area brokerage house; only brokerage firm
    headquartered in Bay Area, with 12 offices here.

**E.F. Hutton & Co. Inc.** (415) 362-3212
400 California St.
San Francisco, CA 94104
*Contact:* Branch Manager.
*Employs:* Approximately 50 in San Francisco Bay Area.
*Description:* One of the top 10 brokerage houses in the United States.

**Goldman Sachs & Company** (415) 393-7500
555 California St.
San Francisco, CA 94104
*Contact:* Branch Manager.
*Employs:* Approximately 70 in the San Francisco office.
*Description:* Old-line investment banking house.

**International Trading Group** (415) 433-6200
120 Montgomery St.
San Francisco, CA 94104
*Contact:* Larhonda James, Personnel, at San Mateo office, 60 East 3rd Street, San Mateo, CA, 94402.
*Description:* Commodity broker.

**Kidder Peabody & Co. Inc.** (415) 398-6400
555 California St.
San Francisco, CA 94104
*Contact:* Stewart Spence, Branch Manager.
*Employs:* Approximately 150.
*Description:* One of the largest investment banking and brokerage houses in the United States.

**Merrill Lynch, Pierce, Fenner, & Smith Inc.** (415) 445-7000
300 California St.
San Francisco, CA 94111
*Contact:* Sales Manager at branch office.
*Employs:* 325 in Bay Area.
*Description:* Biggest brokerage house in the United States.

**Pacific Stock Exchange** (415) 393-4000
301 Pine St.
San Francisco, CA 94111
*Contact:* Ann Buckley, Director of Personnel.
*Description:* Headquarters of Pacific Stock Exchange. Employs finance, accounting, marketing, personnel, and data processors. Entry level is as a runner on the trading floor. Brokerage firms are members and employ clerks and floor brokers. There is also a trading floor in Los Angeles.

**Paine Webber Inc.** (415) 954-6700
555 California St.
San Francisco, CA 94104
*Contact:* James Klein, Branch Manager.
*Employs:* Approximately 40 in San Francisco.

*Description:* Full-service investment brokers handling stocks, bonds, annuities, tax shelters, etc.

**Salomen Bros.**   (415) 951-1777
555 California St., Ste. 3900
San Francisco, CA 94104
*Contact:* Kris McLay, Operations Manager.
*Employs:* Approximately 60 in San Francisco.
*Description:* Oldline investment banking house.

**Charles Schwab & Co. Inc.**   (415) 546-1777
1 2nd St.
San Francisco, CA 94105
*Contact:* Charles Schwab, President.
*Employs:* Approximately 65 in Bay Area.
*Description:* Discount brokerage house, recently acquired by Bank of America. Hires only licensed brokers.

**Shearson-American Express, Inc.**   (415) 362-7440
555 California St., Ste. 3500
San Francisco, CA 94104
*Contact:* Branch Manager.
*Employs:* Hires only licensed brokers.
*Description:* One of the top 10 brokerage houses in the United States.

**Smith, Barney, Harris, Upham & Co. Inc.**   (415) 955-1500
350 California St.
San Francisco, CA 94104
*Contact:* Louise Vogel, Branch Manager.
*Employs:* Approximately 30 in San Francisco.
*Description:* One of the top 10 investment brokerage firms; private, international.

**Sutro & Company, Inc.**   (415) 445-8550
201 California St.
San Francisco, CA 94111
*Contact:* Astrid Broess, Personnel.
*Employs:* 225 in Bay Area.
*Description:* Full service financial investment house with eight Bay Area branches.

## Insurance

The Bay Area has a high concentration of insurance companies. Most of the big eastern firms have branch offices here, and two insurance firms, Fireman's Fund and Industrial Indemnity, were founded and have headquarters here.

Most job seekers have a misconception of the opportunities in insurance. People tend to think in terms of only three kinds of jobs in insurance: the insurance salesman who sells individuals or corporations an insurance program; the underwriter, who evaluates the risk of a potential client and prices the premium; and the claims adjuster, who determines the validity of claims and authorizes payments. In reality there are available jobs in insurance firms in advertising, corporate communications, engineering, law, health, data processing, personnel, and accounting, to name just a few.

There is a world of difference between firms that specialize in property and casualty and those who specialize in life. These companies have different philosophies and different career paths. Basically, the training period is longer for certain lines of business in property and casualty than in life, and there is some opportunity to select a line of insurance for which you may have a real aptitude, interest, or background (e.g., ocean marine, auto, workmen's compensation, health, individual or group life).

There are two kinds of insurance companies: stock companies such as Fireman's Fund and Hartford, whose business comes from licensed insurance brokers or general agencies; and mutual companies such as State Farm and ALLSTATE, which have their own direct sales force.

The largest professional category in insurance is the sales force. Insurance agents sell and service customers for one insurance company, while an insurance broker is a sales representative for several companies. Agents are paid commissions, whereas most brokers are independent businesspeople.

For background on the industry, read the fine book *The Invisible Bankers*, by Andrew Tobias.

Then go to the library and ask for the monthly journals that discuss and describe what is happening in various segments of the industry, including specific types of insurance (life, health, casualty and property). For example, look for:

- *Underwriters' Report*, 667 Mission St., San Francisco, CA 94105
- *National Underwriter*, 420 E. 4th St., Cincinnati, OH 45202

Further information about the industry, including training programs, etc., can be obtained by contacting organizations such as the following.

American Insurance Association
465 California St.
San Francisco, CA 94104
(415) 957-0711

California Association of Life Underwriters
333 Hegenberger Rd.
Oakland, CA 94621
(415) 638-2450

Chartered Property & Casualty Underwriters' Association
President is currently:
Sharon Jakobi
Poulton & Associates
140 Franklin St.
Oakland, CA 94607
(415) 444-5353

Insurance Educational Association
300 Montgomery St.
San Francisco, CA 94104
(415) 986-6356

The Insurance Information Institute
400 Montgomery St.
Ste 720
San Francisco, CA 94104
(415) 392-3185

Insurance Services Office
550 California St.
San Francisco, CA 94104
(415) 781-8828

Insurance Women's Association of San Francisco
(415) 576-8335
*Contact:*   Mary Annswahen

The Life Office Management Association
100 Colony Sq.
Atlanta, GA 30361
(404) 892-7272

San Francisco Life Insurance Brokers
22 Battery St.
San Francisco, CA 94126
(415) 392-1625

Surety Underwriters' Association
PO Box 2045
San Francisco, CA 94111
(415) 935-1297

Western Association of Insurance Brokers
235 Montgomery St.
San Francisco, CA 94104
(415) 392-5383

Most of the large insurance companies (e.g., Aetna) have excellent brochures and pamphlets they will send you along with their annual report. These booklets provide an in-depth look at the job skills and career opportunities in insurance.

As you review the Bay Area insurance company listings, keep in mind that in the insurance business there's a very good chance that you will spend some time training in other U.S. cities. And your progress or promotions may depend on your willingness to relocate.

## INSURANCE JOB TITLES AND SALARY RANGES

### Sales

About a third of the jobs in insurance are in sales. Sales jobs may be full-time or part-time.

Companies usually provide a salary while their new salespeople build up a commission base. Then, after commissions build, income is derived completely from commissions. Many salespeople earn at least $18,000–$22,000 a year and because it is a commission business the opportunities for more income are wide open.

To sell insurance in the state of California, you must be licensed by the California State Insurance Department. Most big insurance companies will hire college graduates and train them to their own selling techniques while they are applying for a license. However, a college degree is not necessary, especially if you have sales experience or have studied insurance at a trade school or junior college.

### Nonsales Jobs

The majority of insurance jobs are not in sales. These other positions may include that of underwriter, actuary, field representative, employee benefit representative, and marketing, public relations, and legal experts, to name just a few.

For example, you may begin your career as an *associate casualty* or *property underwriter* earning $14,000–$16,000. Then you may advance to *underwriter* and earn $16,000–$20,000. Next comes *regional underwriter* at $20,000–$24,000 and then *senior underwriter* at $25,000–$33,000. *Top executive underwriters* may earn $38,000–$60,000.

If you are interested in forecasting, planning, and statistical analysis, you might choose an actuarial career path, beginning as an actuarial trainee earning about $10,000–$13,000. You must pass various exams leading to membership in the Society of Actuaries. This can take five or more years, but salaries increase with each step of the process. As a full *fellow* you may earn $30,000–$45,000.

Below are salary ranges for some of the senior level insurance jobs. Of course, salaries vary widely by the size of the insurance company or office.

- Public Relations: $33,000–$43,000
- Marketing Executive: $65,000–$74,000
- Legal Executive: $47,000–$67,000
- VP Administration: $52,000–$62,000
- Top Insurance Agency Executive: $56,000–$59,000
- Top Group Executive: $54,000–$58,000
- Data Processing Executive: $50,000–$64,000
- Chief Executive Officer: $100,000–$150,000

## INSIDERS' ADVICE

Employers advise that persistence and patience are two of the most important qualities they look for in recruiting sales and service representatives for the insurance field. Of course, good quantitative and selling skills are also needed, but patience is very important because only three of every 10 interviews may result in a sale.

Maturity and community involvement are other qualities that are often mentioned as a major plus by Bay Area insurance firms. Since insurance salespeople's incomes depend on their contacts and the trust others develop in their integrity and judgment, the contacts they make in the community are very important to their work.

## INSURANCE COMPANY DIRECTORY

**Aetna Life and Casualty**    (415) 445-8700
1 Post St.
San Francisco, CA 94106
*Contact:* Donna Smith, Personnel.
*Employs:* 40,000 nationwide, 400 in Bay Area
*Training:* For underwriters, claims representatives, premium auditors.
*Possible Entry Level Positions:* Need college degree to become a claims
    representative, an underwriter, a safety engineer, a premium auditor, or a
    bond representative.
*Description:* One of the oldest and largest insurance companies in the
    nation . . . has three divisions: commercial insurance, employee benefits,
    personal financial security.

**ALLSTATE Insurance Company**    (415) 329-7000
2882 San Hill Rd.
Menlo Park, CA 94025

*Contact:* Personnel Manager or John Kehoe, Regional Director.

*Employs:* 4,000 in northern California region.

*Training:* For underwriters, claim representatives, and sales agents, at Menlo Park facility.

*Possible Entry Level Positions:* Need a college degree to become a unit supervisor trainee, an underwriter, an associate claim representative, or a sales agent.

*Description:* Subsidiary of Sears and one of the leading multiline insurance firms in United States.

**Blue Cross of California**   (415) 645-3000

1950 Franklin St.

Oakland, CA 94059

*Contact:* Noel Smith, Professional Recruiting.
  Sheila Clark, Data Processing.

*Employs:* Approximately 1,350 in Bay Area.

*Training:* For service representatives and managerial positions.

*Possible Entry Level Positions:* Assistant analyst, junior accountant; approximately 80 percent of positions require experience.

*Description:* Largest health insurance company on West Coast.

**Blue Shield of California**   (415) 445-5532

Blue Shield Plaza

2 Northpoint

San Francisco, CA 94119

*Contact:* Robin Atlas, Personnel.

*Employs:* Approximately 900 at San Francisco office.

*Training:* At Lodi office for management training.

*Possible Entry Level Positions:* Customer service, sales/marketing, financial analysis, word processing, auditing, underwriting, compensation/benefits.

*Description:* General health insurance.

**Fireman's Fund Insurance Companies**   (415) 899-2000

777 San Marin

Novato, CA 94998

*Contact:* Arlene Lumba, Personnel, or Patti Hoffman, Personnel for San Rafael office

*Employs:* 4,000 in San Francisco; 14,000 nationwide.

*Training:* For claims, systems, underwriting, and management; hires primarily experienced personnel.

*Possible Entry Level Positions:* financial analysis, word processing, data processing.

*Description:* Largest property and casualty insurance company on the West Coast, but operates nationwide

**Industrial Indemnity Co.**   (415) 986-3535

255 California St.

PO Box 7468

San Francisco, CA 94120

*Contact:* Meryl Dorey, Personnel Manager.

*Employs:* 800 in San Francisco office.

*Training:* Hires primarily experienced employees and offers advanced casualty, property, and underwriting training.

*Possible Entry-Level Positions:* Word processing, financial analysis.

*Description:* 11 types of commercial and personal insurance.

**Metropolitan Insurance Co.**    (415) 546-3000

425 Market St.

San Francisco, CA 94108

*Contact:* District or Office Manager at office you select; 425 Market is head office for western states region.

*Employs:* Approximately 1,000.

*Training:* "Career success school" for sales reps.

*Possible Entry Level Positions:* Always recruiting for sales reps.

*Description:* Second-largest insurance company in the United States. Property, casualty, annuity, life, health, and group insurance.

**Prudential Insurance Co. of America**    (415) 468-0650

San Francisco District Office

5 Thomas Mellon Circle

San Francisco, CA 94134

*Contact:* Branch office personnel or manager.

*Employs:* 50 in San Francisco branch.

*Training:* For sales agents.

*Possible Positions:* Sales agent and clerical only in Bay Area. Data processing, customer service.

*Description:* Largest insurance company in United States

**Transamerica Insurance Group**    (415) 983-4700

600 Montgomery St.

(7th floor, Pyramid Bldg.)

San Francisco, CA 94111

*Contact:* Catherine Cunningham, Personnel Director.

*Employs:* Approximately 200 in Bay Area.

*Training:* Hires primarily experienced personnel but trains in underwriting and claims.

*Possible Positions:* Claims adjuster, underwriter, managerial.

*Description:* Property and casualty insurance; Occidental Life (Transamerica's largest subsidiary) is leading group life and health insurance company in the country.

**Travelers Insurance**    (415) 928-1390

2835 Mitchell

Walnut Creek, CA 94596

*Contact:* Dan Bendor, Personnel Director

*Employs:* Approximately 50

*Training:* 6 months–1 year of training for entry level positions; high turnover rate.

*Possible Positions:* Field assistant, casualty claims representative trainee, group insurance trainee.

*Description:* One of the top five insurance firms; offers all kinds of insurance.

# 7

# Business Services

Business services are the leading employers in the Bay Area. This chapter focuses on businesses that provide services to their client companies for a fee or a commission. These companies include specialists in advertising, public relations, sales promotion, direct mail, corporate communication and design, market research, and consulting.

If you have an interest in communications or marketing, you will want to consider several of these related fields to determine the best career prospects for you.

## *Advertising*

"Advertising seems so exciting." That is the reason most people give for choosing advertising as a future career. But what do they mean? Is it true? What else should you know about it?

Advertising is rarely boring: it is fast-paced, challenging, complicated, and often exhausting. There's a very glamorous side as well as a very grubby, roll-up-your-sleeves aspect to advertising. It's tough, risky, contemporary, and fun.

In how many other businesses can you switch from working on a shampoo account to working for a motorcycle manufacturer? In the advertising business it's possible to make that kind of change within the same ad agency every few years. So you can have broad intellectual variety but still build your career within one company or along one career path.

Since advertising is an aspect of marketing, it is ever changing and challenging. Your job as an advertising specialist is to analyze the market and steer your client's business on the best course for success. This often requires a complicated effort over long hours of concentrated work. And because advertising agency work is a service performed for the client marketing company, you must forever adapt to the client's timetables and demands.

The people in advertising are generally lively and the work environment somewhat relaxed in style. It's tough in that it is highly competitive and politically charged. Job security is low since your job may vanish if a client decides to change agencies. The stress may age you, but the focus of advertising is on new technology, new styles, and new attitudes. Yes, advertising is an exciting business. *Advertising,* as defined in this chapter, will include only a discussion of advertising agency jobs. But keep in mind that the advertisers or clients—banks, services, and manufacturing firms in the Bay Area—may also hire you.

In the Bay Area the advertising business has some rather unusual characteristics that make it both more pleasant and more difficult to work in advertising here.

The San Francisco advertising community is tiny relative to major urban advertising centers such as New York City and Chicago. It is also small relative to Los Angeles, where the headquarters of some West Coast agency firms are based.

Competition for new business to expand the size and billings of San Francisco agencies is fierce. Both the small size of Bay Area business in general and the lower incidence of outside (non–Bay Area) clients contribute to keeping Bay Area agencies rather small.

This small size has several direct effects on the character of the ad business here and on your chances of success in a job search:

- San Francisco ad agencies are not as burdened by the many policies common to big firms and can perhaps be more creative, flexible, and innovative about career paths.
- There are fewer staff levels, and your chances of working closely with excellent, seasoned ad professionals may be greater.
- The competition for entry level jobs, as well as for promotions to more senior-level jobs, is severe. The small size of the business keeps the total number of new opportunities down, so perseverance and timing will make a difference in your job search.

Here are a few facts and figures to help you picture the ad agency business in San Francisco and the Bay Area.

- There are approximately 100 separate advertising agencies in the Bay Area (the largest of which are in San Francisco).

- Bay Area agencies employ approximately 2,500 people at all levels, from clerical to management.
- Advertising billings for the Bay Area are estimated at $700 million per year.

If you have little or no experience in advertising, you should begin your preparation by reading a few key books. These are recommended and are easy to find at libraries:

- *Confessions of an Advertising Man*, by David Ogilvy.

- *From Those Wonderful Folks Who Brought You Pearl Harbor*, by Jerry Della Femina.

These will familiarize you with the kind of business advertising really is. (Ignore the old-fashioned sexist tone in Ogilvy's book. It is not the industry attitude.) These books are enjoyable reading and give you a hands-on feeling for advertising.

You should also read trade journals, especially:

- *Advertising Age*
- *Adweek* (West Coast edition)

These will give you an idea of current advertising perspective so you can converse intelligently in interviews.

Anytime you approach an agency, arrive armed with knowledge of their client account list and the advertising campaigns they have done for these clients. Use these resources:

- *Standard Directory of Advertising Agencies* (known as the "Red Book")
- *Advertising Age—Yearly Agency directory* (western edition)
- *Adweek Agency Directory* (western edition)

These resources list ad agencies and their account billings and discuss "hot" agencies of the year. The San Francisco Business Library at 530 Kearny has these books.

Recruiters cannot be particularly helpful to entry level job seekers since almost all of their search assignments are for experienced people. If you have advertising experience and want to make a job change or are new to San Francisco, however, these recruiters may be able to help you. They are paid by their clients, so no fee is charged to you.

Best bet for executive level jobs:

Harreus and Strotz
Transamerica Pyramid, 31st fl.
San Francisco, CA 94111
(415) 461-9100

A possible source for entry level jobs:

Advertising Careers
681 Market St.
San Francisco, CA 94104
(415) 957-9525

Other agency executive recruiters:

Richard Torretto & Associates
PO Box 265
Sausalito, CA 94965
(415) 332-9420

Vito Bialla & Associates
631 Bridgeway
Sausalito, CA 94965
(415) 332-7111

## ADVERTISING ORGANIZATIONS

There are several San Francisco organizations set up to serve the local advertising community. These organizations can be of some help to newcomers by providing contacts, advice, and, sometimes, job leads. Please note that in every case the local advertising organizations prefer that you write or telephone for information rather than going directly to their business offices.

**San Francisco Ad Club**    (415) 986-3878
681 Market St., Rm. 898
San Francisco, CA 94104
*Executive Director:* Paula Byrons
*Ad Club:* Meets first and third Wednesday for lunch; current employment in
    advertising not required; luncheons open to public for a fee; membership is
    $70 per year and $20 initiation fee.
*Ad Club II (for professionals under age 30):* Meets first and third Thursdays
    for an evening cocktail party; employment not required; membership is $35
    per year and $10 initiation. Ad Club II can be very helpful to newcomers in
    the ad business. For example, it provides seminars of interest to young or
    junior advertising people, and each spring it conducts a one-day symposium
    on how to get a job in advertising. It also conducts fundraisers for
    scholarship intern programs at ad agencies. Occasionally, the Ad Club will
    know of San Francisco job openings. However, they are not a placement
    service, so all referrals of this sort are very informal.

**The American Association of Advertising Agencies of Northern California (The Four As)** (213) 657-3711
There is no northern California Four As office. The West Coast is covered by the Los Angeles office.
8500 Wilshire Blvd.
Beverly Hills, CA 90211
*Description:* A management-oriented trade organization whose goals are to help agencies manage their businesses better and to represent agency business to the government, media, and client organizations. Northern California chapter has 54 member agencies, large and small. Educational booklets published by the association are available at the San Francisco business library (530 Kearny Street).
*Internship Program:* Summer jobs at participating ad agencies for qualified advertising students from California universities (estimated salary is $500 per month).
*Advanced Studies Program:* For junior agency personnel, using case method.

**American Advertising Federation** (415) 421-6867
251 Post St.
San Francisco, CA 94120
*Description:* A national advertising lobbying organization which is headquartered in Washington, D.C.; 190 advertising clubs nationwide. Sponsors "Best in the West" awards program once a year.

**San Francisco Women in Advertising** (415) 957-1264
681 Market St.
San Francisco, CA 94105
*President:* Katheryn Van Dyke.
*Description:* This organization is designed as a forum for women in advertising with the goal of furthering their success. The club sponsors monthly seminars, runs classes on basic advertising skills, and publishes a monthly newsletter of club activities. Annual membership is $35. The public is welcome to attend a monthly seminar session on the second Thursday evening of the month.

**San Francisco Society of Communicating Arts** (415) 777-5287
445 Bryant St.
San Francisco, CA 94107
*Communications Director:* Kathryn Braun.
*Description:* This club's purpose is to provide a showcase for local commercial art talent and to promote professional growth for its members. It also publishes a monthly newsletter, sponsors an art directors' show and awards ceremony, sponsors meetings and lectures for members, provides a direct mailing list for use by members for free-lance work or other employment searches, and occasionally will exchange job information on an informal basis but is not a job consulting service.

## IF ALL ELSE FAILS

Because the competition for agency jobs is fierce, here are some additional things to try.

### Temporary Agencies

Consider working for a few temporary help companies that specialize in agency placement in San Francisco:

Sally Walters Placement
320 Market St.
San Francisco, CA 94105
(415) 981-1414

McCall Associates Personnel
303 Sacramento
San Francisco, CA 94104
(415) 981-0687

Abar Temporary Service
690 Market St.
San Francisco, CA 94105
(415) 434-0400

### Retail Advertising

Retail department stores are often a good place to gain experience in advertising. If you want a job as a copywriter or an art director, you must have a book (portfolio) and some experience. A year spent in department store advertising can give you a better chance for an agency job.

### Work For a Freelancer or a Small Agency

If experience is what you need, be creative about how to get it. For example, you can offer your services to freelance artists or copywriters to do "grunt" or administrative work. (Find them through the San Francisco Society of Communicating Arts, listed earlier.)

Identify the smaller agencies not in San Francisco as your first job target. You might end up learning more in a variety of advertising jobs there anyway. (Find them in the industry source books listed earlier.)

## ADVERTISING AGENCY JOB TITLES AND SALARY RANGES

Ad agencies work with the marketing departments of their client manufacturing or service companies. This diagram shows how this interaction takes place.

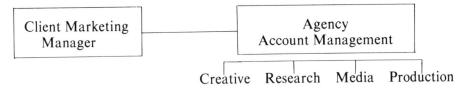

### Agency Account Managers

These individuals represent the agency to the client and represent the client to the other agency departments. The career path may begin with a job as *account coordinator* or *traffic manager* or sometimes as *assistant account executive.* Next you progress to *account executive,* then to *account supervisor,* and then to *vice-president, management supervisor.*

Account managers handle the marketing and business management function of the agency. They are responsible for generating a profit on their accounts for the agency and must analyze client marketing issues so that the client will generate sales and profit through the advertising that is developed.

Salary ranges are estimated here, but note that they depend on the size of the agency and the size of the account responsibility.

- Account Coordinator: $11,000–$16,000
- Assistant Account Executive: $15,000–$25,000
- Account Executive: $18,000–$40,000
- Account Supervisor: $25,000–$50,000
- Management Supervisor: $40,000–$70,000
- Management Group Director: $65,000–$80,000

### Creative Department

This is the department in which advertising ideas are conceived, written, and designed by *copywriters* and *art directors.*

The career path may begin with *junior writer* or *junior art director* and progress to *writer* and *art director.* Then you may move on to *group head* or *associate creative director* and then *creative director.* Here are salary ranges for these positions.

- Assistant Art Director/Writer: $10,000–$15,000
- Art Director/Copywriter: $15,000–$55,000
- Associate Creative Director: $45,000–$70,000
- Creative Director: $45,000–$100,000

## Media

Media managers plan, purchase, monitor, and analyze media decisions regarding allocation of advertising funds to TV, radio, newspapers, magazines, billboards, etc.

The career path is generally divided into two broad functions of planning and buying. And buying is further divided into local and regional buyers versus national network media buyers.

In general, the planners are more senior than the buyers. However, network buyers play an extremely important role due to the ceiling on network broadcast time that is available (only so many minutes on prime time on three networks) and the negotiable prices for broadcast time. Salary ranges are listed below.

- Media Estimator: $8,000–$13,000
- Assistant Media Buyer: $9,000–$14,000
- Assistant Media Planner: $9,000–$14,000
- Media Planner: $12,000–$22,000
- Media Supervisor: $20,000–$35,000
- Media Director: $30,000–$65,000

## Research

This department provides information that is vital to the strategic decisions underlying marketing. Researchers study consumer attitudes, habits, purchase patterns, and responses to advertising. Salary ranges follow.

- Research Assistant/Analyst: $12,000–$17,000
- Research Supervisor: $18,000–$35,000
- Research Director: $35,000–$60,000

## Production

This department is responsible for the execution of an advertising concept, transforming it into a finished product. Broadcast and print production are the two broad areas.

*Broadcast Salary Ranges*
- Projectionist: $9,000–$15,000
- Production Assistant: $15,000–$20,000
- Producer: $20,000–$60,000
- Production Manager: $40,000–$65,000

*Print Salary Ranges*
- Print Production Assistant: $9,000–$20,000
- Print Production Supervisor: $20,000–$28,000
- Print Production Manager: $20,000–$28,000

## INSIDERS' ADVICE

Advertising professionals are continually confounded by the general lack of preparation, creativity, and persistence of job seekers who claim to be interested in this highly competitive field. Employers meet a great number of somewhat articulate, charming people who have not bothered to do even the most superficial homework on the agency with whom they are interviewing or even on the advertising field in general.

Advertising professionals say they look for subtle clues as to how job hunters market themselves, how interested they are in current events or cultural trends, and how persevering they will be in demonstrating a commitment to the job.

Hiring managers also look for signs that an individual can process information quickly, maintain high energy in a fast-paced environment, work well as part of a team and, handle a great deal of pressure.

### Developing a Portfolio

You may need assistance in working up a portfolio, which you will need to get a job in an agency creative department. The Bay Area offers courses that focus on portfolio development. Consider these:

"How to Make Money in Advertising and Public Relations"
Norman Wilner
San Francisco State University
(415) 469-2176

Academy of Art College
540 Powell St.
San Francisco, CA 94108
(415) 673-4200

Also, be sure to read *How to Put Your Book Together and Get a Job in Advertising* by Maxine Pietro.

### Misconceptions About Bay Area Advertising

There are some popular myths about Bay Area advertising that job seekers should recognize as false.

1. *Agency jobs in San Francisco are impossible to get.* This simply is not true. In fact, top agencies regularly have to recruit outside the Bay Area for experienced account managers and media supervisors. So, if you have experience, you stand a good chance for a top job.
2. *Working in the agency business in San Francisco is a dead end.* This is also not true. Many San Francisco agency people actually have the responsibility for larger chunks of business than do their peers in other cities. It is also possible, of course, to return to the bigger advertising centers (New York, Chicago, Los Angeles, etc.) and continue a fast-moving career.

## AD AGENCY DIRECTORY

Some of the top Bay Area full-service advertising agencies are included here.

Entry level positions are defined as those positions you may realistically expect to get with little or no advertising experience.

This list should not stop you from naming a higher-level job as your goal, but you may have to consider a less direct route to get there. For example, if it is your goal to become an account executive, a stint as account coordinator or media buyer may be your best approach.

In all cases where clerical or mailroom jobs are listed as entry level you may realistically expect a chance to move into other agency jobs. Be sure to state right from the beginning that this is your goal.

Most of the agencies listed here are enthusiastic supporters of the Four A's internship program for training new advertising people. Some of the larger agencies indicated their hopes of starting their own training programs in the future, so be sure to ask about that.

In the Bay Area the top three agencies are Foote, Cone & Belding/Honig, Ketchum Advertising, Inc. (formerly known as Botsford Ketchum), and J. Walter Thompson.

### San Francisco

**BBDO West**   (415) 397-0346
825 Battery St.
San Francisco, CA 94111
*Contact:* Bob Imel, Senior Vice-President, Client Services.
*Employs:* 15.
*Billings:* $15 million.
*Training:* No formal program.
*Possible Entry Level Positions:* Account coordinators, media estimators, clerical.
*Some Major Clients:* Del Monte Foods (Hawaiian Punch), Hunt Wesson, Specialty Brands, Strawberry Board.

**Chiat Day, Inc.** (415) 445-3000
414 Jackson Sq.
San Francisco, CA 94111
*Contact:* Fred Goldberg, Senior Vice-President, Client Services.
David Yoder, Vice-President, Media Director.
Marian McBride, Print Production Director.
William Foote, Research Director.
Tom Tawa, Creative Director.
*Employs:* 60.
*Billings:* $25 million.
*Training:* No formal program.
*Possible Entry Level Positions:* Media estimators, clerical, mailroom.
*Some Major Clients:* Apple Computers, American Motors, Intel (computers),
Genstar (building conglomerate), Transamerica Corporation.

**Cunningham & Walsh** (415) 981-7850
500 Sansome St.
San Francisco, CA 94111
*Contact:* Joseph Therrien, Senior Vice-President, General Manager.
Frank Martin, Vice-President, Media Director.
Bruce Gale, Creative Director.
Richard Wall, Research Director.
*Employs:* 70.
*Billings:* $22 million.
*Training:* No formal program.
*Possible Entry Level Positions:* Account coordinator, assistant media buyers,
clerical.
*Some Major Clients:* Fireman's Fund, Qantas Airways, Pendleton Woolen
Mills, Royal Viking Cruise Lines.

**Dailey & Associates** (415) 981-2250
574 Pacific Ave.
San Francisco, CA 94133
*Contact:* Eugene Stokes, Executive Vice-Chairman/Managing Director.
Jerry Keller, Senior Vice-President, Director of Travel Accounts.
Jim Kong, Vice-President, Media Director.
*Employs:* 80.
*Billings:* $142 million (for San Francisco and Los Angeles).
*Some Major Clients:* Crown Zellerbach, Mexicana Airlines, New Zealand
Tourism, Northern California Honda, Philippine Airlines and Tourism.

**Dancer Fitzgerald Sample** (415) 982-8400
1010 Battery St.
San Francisco, CA 94111
*Contact:* Burtch Drake, President.
Joan Levine, Creative Director.
Laura Dearborn, Media Director.
George Dunn, Research Director.
*Employs:* 70.

*Billings:* $30 million.
*Training:* No formal program.
*Possible Entry Level Positions:* Media buying/planning,
    administrative/clerical.
*Some Major Clients:* Almaden Vineyards, Barclays Bank, General Mills,
    Amdahl Computers, *Sunset Magazine.*

**D'Arcy-MacManus and Masius Inc.**   (415) 391-2750
433 California St.
San Francisco, CA 94104
*Contact:* Linda Whiting, Manager of Personnel.
*Employs:* 60.
*Billings:* $25 million.
*Training:* No formal program.
*Possible Entry Level Positions:* Traffic, administrative/clerical.
*Some Major Clients:* Crown Zellerbach, Idaho Potato, California Canners and
    Growers.

**Foote, Cone & Belding/Honig**   (415) 398-5200
55 Francisco St.
San Francisco, CA 94133
*Contact:* Barry Ansell, Associate Director of Human Resources.
*Employs:* 300.
*Billings:* $120 million.
*Training:* For assistant account executives and creative assistants.
*Possible Entry Level Positions:* Two to four assistant account executives per
    year, one or two market research assistants, account coordinator.
*Some Major Clients:* Levi Strauss & Company, Clorox, Armour Dial,
    C & H Sugar, California Milk Advisory Board, Eddie Bauer, Inc.

**Grey Advertising**   (415) 421-1000
50 California St.
San Francisco, CA 94111
*Contact:* Hank McWhinney, Executive Vice-President, Managing Director.
    Warren Peterson, Executive Vice-President, Creative Director.
    Dianne Barnes, Vice President, Media Director.
    Warren Houston, Vice President, Director of Marketing Research.
*Employs:* 60.
*Billings:* $20 million.
*Training:* For assistant account executives.
*Possible Entry Level Positions:* Two or three media openings per year, two
    assistant account executive trainees, clerical.
*Some Major Clients:* Bank of America, Kikkoman Sauces, Computerland
    Retail Computer Stores, San Miguel Beer, Westin Hotels.

**Ketchum Advertising Inc.**   (415) 781-9480
55 Union St.
San Francisco, CA 94111

*Contact:* Susan Engle, Vice President, Personnel Manager.
*Employs:* 250.
*Billings:* $75 million.
*Training:* For assistant account executives.
*Possible Entry Level Positions:* Assistant account executive, media buying or planning, account coordinator, clerical.
*Some Major Clients:* Hunt Wesson, Clorox, Bank of America, Pillsbury, Christian Bros. Wines.

**McCann-Erickson**    (415) 981-2262
201 California St.
San Francisco, CA 94111
*Contact:* Loretta O'Connell, Personnel Manager.
*Employs:* 125.
*Billings:* $50 million.
*Training:* No formal program.
*Possible Entry Level Positions:* Media assistants, account coordinators, clerical, mailroom.
*Some Major Clients:* Bechtel, Wells Fargo Bank, Chevron Chemical Co., Del Monte Corporation, Levi Strauss & Co. (Activewear Division), Specialty Brands.

**Ogilvy and Mather**    (415) 981-0950
735 Battery St.
San Francisco, CA 94111
*Contact:* Ann Martin, Director of Office Administration.
*Employs:* 80.
*Billings:* $40 million.
*Training:* No formal program.
*Possible Entry Level Positions:* One assistant account executive per year, administrative assistants, clerical.
*Some Major Clients:* Blitz Weinhard Brewing Co., Pabst Brewery, Oakland Athletics Baseball, California First Bank, E. & J. Gallo Winery.

**J. Walter Thompson**    (415) 955-2000
4 Embarcadero Center
San Francisco, CA 94111
*Contact:* Joe Ries, Vice-President, Director of Personnel.
*Employs:* 170.
*Billings:* $60 million.
*Training:* For one assistant account executive and one creative person per year.
*Possible Entry Level Positions:* Assistant account executive, media buying and estimating, research analyst, traffic, production dept. assistant, clerical.
*Some Major Clients:* Chevron, Jacuzzi Whirlpool Bath, Oregon Farms, Sprint Communications, Hewlett-Packard, Activision.

**Wilton, Coombs and Colnett, Inc.**    (415) 981-6250
855 Front St.
San Francisco, CA 94111

*Contact:* Marilyn Aries, Office Manager.
*Employs:* 40.
*Billings:* $15 million.
*Training:* No formal program.
*Possible Entry Level Positions:* Clerical, art assistant (paste-up), media billing
   coordinator.
*Some Major Clients:* Hewlett-Packard Computer Systems, Signetics
   Corporation, GTE.

**Young and Rubicam West**    (415) 393-0600
753 Davis St.
San Francisco, CA 94111
*Contact:* Christine Osborne, Personnel Director.
*Employs:* 75.
*Billings* $20 million.
*Possible Entry Level Positions:* Assistant account executive interns, assistant
   media planners, administrative, traffic, clerical.
*Some Major Clients:* Clorox, Lincoln-Mercury Dealers, Pacific Stereo,
   Harrah's Hotel, United Vintners, Atari.

## The Peninsula

The largest ad agencies on the Peninsula are listed below.

**Bergthold, Fillhardt & Wright, Inc.**    (408) 287-8500
190 Park Center Plaza
San Jose, CA 95113
*Contact:* Curtis L. Wright, President.

**Bozell & Jacobs, Inc.**    (415) 856-9000
2440 Embarcadero Way
Palo Alto, CA 94303
*Contact:* Jack Anderson, Sr., VP General Manager.

**The Coakley, Heagerty Cos., Ltd.**    (408) 249-6242
122 Saratoga Ave.
Santa Clara, CA 95050
*Contact:* John D. Heagerty, President.

**Commart Communications**    (408) 727-1943
3350 Scott Blvd.
Santa Clara, CA 94051
*Contact:* Agnieszka Winkler, President.

## AD AGENCIES SPECIALIZING IN OUTDOOR ADVERTISING

**Foster and Kleiser**    (415) 835-5900
1601 Maritime St.
Oakland, CA 94607

**Gannett Outdoor of Northern California**   (415) 527-3350
1695 Eastshore Highway
Berkeley, CA 94710


AD AGENCY SPECIALIZING IN RECRUITING/PLACEMENT ADVERTISING

**Bernard Hodes**   (415) 391-9123
222 Vallejo St.
San Francisco, CA 94105

**Deutsch Shea & Evans**   (415) 434-0104
55 Francisco St.
San Francisco, CA 94133


## Public Relations

Much of the news you read or hear began as a press release from one of the nation's corporate public relations departments or PR agencies. The primary distinction between PR and advertising is that PR is information and image conveyed through editorial news coverage, while advertising is communication via paid media. Public relations has a lot of different titles, including corporate communications, publicity, public information, and investor relations. And in the Bay Area the competition for all of these jobs is fierce but not totally prohibitive.

PR jobs run the gamut from in-house corporate departments in large Bay Area companies to free-lance writing opportunities with smaller companies. This chapter will focus primarily on employment with PR agencies. However, Chapter 22, with resources and organizational listings, will be helpful in making contacts for a whole range of PR jobs you may want to consider.

To increase your chances for landing a PR job you should have the following.

*Degree:* A journalism, marketing, or business background is preferred. Advertising, technical writing, education, and English are OK.

*Portfolio:* A portfolio is not absolutely necessary but writing samples are, so you may as well present them in portfolio form and make a better impression. Your presentation should cover a broad range of writing samples, including published articles, press kits, speeches for senior executives, employee publications, technical writings, etc.

In the Bay Area there will tend to be more opportunity for public relations people with expertise in high-tech businesses and financial writing, including financial portions of annual reports and press releases sent to the investment community. The newer-technology companies need PR people who understand their products and can make them understandable to others. And the financial community is changing rapidly and needs more consumer communication of the supermarket of investment services now being offered. A proven knowledge of the Bay Area community and current events, plus solid experience in business or the news media, would also help distinguish you from other job applicants. Most PR employees are comfortable writing and composing on word processors, so this skill is also a benefit. Knowledge of video or film production and photography is also a benefit since so much communication is now in broadcast form.

## PR PUBLICATIONS

### Books for General Background:

- *Getting Back to Basics of Public Relations and Publicity,* by Culligan and Greene.
- *How to be Heard,* by Klein and Danzig.
- *Excellence in Communication.* Case histories, available through International Association of Business Communications (IABC), 870 Market St., San Francisco, CA 94102; (415) 433-3400.
- *O'Dwyer's Directory of Public Relations Firms.* A full list of PR agencies in the United States.

### Resources

- *Communication World.* Published monthly by IABC, 870 Market St., Ste. 940, San Francisco, CA 94102; (415) 433-3400.
- *Bull Dog, Insiders' Report on PR and Communications in the West.* Available from Art Garcia, 500 Sutter St., Ste. 405, San Francisco, CA 94102; (415) 421-3804.
- *Business Wire.* Available from Larry Lokey, 235 Montgomery St., San Francisco, CA 94102; (415) 986-4424. Lokey owns a private wire service that "telexes" press releases directly to business editorial departments of the media. He is also willing to forward resumes on to clients if he knows of opportunities.
- *Adweek West,* 514 Shatto Pl., Los Angeles, CA 90020; (213) 384-7100.

## PUBLIC RELATIONS ASSOCIATIONS

Bay Area public relations people are generally friendly and helpful to job seekers. They are quick to admit that, locally, PR is a small field of opportunity, and they seem eager to lend newcomers a hand. You may be able to make public relations contacts through these organizations:

Public Relations Society of America
Bay Area Chapter
55 Sutter St.
Ste. 792
San Francisco, CA 94104
(415) 861-7559

Nonmembers of the PRSA are welcome at luncheon meetings held every third Thursday at the Metropolitan Club. They also publish a membership list.

Press Club of San Francisco
555 Post St.
San Francisco, CA 94102
(415) 755-7800

International Association of Business Communicators
870 Market St.
San Francisco, CA 94102
(415) 433-3400

IABC publishes helpful materials (described above) and offers a reference library, seminars, and a 24-hour job hotline at (415) 421-9342. For information about the Peninsula branch of IABC, contact Heidi Ericson, (415) 941-4305.

## EXECUTIVE RECRUITER

For middle or senior level public relations managers an executive recruiter may be of help. Contact:

Judy Cushman
Marshall Consultants
Seattle, WA 98027
(206) 392-8660

## PUBLIC RELATIONS JOB TITLES AND SALARY RANGES

A public relations agency career path may start with the job of *assistant account executive* ($12,000–$15,000), followed by that of *account executive* ($18,000–$22,000), then *senior account executive* or *account supervisor* ($25,000–$38,000). *Group supervisor* ($40,000–$48,000) is the next step and finally *vice-president* (approximately $50,000–$60,000).

The corporate public relations career path, on the other hand, usually starts with the position of *assistant editor* ($15,000–$18,000) and moves to *editor* ($20,000–$24,000), then to *media relations associate* ($25,000–$30,000). Next is *media relations manager* ($30,000–$45,000) and then *vice-president, public relations director* ($50,000–$65,000).

## INSIDERS' ADVICE

Public relations managers and PR recruiters advise that the best way to get a job may be to volunteer or do free-lance work for the firm. That way they know the quality of your work and may come to depend on your knowledge and experience in their field, and you'll know when an opening is available or if a permanent job can be created for you.

The best way to get free-lance PR work in the Bay Area is by networking via the PRSA. There are a lot of free-lance opportunities for those who can work quickly under tight deadlines to "rescue" the PR person at a large local firm who did not have the time to write a needed press release or magazine article.

Free-lancers are paid based on their experience and reputation. A writer could expect to earn $20–$60 per hour or perhaps $250–$1000 for an article or press release. For more information on free-lancing you may wish to read *Freelance Forever* by Marietta Whittlesey.

Hiring managers look for individuals who can write and speak effectively. Prior experience with newspapers, magazines or broadcast is a distinct advantage. Experience in sales of any kind and courses in public speaking will be considered positively.

## PUBLIC RELATIONS DIRECTORY

**Beyl and Boyd**    (415) 434-3900
177 Post St.
San Francisco, CA 94108
*Contact:* William Boyd, Partner
*Employs:* 10.
*Description:* Corporate, real estate, travel, public relations, product identity
    programs, and marketing support. Recently started technical writing division
    and expects to grow in this area.

**Burson-Marsteller**    (415) 392-9200
755 Davis St.
San Francisco, CA 94111

*Contact:* Steve Pisinski, Vice-President
*Employs:* 6.
*Description:* Marketing support and PR, part of Young and Rubicam
  Advertising.

**Carl, Byoir, Arnold, Palmer & Noble**   (415) 957-9405
181 Fremont St.
San Francisco, CA 94105
*Contact:* Gerald Noble, Sr. Vice President
*Employs:* 20.
*Description:* Specializes in marketing support and publicity, especially
  "problem" public relations. Subsidiary of Foote, Cone & Belding
  Advertising.
*Some Major Clients:* Crocker Bank, Fireman's Fund, VISA International,
  Southern Pacific, Embarcadero Center, PG&E, Peat Marwick & Mitchell,
  Sumitomo Bank, Grubb & Ellis, Hill & Co.

**Carter Callahan & Associates**   (408) 998-5433
607 N. 1st St.
San Jose, CA 95112
*Contact:* Edna Markham, Chief Financial Officer
*Employs:* 31.
*Description:* Full-service PR firm specializing in high-tech, commercial
  industrial developers, and banks.

**Cunningham & Walsh**   (415) 981-7850
500 Sansome St.
San Francisco, CA 94111
*Contact:* Adri Boudewyn, Director, Western Region.
*Employs:* 10.
*Description:* Broad-based PR agency specializing in public and community
  issues.

**Dailey & Associates**   (415) 981-2250
574 Pacific Ave.
San Francisco, CA 94133
*Contact:* Robert Kenney, Manager
*Employs:* 14.
*Description:* Full-service public relations specializing in consumer marketing,
  strategic focus.
*Some Major Clients:* Mexican Airlines, Guild Wineries, Philippine Airlines,
  Fairmont Hotels, Hertz.

**Hill & Knowlton, Inc.**   (415) 781-2430
177 Post St.
Ste. 500
San Francisco, CA 94108
        or
4000 Moorpark Ave.   (408) 246-2187
San Jose, CA 95117

*Contact:* Donald Winks, San Francisco Office Manager
  Bruce Bough, San Jose Manager.
*Employs:* 10 in San Francisco; 7 in San Jose
*Description:* Largest PR agency in the world; division of J. Walter Thompson
  Advertising. Full-service, including corporate financial relations, investor
  relations, community affairs, marketing, promotion, and publicity.
*Some Major Clients:* Foremost-McKesson, Southern Pacific, Homestake
  Mining, Callagen Corporation.

**Hoefer-Amidei**   (415) 788-1333
426 Pacific Ave.
San Francisco, CA 94133
*Contact:* L. Neal Amidei, President
*Employs:* 20.
*Description:* Marketing and communication support.
*Some Major Clients:* California Brandy Advisory Board, U.S. Leisure Corp.,
  Eastmont Mall, California Nickel Corporation.

**Ketchum Public Relations**   (415) 781-9480
55 Union St.
San Francisco, CA 94111
*Contact:* Susan Engle, Vice-President, Personnel
*Employs:* 270 total (including advertising).
*Description:* Full-service marketing and communications firm.

**Lowry & Partners**   (415) 392-3010
921 Front St.
San Francisco, CA 94111
*Contact:* Robert Lowry, President
*Employs:* 15.
*Description:* Full-service public relations for local, national, international
  accounts.
*Some Major Clients:* Include AmFac Hotels, Hexel Corporation, McDonald's,
  PLM, Pearl Cruises.

**Pinne Garvin Hock**   (415) 421-3300
222 Vallejo
San Francisco, CA 94111
*Contact:* Stew Maltow, Public Relations Manager
*Employs:* 50.
*Description:* PR and advertising for computer-related, transportation, and real
  estate business.
*Some Major Clients:* Bolle & Babbage, Pacific Software, Peterbilt Trucks,
  Deutz.

**The Public Relations Bank**   (415) 397-4090
921 Front St.
San Francisco, CA 94111
*Contact:* Jenna Haney, Project Manager
*Employs:* A "bank" of freelancers.

*Description:* Marketing support firm; specializes in marketing and PR for hotels and restaurants.

**Regis McKenna Public Relations**    (415) 494-2030
1800 Embarcadero Rd.
Palo Alto, CA 94303
*Contact:* Gail Holste, Office Manager
*Employs:* 50.
*Description:* Full-service PR firm that specializes in marketing positioning, corporate communications and PR for high-tech firms, start-up companies, and genetic engineering firms.
*Some Major Clients:* Apple Computer, Intel, Cetus, National Advanced Systems, Televideo.

## Sales Promotion

Sales promotion is fast becoming an important facet of marketing programs for an increasing number of American companies. Because of the rising costs of promotion and media vehicles, the need for short-term sales impact, the decrease in retail sales clerks to provide product information, and a desire to cut through "media clutter," many companies are approaching sales promotion planning more than ever before. It is a growing segment of Bay Area marketing communications, and though it accounts for only a small portion of Bay Area marketing investments, it offers a very creative and fast-paced career opportunity.

*Sales promotion* is a very broad term and is used here to refer to sales and consumer motivation programs and events, awards, contests, trading stamps, coupons, giveaways, sweepstakes, point-of-sale displays, sampling, direct mail offers, slide shows, presentations, and promotional films.

As in the fields of advertising and public relations, the Bay Area is a small market for sales promotion. However, the professionals here are very willing to help job seekers.

There are essentially two kinds of career opportunities in sales promotion: (1) those that involve marketing decision making and client contact and (2) those that involve creative ideation, execution, and production (writing, art, photography, videotape, film, print, and visual production). For the first, a background in marketing or business, especially sales, is preferred, but you could probably also market your background in education, retailing, or social science fairly well. For the second, a background in journalism, creative writing, computer graphics, commercial art, design, photography, or production are important. And you'll need a portfolio of writing samples or a videotape or film "reel" or other samples of your work.

Here are two good ways to increase your chances of landing a good sales promotion job:

1. Do freelance work for the companies with whom you want a job. That way, they will know your work and you'll know about any openings that become available.
2. Become skilled in video production techniques and computer graphics. The demand for these is ever increasing.

### Sales Promotion Publications

Some of the publications that cover the field and may sometimes advertise job openings are listed below.

* *Audio Visual Communications*
* *Photo Methods*
* *Business Screen*
* *Adweek*
* *Advertising Age*
* *California Business*
* *Premium Marketing*

## SALES PROMOTION ORGANIZATIONS

In the Bay Area you may meet sales promotion professionals by contacting these organizations.

Association for Multi-Images (AMI)
Northern California Chapter
1033 Battery St.
San Francisco, CA 94111
(415) 433-2005

AMI also offers seminars, a journal, and a placement service. Meetings are held every other month and are open to nonmembers.

American Institute of Graphic Arts (AIGA)
c/o Michael Vanderbyl
1000 Sansome St.
San Francisco, CA 94111
(415) 397-4583

This organization has chapters in all major U.S. cities and sponsors events and exhibits of graphic design.

Artists in Print
Fort Mason Center
Bldg. D
San Francisco, CA 94123
(415) 673-6941
*Contact:* Elsa Manley
This organization offers job placement for full-time and freelance production artists, photographers, and graphic artists.

There is one excellent employment agency that specializes in permanent and freelance placement for these fields. Try Art Jobs Agency, 622 Washington Ave., San Francisco, CA 94111, (415) 392-2186.

## SALES PROMOTION JOB TITLES AND SALARY RANGES

The titles in full-service sales promotion agencies are similar to those in advertising and public relations agencies, including *account executives* ($17,000–$30,000), *copywriters* ($14,000–$35,000), and *media buyers* $14,000–$35,000).

Sales promotion agencies may also hire *photographers* ($16,000–$26,000), *technical writers* ($16,000–$27,000), and *artists/art directors* ($14,000–$30,000).

## INSIDERS' ADVICE

Sales promotion managers say they want to hire experienced professionals who are knowledgeable about merchandising promotion offers, sales presentations, trade deals, and even co-op advertising.

Most sales promotion managers mention a sales background as a great way to gain experience, especially detail sales such as you'd learn in selling for a large drug chain or a large food corporation.

## SALES PROMOTION DIRECTORY

The largest Bay Area full-service sales promotions firms include Impact, Merchandising Factory, and Flair Communications.

**Carlson Marketing Group/E. F. MacDonald**   (415) 945-1560
2950 Camino Diablo
Ste. 200
Walnut Creek, CA 94596
*Contact:* Bruce Fredrickson, Division Manager.
*Employs:* 8.
*Description:* Growing branch of a broad-based marketing support company

(headquarters in Minneapolis) specializing in sales incentives, promotions, meetings, and events.

**J.K. Carlton Inc.**   (415) 986-2234
2222 Irving St.
San Francisco, CA 94121
*Employs:* 5.
*Description:* One-man direct mail firm; hires free-lancers.

**Chart Masters**   (415) 421-6591
1 Holland Court
San Francisco, CA 94103
*Contact:* John Lyons, President.
*Employs:* 50
*Description:* Creates multimedia slide presentations for meetings using computer graphics, photography, and music.
*Some Major Clients:* Levi Strauss & Company and sales promotion firms in this directory.

**Flair Communications**   (415) 989-4845
350 Pacific Ave.
San Francisco, CA 94111
*Contact:* Richard Kiechle, Vice-President.
*Employs:* 10.
*Description:* Largest national sales promotion agency; also does direct mail.
*Some Major Clients:* Mattel, Christian Brothers, Memorex.

**Impact**   (415) 398-5200
55 Francisco St.
San Francisco, CA 94133
*Contact:* Constantine Camamis, Director.
*Employs:* 25.
*Description:* Full-service sales promotion, corporate identity, packaging, new product positioning, and direct response company.
*Some Major Clients:* Levi Strauss & Company, State of Alaska Division of Tourism, C & H Sugar, Pacific Telephone, Adia Temporary Service, Wallpapers To Go, Ore-Ida Foods, Inc., Codart.

**The Meeting Makers**   (415) 536-1288
19 Embarcadero Cove
Oakland, CA 94606
*Contact:* Dick Strain, Vice President, Marketing.
*Employs:* 10 professionals.
*Description:* Planners and designers of meetings, tradeshows, presentations and seminars. Specialize in advertising and finance clients.

**The Merchandising Factory**   (415) 956-4990
222 Front St.
San Francisco, CA 94111
*Contact:* Joel Lewis, President.
*Employs:* 15.

*Description:* Total marketing communications firm specializing in planning and execution of trade and consumer programs, including introduction of new products, national sales promotion events, and consumer advertising.
*Some Major Clients:* Bank of America, Clorox, Carnation, Activision, Laura Scudder Potato Chips.

**Merchandising Methods Inc.**   (415) 957-1555
274 Brannan St.
San Francisco, CA 94107
*Contact:* John Goetz, Purchasing Manager
*Employs:* 100.
*Description:* Direct mail advertising and production, sales promotion.
*Some Major Clients:* Bank of America, Wells Fargo, Crocker, American Cancer Society, Symphony Foundation.

**Netcom International**   (415) 921-1441
1702 Union St.
San Francisco, CA 94123
*Contact:* Paula Nunas, Vice President, Special Projects
*Employs:* 25.
*Description:* Video conferencing via satellite, live TV broadcast special events.

**Pollaks**   (415) 873-3232
170 Associated Rd.
South San Francisco, CA 94080
*Contact:* A.A. Heller, President
*Employs:* 30.
*Description:* Specializes in contest development, materials, and prize fulfillment.
*Some Major Clients:* Pepsi, Seven-Up, Del Monte, Clorox.

**The Register Mark/The Second Company**   (415) 392-3757
1033 Battery St.
San Francisco, CA 94111
*Contact:* Donna Schantz, President.
*Employs:* 15.
*Description:* Specializes in multimedia presentations for meetings.

**Serigraphics Displays**   (415) 861-2600
110 Gough St.
Ste. 401
San Francisco, CA 94102
*Contact:* Rabun Wilson, Sales Manager
*Employs:* 10.
*Description:* Printing, design, point-of-sale, and sales promotion specialists.
*Some Major Clients:* Levi Strauss & Company, Clorox, Wilson Foods, Penzoil.

**Slide Factory**    (415) 957-1369
300 Broadway
San Francisco, CA 94133
*Contact:* Paul Snyder, President
*Employs:* 5.
*Description:* Specializes in 35mm slide production for presentations.

**Walters Hansen Associates**    (415) 777-3217
85 Bluxome St.
San Francisco, CA 94107
*Contact:* Walters Hansen, President
*Employs:* 10.
*Description:* Presentation design, graphics, charts, animatics, photography.

**Wunderman, Ricotta & Kline**    (415) 398-3244
755 Davis St.
San Francisco, CA 94111
*Contact:* Christine Osborne, Personnel.
*Employs:* 8.
*Description:* Direct mail advertising specialists, subsidiary of Young & Rubicam.

## Corporate Communication and Design

Corporate communication and design companies specialize in personalizing companies and products. This is done in order to distinguish them from their competition and to communicate more efficiently the essence of the company or product. As more companies diversify or become part of a huge conglomerate, the job of communicating a firm's personality has become more complex and challenging than ever before.

Communication researchers say that 80 percent of the information we receive is gathered through our visual senses. And given the vast amount of visual marketing messages assaulting our senses, it is easy to see why corporate communications and design firms have been growing rapidly in the past decade.

Two of the nation's largest corporate communications firms (Landor Associates and S&O Consultants, Inc.) are here in the Bay Area. These firms may employ designers, art directors, architects, audiovisual specialists, photographers, writers, researchers, and consumer marketing specialists.

As in the other communications fields, job openings are relatively scarce. However, the design field is still very much in a growth phase, so job prospects are expected to be brighter than in other communication fields.

Because of the Bay Area's position as the West Coast high-tech and finance capital, job seekers with marketing or design experience in technology or finance may have an advantage. There are many high-tech start-up companies that will need corporate positioning and logo development. And the financial community is changing quickly due to deregulation and diversification so that banks and other financial institutions need to reexamine their corporate communications in order to communicate their new services and a new aggressive attitude.

The Bay Area's location also provides an opportunity to serve many foreign companies, especially from "Pacific Basin" countries such as Japan and China. Therefore, international experience or another language may be a benefit to your job search.

Many of the resources listed in this chapter under Sales Promotion will be helpful to job seekers considering design companies.

Bay Area designers particularly mentioned (415) 326-6040 *Communication Arts* magazine and the *American Institute of Graphic Artists* (415) 397-4583 as good resources for job hunters.

## CORPORATE COMMUNICATION AND DESIGN JOB TITLES AND SALARY RANGES

Job titles and career paths tend to be somewhat similar to those of ad agencies and sales promotion firms.

The basic functions include strategic marketing, creative (art and writing), research, and production. The following are salary ranges.

### Strategic Marketing

- Account Manager: $25,000–$40,000
- Management Supervisor: $40,000–$65,000
- Vice-President: $65,000–$100,000

### Creative

- Package Design: $20,000–$80,000
- Retail, Corporate Identity: $20,000–$80,000

### Research

- Analyst: $18,000–$25,000
- Manager: $25,000–$40,000

### Production

- Production Assistant: $12,000–$22,000
- Production Manager: $23,000–$32,000

## INSIDERS' ADVICE

Corporate communication and design companies say they are primarily interested in hiring experienced marketing and graphics design people. They look for individuals with a lot of past experience in marketing, client service, packaging or graphics decisions or those who have worked on brands for which the visual projection of the brand image was given important consideration.

It is difficult to get an entry level job at a design firm. Assistant art directors with a good portfolio and some experience may have a chance to be hired as a "wrist" to do art renderings of others' ideas and work their way up.

## CORPORATE COMMUNICATION AND DESIGN DIRECTORY

**Cato Yasumura Behaeghel (CYB)**    (415) 393-0689
753 Davis St.
San Francisco, CA 94111
*Contact:* Renaldo Gonzalez, Vice-President, General Manager.
*Employs:* 25.
*Description:* Formerly named Cato-Johnson; a subsidiary of Young and
   Rubicam. Specializes in corporate identity and communications,
   environmental design, graphic and package design.
*Some Major Clients:* Atari, Clorox, Oregon Farms, Specialty Brands,
   Foremost-McKesson.

**Landor Associates**    (415) 955-1200
Ferryboat Klamath
Pier 5
San Francisco, CA 94111
*Contact:* John Diefenbach, President.
*Employs:* 100.
*Description:* Headquarters of largest United States design firm; full-service
   marketing and communications consultants specializing in design, corporate
   identification, packaging, product development, space planning, and
   communications research.
*Some Major Clients:* Westin, Cotton, Inc., Levi Strauss & Company, Coca-
   Cola, Del Monte, Sara Lee, Bank of America, Phillip Morris.

**S & O Consultants, Inc.**    (415) 956-7575
575 Sutter St.
San Francisco, CA 94102
*Contact:* William A. Schneider, Vice President
*Employs:* 60.
*Description:* Second largest design firm in United States; marketing
   consultants specializing in new product positioning, packaging, brand name
   development, corporate identification, and design research; includes Nova
   design research company.

*Some Major Clients:* Transamerica, Clorox, Hunt-Wesson, Taco Bell, Mrs. Fields, First Interstate Bank, Burger King, Atari.

**Sidjakov, Berman and Gomez**    (415) 543-9962
10 Hawthorne St.
San Francisco, CA 94105
*Contact:* Lessley Berry, Traffic Manager
*Description:* Local graphics design firm.

## Market Research

The field of market research offers the opportunity to combine an interest in human behavior and attitudes with business and marketing. Market researchers generally measure consumer activity and opinion through mail, phone, or personal surveys; attitude and awareness studies; focus group discussions; and quantitative techniques such as multivariate analysis, conjoint analysis, and computer-based modeling.

The usual positions in research may include those of research director or analyst at a manufacturing/marketing company, research supervisor or research account executive at an ad agency, and research project director or analyst at a market research company. Market research companies are generally hired to design and conduct research studies by manufacturing firms or by ad agencies on behalf of their clients. For research jobs in manufacturing/marketing companies or in ad agency research departments, refer to the manufacturing and advertising sections of this book. Only the Bay Area market research companies are listed here.

In the Bay Area market research is quite competitive. There are many experienced, qualified researchers who have chosen to live here for the lifestyle the Bay Area offers.

A background in marketing and business, especially with an MBA, is preferred. Graduate work in social science, especially with a focus on statistics, may also be a plus. Skills in using home computers and word processing will be viewed positively. But actual experience in doing research design or field work will give you the best chance of finding a job. If you have a specialty—e.g., sampling experimental design—this is even more of an advantage.

The two biggest names in market research in the U.S. have offices here, but job searching with them is pretty futile.

- Burke Marketing Research primarily hires and trains people at its Cincinnati headquarters. All the professionals in their Bay Area office started in Cincinnati and were transferred here.
- A. C. Nielsen has a small branch office but hires only clerical staff here.

## MARKET RESEARCH PUBLICATIONS

As is characteristic of the marketing research supplier business, the Bay Area has a large number of small (i.e., two to four professionals) independent research suppliers. A complete list of the names and descriptions of these firms can be found in the *International Directory of Market Research,* often called "The Green Book."

## MARKET RESEARCH ORGANIZATIONS

The best overall source of market research jobs is the American Marketing Association (AMA), 681 Market St., San Francisco, CA (415) 495-4036. This is a very active organization with more than 600 members in the Bay Area. It sponsors monthly lunches featuring research speakers. Nonmembers are welcome, and this is a very good way to meet the leading research professionals in the Bay Area. Also, the AMA has a job placement service with job listings and a resume file. Ask the AMA for the name of the volunteer researcher who is currently running the job placement program.

In addition to the AMA, women may consider contacting an informal market research network called WC Fields. Call Betsy Canapary (415) 397-1200, principal at the firm of Corey, Canapary & Galanis, and ask if you can join one of the group's luncheon discussions.

Another small informal Bay Area research network is the Market Research Association. This group holds monthly evening sessions with research speakers. Call Toni Berke (415) 951-5054, Research Director at Crown Zellerbach, and ask for an invitation to one of their sessions.

Most of the listings provided in this chapter are full-service market research companies. In addition to these, there are small field research or focus group facilities that might be able to give you some freelance research work:

Ecker Consumer Recruiting
347C Serramonte Plaza
Daly City, CA 94015
(415) 755-4182

Far West Research
1315 23rd Ave.
San Francisco, CA 94122
(415) 564-8923

Yarborough & Associates
Claremont Hotel
Oakland, CA 94705
(415) 531-9099

Experienced research managers with excellent academic and business credentials may find a job through executive recruiters. Your best bet is to contact:

Harreus and Strotz
Transamerica Pyramid Bldg.
600 Montgomery St.
San Francisco, CA 94115
(415) 461-9100

## MARKET RESEARCH JOB TITLES AND SALARY RANGES

The entry level job at a market research firm is that of *research assistant* ($13,000–$18,000). (Sometimes in small firms this means you may have to start by doing some clerical tasks and "number crunching.") Next is the position of *market research analyst* ($16,000–$24,000) and then that of *research manager* ($20,000–$35,000). Many researchers start their own firms and become *partners* or *presidents* ($45,000–$100,000) as the next step in the career path.

## INSIDERS' ADVICE

Almost without exception, every market research professional in the Bay Area mentions the importance of making contacts as the way to get one of the few market research jobs here. This means you should definitely go to the organizational lunches mentioned earlier and try to meet as many local researchers as possible.

You may also consider attending a research conference or seminar given in San Francisco as another way to make contacts with Bay Area researchers.

According to insiders, competition among middle-level researchers seems high. This suggests that focused training or knowledge in a specialty may help distinguish you from others. For example, you could choose market segmentation, advertising copy testing, or computer modeling and get some advanced knowledge in this area as a way of marketing you and your research skills.

Bringing along samples of past research analysis and written presentation style will also distinguish you from other interviewees. The ability to apply market research analysis skills to overall marketing problems and think strategically (not just as a technical research statistician) is highly desirable.

## MARKET RESEARCH DIRECTORY

**BBW Research**    (415) 392-0365
690 Market St.
San Francisco, CA 94104
*Contact:* Charles Hemmingson, Research Director.
*Employs:* 15.
*Description:* Full-service market research firm specializing in public affairs.

**Communications Research**    (415) 955-1300
Ferryboat Klamath
Pier 5
San Francisco, CA 94111
*Contact:* Francois Christian, Director.
*Employs:* 8.
*Description:* Affiliate of Landor Associates. Specializes in packaging and
corporate identity research.

**Corey, Canapary & Galanis Research**    (415) 397-1200
447 Sutter St.
San Francisco, CA 94108
*Contact:* Ed or Elizabeth Canapary, Principals
*Employs:* 12 full-time, 100 part-time.
*Description:* Full-service market research firm specializing in political polls
and entertainment research.

**Decision Research Institute**    (415) 929-7474
2504 Pacific Ave.
San Francisco, CA 94115
*Contact:* Richard Mickley, President
*Employs:* 10.
*Description:* Service-related research, e.g., health care, recreation, culture.

**Elrick & Lavidge**    (415) 434-0536
240 Stockton St.
San Francisco, CA 94108
*Contact:* Brad Woolsey, Vice-President.
*Employs:* 10.
*Description:* Full-service market research firm specializing in design, data
collection, analysis, and presentation.

**Field Research Corporation**    (415) 781-4921
234 Front St.
San Francisco, CA 94111
*Contact:* Aaron Levy, President.
*Employs:* 25.
*Description:* Full-service market research firm.

**Management Decision Systems**   (415) 391-2041
4 Embarcadero Center
Ste. 2440
San Francisco, CA 94111
*Contact:* Michael Thoma, Western Regional Manager.
*Employs:* 10.
*Description:* Headquarters in Boston; creates market research consulting and decision support systems using computer software.

**Management Research Information Associates Inc.**   (415) 472-4811
PO Box 4334
San Rafael, CA 94913
*Contact:* A. M. Buckelew, Executive Vice-President
*Employs:* Eight
*Description:* Does political economic risk analysis and special research studies.

**Marketing and Research Counselors**   (415) 697-2923
1860 El Camino Real
Burlingame, CA 94010
*Contact:* John Uhles, Manager
*Employs:* Five
*Description:* Full-service market research firm specializing in consumer package goods.

**Matheson & Matheson**   (415) 956-4009
1052 Greenwich St.
San Francisco, CA 94133
*Contact:* Richard Matheson, Principal
*Employs:* Five
*Description:* Specializes in new products and new companies; also provides financial business development advice.

**Nova Research Corporation**   (415) 391-3090
575 Sutter St.
San Francisco, CA 94102
*Contact:* Frank Sutton, Vice-President.
*Employs:* 12.
*Description:* Affiliated with S & O Designs. Specializes in design package and corporate identity research.

**Opinion Research Corporation**   (415) 421-1198
4 Embarcadero Center
San Francisco, CA 94111
*Contact:* Tim Ellard, Senior Vice-President.
*Employs:* Approximately five.
*Description:* Does a broad range of field research and computer-based modeling.

## Consulting and Recruiting

There are as many types of consulting as there are businesses; e.g., technical, managerial, financial, and so forth. Companies may have internal consulting departments or may hire outside consulting firms to assist in problem solving.

It is generally agreed that truly successful consultants tend to have these characteristics: flexibility, good communication and presentation skills, creative problem-solving ability, confidence, assertiveness, and intellectual mastery of their field. If you think this describes you, then perhaps you should consider the consulting business.

As a consultant you may do a lot of traveling and will compete with other individuals for the chance to work on client problems. It can be exciting work and offers lots of variety in both the kinds of client companies and the intellectual challenges you will face. Consulting is often considered a young person's field because of the high energy level and amount of travel that is required and because once they have gained the client's confidence, consultants often move from their consulting firm to take over key positions at the client company. Consulting is also a popular field for those who have retired from a full–time position but have experience and knowledge to offer to other companies on a project basis.

In this section three kinds of consultants are covered:

- *Technical, environmental, and engineering firms,* which hire engineers, geologists, chemists, physicists, economists, social scientists, strategic planners, and decision analysts, most of them with advanced degrees and some experience.
- *Management consulting firms,* who hire MBAs, strategic planners, economists, financial analysts, and marketing managers. Note that all of the "Big Eight" accounting firms (listed in Chapter 6, "Accounting") have management consultancies as well as financial services. Most of the large management consulting firms have formalized training programs for newly recruited MBAs.
- *Executive recruiters,* who hire primarily experienced business managers who are knowledgeable enough to recruit other executives ($40,000 annually and up) for key jobs in marketing, finance, operations, and general management.

Of these three rather diverse kinds of consulting, the management consulting business seems to benefit, rather than suffer, from difficult economic times. As one consultant said, "It is then that large corporations see the wisdom of getting some outside counsel to help identify and recommend solutions to complex problems."

The hazardous waste field is one of the strongest growth areas in environmental consulting today, for those interested in this type of consulting.

## PUBLICATIONS ON CONSULTING

For some background reading and more information on consulting, read these books:

- *The Howard L. Shenson Consulting Handbook,* by Howard Shenson, $39; and *Principles and Practices of Professionalism in Consulting,* by Steven Styker, $29. Both of these books can be ordered by writing to Howard Shenson, Inc., 20121 Ventura Blvd., Ste. 245, Woodland Hills, CA 91364.
- *Consultants and Consulting Organizations Directory: A Reference Guide to Concerns and Individuals Engaged in Consultation for Business and Industry,* by Wasserman and McLean. Check your library for this massive volume, which lists more than 7,000 consulting firms in 135 fields. Information is arranged geographically.
- *Directory of Executive Recruiters,* Consultants News, Templeton Rd., Fitzwilliams, NH 03447.

## CONSULTING ORGANIZATIONS

If you are considering consulting as a career, some organizations that may be worth investigating are listed below.

Association of Consulting Management Engineers (ACME)
342 Madison Ave.
New York, NY 10017

Association of Executive Recruiting Consultants, Inc. (AERC)
30 Rockefeller Plaza
New York, NY 10020

## CONSULTING JOB TITLES AND SALARY RANGES

### Technical, Environmental, and Engineering

The technical consulting field has such a wide variety of titles and professions that not all job titles can be listed here. Some examples are listed to provide some guidance and comparisons for Bay Area job seekers.

Salary ranges vary according to the size of the firm, and your education, experience, and technical reputation in your field. Below are ranges for starting salaries in the Bay Area.

## Engineering

|  | *BS* | *MS* | *PhD* |
|---|---|---|---|
| Civil | $15,000–$20,000 | $20,000–$22,000 | $22,000–$30,000 |
| Chemical | $24,000–$26,000 | $32,000–$35,000 | $35,000–$42,000 |
| Electrical | $14,000–$20,000 | $20,000–$26,000 | $29,000–$42,000 |

## Science

|  | *BS* | *MS* | *PhD* |
|---|---|---|---|
| Chemistry | $18,000–$21,000 | $22,000–$26,000 | $27,000–$35,000 |
| Computer | $19,000–$21,000 | $21,000–$23,000 | $24,000–$28,000 |
| Physics | $21,000–$24,000 | $24,000–$26,000 | $28,000–$35,000 |
| Geology | $21,000–$23,000 | $23,000–$26,000 | $27,000–$35,000 |

## Management

The salary opportunities in management consulting depend on the size of the firm and the firm's general reputation in the business community.

Although titles may vary slightly, this is the general career path:

- Junior Consultant: $30,000–$50,000
- Senior Consultant: $40,000–$60,000
- Manager: $45,000–$75,000
- Partner: $60,000–$125,000
- Senior Partner: $100,000 +

Most management consultancies offer the opportunity for an annual bonus at the senior consultant level and above. However, because of competition to hire top business school graduates, recently some firms have begun to offer bonuses to first-year consultants, thus allowing for the possibility of $50,000 year for a newly minted MBA.

## Executive Recruiting

Job titles and salary ranges vary widely depending on the reputation of the firm, its style of fee collection, and whether a bonus or commission is given for new business development.

## LARGE FIRMS

- Researcher (may do clerical, similar to paralegal at law firm): $15,000–$25,000
- Associate Recruiter or Consultant: $22,000–$36,000
- Senior Associate: $28,000–$45,000
- Managing Associate: $35,000–$52,000
- Vice-President: $40,000–$65,000
- Vice-President, Managing Partner: $70,000–$150,000

## SMALLER FIRMS

Smaller firms generally have fewer titles, and the salary ranges are therefore broader for the titles they do use.
- Researcher: $15,000–$25,000
- Associate Recruiter: $30,000–$60,000
- Senior Vice-President or Partner: $50,000–$130,000

## INSIDERS' ADVICE

### Technical And Management Consulting

One of the ways mentioned by consultants to increase your job options is to be published in your area of expertise. This is especially true in the technical fields where, as in academia, it is expected that professionals will contribute to the literature of the field. However, marketing consultants who are just starting out may find that an article published in the *Harvard Business Review* will noticeably affect their visibility and career prospects. A good way to get started on this is to offer to give a verbal presentation of a paper at a professional meeting or association. Then you can adapt your paper for potential publication in a journal.

Bay Area hiring managers say that when considering job candidates for consulting jobs they look for high intelligence, excellent written and verbal communication ability, curiosity, and stamina.

### Executive Recruiting

When considering a career in recruitment it is important to take into account the implications for workstyle of the firm's fee collection method.

There are three basic kinds of search or recruitment companies. First are the job placement or employment firms, which focus on a fairly junior level or may place temporary help. Often they work for a fee, which the job seeker must pay when placed in a job. Second are the recruitment firms that work on a contingency basis, receiving payment only when they place a person in a job opening. This method of payment has sometimes caused concern, on the part of both firms and individuals, regarding the true motivation of the recruiter. (Is this really the right candidate? Is this really the right job for me?)

Finally there are executive recruitment consultants, who are retained by a company and paid a fee (usually over three months) to locate the best candidates for a job. In general these companies are the most well respected and work on the most senior level searches.

## CONSULTING DIRECTORY

### Technical, Environmental, And Engineering Consultants

**Bechtel Corporation**   (415) 768-7080
50 Beale St.
San Francisco, CA 94119
*Contact:* Iris Mahon Supervisor of Personnel
*Employs:* 9,000 in Bay Area.
*Description:* Nation's largest engineering and construction firm provides
consulting as part of engineering contracts. Privately held firm, owns Dillor
Read and Co., investment bankers, and Peabody Coal, largest U.S. coal
producer.

**Dames and Moore**   (415) 433-0700
500 Sansome St.
San Francisco, CA 94111
*Contact:* Kaye Godwin, Business Development Specialist
*Employs:* 60 in Bay Area.
*Description:* Environmental engineering consulting firm specializing in soils
investigation.

**Ecology and Environment, Inc.**   (415) 777-2811
120 Howard St., Ste. 640
San Francisco, CA 94105
*Contact:* Ron Karpolwics and Mark Bradford, Managing Partners.
*Employs:* 500 nationally, 20 in Bay Area.
*Description:* Does environmental consulting, including environmental impact
studies, hazard and risk assessment, and environmental planning.

**Environmental Science Associates**    (415) 552-4775
1291 East Hillsdale Blvd.
Foster City, CA 94404
*Contact:* Paul Zigman, President
*Employs:* 75
*Description:* Urban and regional planners, transportation, engineering, and
science, offices in San Francisco and Novato.

**Jefferson Associates**    (415) 931-3001
683 McAllister St.
San Francisco, CA 94109
*Contact:* Bill Ziebron, Vice President Management and Planning
*Employs:* 16 and uses outside consultants
*Description:* Environmental planning impact assessments, transportation and
engineering planning, applied economics and survey research.

**SRI International**    (415) 326-6200
333 Ravenswood Ave.
Menlo Park, CA 94025
*Contact:* Dave Glockar, Employment.
    Dr. William Miller, President, CEO.
*Employs:* More than 3,000.
*Description:* Nonprofit problem-solving consultancy and research organization.

**Woodward-Clyde Consultants**    (415) 434-1955
1 Walnut Creek Center
Walnut Creek, CA 94596
*Contact:* Adelle DiGiorgio, Employment, or Douglas C. Moorhouse,
    Chairman, at Woodward-Clyde Corporate Office, 600 Montgomery St., San
    Francisco, CA 94111; (415) 434-1955.
*Employs:* 400 in Bay Area.
*Description:* Does geotechnical environmental consulting, including
    engineering, earth, and environmental sciences.

## Management Consulting

**Bain and Company**    (415) 854-0660
3000 San Hill Rd.
Menlo Park, CA 94025
*Contact:* Deborah Brayton, Recruiting Manager.
*Description:* International management consulting firm for Fortune 500
    companies; headquartered in Boston.

**Booz Allen Hamilton, Inc.**    (415) 391-1900
555 California St.
San Francisco, CA 94104
*Contact:* Christian L. Rust, Vice-President.
*Employs:* 50 professionals.

*Description:* Does general management consulting, including finance, strategy, operations, organization and compensation.

**Boston Consulting Group**    (415) 854-5515
2180 Sand Hill Rd.
Menlo Park, CA 94025
*Contact:* Sandy Newton, Recruiting Director.
*Employs:* 35.
*Description:* Specialization is in financial and economic consulting and in strategic planning and decision making.

**Cresap, McCormick & Paget, Inc.**    (415) 781-8421
650 California St.
San Francisco, CA 94115
*Contact:* Allan J. Preger, Vice President.
*Employs:* 20.
*Description:* Financial, economic, strategic, management consulting.

**Arthur D. Little**    (415) 981-2500
4 Embarcadero Center
San Francisco, CA 94111
*Contact:* David Hurley, Vice-President.
*Employs:* 80 professionals.
*Description:* Commercial business problem solving and scientific technical consulting.

**McKinsey & Company**    (415) 981-0250
555 California St.
San Francisco, CA 94104
*Contact:* John Dowell, Director of Professional Staff and Recruiting.
*Employs:* 70.
*Description:* Management consulting—strategic planning, organization—for very large corporations (for Fortune 500).

## Executive Recruiting

**Bacci, Bennett, Owen, Webb Inc.**    (415) 989-8212
600 Montgomery St.
San Francisco, CA 94111
*Contact:* Frank Bacci, President.
*Description:* Medium-sized regional firm.

**Boyden Associates, Inc.**    (415) 981-7900
1 Maritime Plaza
San Francisco, CA 94111
*Contact:* Julia C. Hirsch, Vice-President.
*Description:* Oldest general recruitment company in the United States.

**William H. Clark Associates**   (415) 421-2325
517 Washington St.
San Francisco, CA 94111
*Contact:* Lynn Bray, Office Manager; Janis M Zivic, Manager.
*Employs:* 2.
*Description:* Large national executive search firm (just starting out in San
Francisco).

**Leon A. Farley & Associates**   (415) 777-2888
1 Market Plaza
San Francisco, CA 94105
*Contact:* Leon A. Farley, President
*Description:* Small regional firm.

**Harreus & Strotz**   (415) 421-0200
180 Montgomery St.
San Francisco, CA 94115
*Contact:* Charles Harreus or Chuck Strotz, Principals
*Description:* Regional firm specializing in marketing, market research, and
advertising recruitment.

**Heidrick & Struggles**   (415) 981-2854
4 Embarcadero Center
San Francisco, CA 94111
*Contact:* David Elliott, Senior Vice-President.
*Employs:* 15–20 in San Francisco.
*Description:* Management consulting and executive recruitment generalists;
second-largest recruiting firm in the world.

**Ward Howell Associates, Inc.**   (415) 398-3900
3 Embarcadero Center
San Francisco, CA 94111
*Contact:* Michelle Hughes, Partner.
*Description:* Large international firm.

**S.L. Jones and Company**   (415) 921-8233
2196 Green St.
San Francisco, CA 94123
*Contact:* Sharon Jones, Principal.
*Description:* Small contingency search firm specializing in banking, computer
sales, computer marketing, and other technical searches.

**Karr, Bartel & Adams**   (415) 956-6700
4 Embarcadero Center
Ste. 750
San Francisco, CA 94104
*Contact:* Lili Pratt, Consultant.
*Description:* Regional firm specializing in middle management finance,

accounting, and administration; 75 percent retained search, 25 percent contingency search.

**Korn-Ferry International**    (415) 956-1834
600 Montgomery St.
San Francisco, CA 94111
*Contact:* Robert Lo Presto, Vice President.
*Employs:* 15 in San Francisco
*Description:* Largest executive recruiting firm in the world.

**David Powell Inc.**   (415) 854-7150
3000 Sand Hill Rd.
Bldg. 2, Ste. 235
Menlo Park, CA 94025
*Contact:* Chris Loker, Consultant
*Description:* Small regional firm specializing in general management and high tech.

**Russell Reynolds Associates**    (415) 392-3130
201 California St.
Ste. 950
San Francisco, CA 94111
*Contact:* John R. Haase, Personnel Director
   Joe Griesedick, Director.
*Employs:* 8-12 in San Francisco
*Description:* One of the largest recruitment firms in the United States, specializing in banking and financial institutions.

**Schlendorf-Allen Associates**    (415) 981-1147
325 Pacific Ave.
San Francisco, CA 94111
*Contact:* Kathleen Allen, Partner.
*Description:* Regional firm conducting searches in consulting, leasing, banking, manufacturing, and transportation.

**Spencer Stuart & Associates**    (415) 495-4141
333 Market St.
San Francisco, CA 94105
*Contact:* Tony Hodge, Consultant
*Description:* Large international firm; third-largest recruiting firm.

# 8

# Communications

The San Francisco Bay Area is truly a communications center. It is fourth nationwide in commercial media revenues and the most competitive market in the nation for cultural broadcasting. There are two commercial classical music stations, four national public radio stations, one foundation radio outlet, four public television stations, and seven college and university radio stations. The Bay Area is also the West Coast's publishing headquarters.

In this chapter broadcast television and radio and film making, newspaper, magazine, and book publishing, and printing and engraving are discussed.

## Broadcast Media

The Bay Area broadcast industry includes approximately 15 commercial television stations and 60 radio stations as well as cable TV networks, public TV stations, and a major film company.

Broadcast stations earn their revenues by selling their audiences to advertisers. They gain that audience by broadcasting programming that consumers will choose to watch or listen to. The bigger the audience they deliver, the more income the station can earn.

In the Bay Area the competition for share of audience is heated. And broadcasters have to balance profit requirements carefully with enough spending to buy or develop programming that audiences will watch.

Bay Area advertising revenues usually come from national advertisers as well as from local car dealerships, retailers, manufacturing firms, and financial institutions.

Of particular interest in this market is cable television. San Francisco's hilly terrain has made cable desirable because it is the best way to improve television reception here. Over 40 percent of the area's 2 million households have cable. Of particular note in the cable TV business is the Gill Cable Company in San Jose. Gill has pioneered an unprecedented arrangement in the cable television business by encouraging rival cable systems to form the "Bay Area Interconnect." This alliance allows the cable companies to compete better for advertising dollars with San Francisco VHF stations because the network delivers a larger viewer audience and makes it easier for media buyers to place orders on the system.

Advertising revenues spent in this region are expected to keep increasing, and Gill Cable and "Interconnect" expect that they will be able to earn half of the local (spot) spending by 1990. Cable television is an exciting new facet of the business and Gill is clearly a company that intends to grow.

As background for your job search, here is a review of the major job categories in broadcasting. Television stations, cable companies, and radio stations, though not identical, have a similar organizational structure. There are six broad categories:

- Program Direction
- Sales
- News
- Promotion and Information
- Engineering
- Business Management


*Program direction* includes responsibility for the daily schedule of shows. Program directors and their production assistants and producers attempt to put together programming that will appeal to both sponsors and audiences. In television this involves decisions about network programs, syndicated shows, local programs, and public service documentaries. In radio the program manager selects the format of the station (contemporary or country or classical music, etc.) and hires the radio personalities. The program department as a whole plans the entire broadcast day-to-day schedule.

*News directors* have the responsibility of getting a fair and factual presentation of the news on the air. This requires balancing available funds and staff and making decisions without a lot of information on which to base them. For example, they have an annual budget for news but have no idea how much reportable news there will be in any one year or how difficult it will be to be on the scene to record it and report on it. The announcers and other on-air personalities at each station usually report to the news director.

*Promotion and information* people encourage the potential audience to tune in to the television station by providing schedules of programs and generating publicity about shows or talent and creating high-interest events. This is really the consumer marketing arm of the stations.

*Engineering* ensures that the signal the stations broadcast can be picked up by consumers' antennas and receivers. They also must watch-dog station compliance with Federal Communications Commission (FCC) regulators. Engineers must pass FCC exams and be licensed.

*Business and general management* have responsibility for the administration and financial aspects of running a profitable business. This function includes personnel, accounting, security, etc.

*Sales* has responsibility for selling broadcast time to advertisers, usually through advertising agencies.

## BROADCAST RESOURCES

- An organization called American Women in Radio and TV sponsors seminars and a career program and has a member job bank. Contact the group through the local president, Marlene Holderbaum, at KTVU, (415) 834-1212 (see listing for address). (The organization is also open to men.)
- Minorities and women can get assistance from the Bay Area Broadcast Skills Bank, 2655 Van Ness Ave., San Francisco CA 94109, by calling Lillian Holford (415) 673-7674. If you send this organization your resume, it will provide telephone counseling.
- Another possibility is the Bay Area Video Coalition, which was set up to help independent film makers and producers. The coalition offers seminars and rents equipment at inexpensive rates. Contact Virginia Van Zandt, Administrative Director, at 1111 17th St., San Francisco CA 94106, or call (415) 861-3282.
- KNBR offers its own training program and also posts all Bay Area broadcast jobs. Call (415) 951-7000 or see listing for address.
- The Media Alliance, which is a support organization for producers, writers, and media workers of all kinds. It has a job bank and a monthly newspaper called *Media File* and is located at Bldg. D, Fort Mason Center, San Francisco CA 94123; (415) 441-2557.

- The *Reel Directory*, PO Box 866, Cotati (Sonoma County), CA 94928, (707) 795-9367 is a guide to film and video production in northern California. This list can be purchased for $10.60 and gives names and addresses of production-related companies.
- The Northern California Broadcasting Association is a trade organization for Bay Area radio. It is planning to offer job bank seminars. Contact Robert Sharon, President, at 680 Beach St., San Francisco, CA 94115; (415) 928-7424.
- Alumnae Resources, at (415) 546-7220, has job listings from KRON-TV on a fairly regular basis.

## BROADCAST JOB TITLES AND SALARY RANGES

Since broadcast jobs are in high demand, you often may have to start as a *mail clerk* or *messenger* ($9,000–$11,000) and move up to *production assistant* ($13,000–$15,500). The next move would be to *associate producer* ($16,500–$24,000), then to *producer* ($25,000–$40,000). This leads to *executive producer, program director* ($40,000–$55,000), or *executive news producer* ($48,000–$60,000).

For a career path in news you might be able to start as a *newswriter* ($20,000–$30,000), moving to *assignment editor* ($28,000–$35,000), to *news editor* ($42,000–$50,000), to *news director* ($55,000–$85,000).

For promotion, information, sales or operations jobs, you might start as traffic clerk ($12,000–$14,000), then move to *traffic scheduler* or *supervisor* ($16,000–$22,000). Later you could move to a *public relations* function ($20,000–$40,000) or the job of *operations manager* ($28,000–$35,000).

Most broadcast sales career paths begin with the position of *sales assistant* ($12,000–$14,000) or *sales researcher* ($12,000–$16,000). The sales assistant coordinates advertising schedules; the sales researcher produces ratings information for programming, promotions, or sales departments to use. The next step up is to *sales account executive* ($16,000–$60,000), selling time on the air to existing clients and developing new clients and income for the station.

## INSIDERS' ADVICE

Almost all the broadcast insiders advise that the San Francisco Bay Area is a fairly tough market for inexperienced broadcast personnel. They advise you to get any experience you can in college and then in smaller cities or towns before trying for broadcast jobs in San Francisco proper.

Local stations encourage job seekers to take any opening they can find and then work their way up. Some of the entry level jobs include traffic personnel, production assistants, grips, secretaries, publicists, designers, news desk assistants, broadcast analysts, sales assistants, and mail room clerks. Most stations are always looking for new writers, especially for the summer, when many employees are on vacation. If you want a chance for a writing job, ask the station to let you take a writing test. Keep in mind that sales experience in any facet of communications is also a plus.

Most of all, be persistent and visible.

## BROADCAST MEDIA DIRECTORY

### Television Stations (Commercial Public, and Cable)

**Gill Broadcast Cable Network**    (408) 998-7333
1302 N. 4th St.
San Jose, CA 95112
*Contact:* Robert Hosfeldt, V P, General Manager
*Description:* Creators of "Bay Area Interconnect," the largest cable network in the country.

**KBHK-TV (Field Communications)**    (415) 885-3750
420 Taylor St.
San Francisco, CA 94102
*Contact:* Darla Bruhns, Personnel.
   Bill White, Vice-President and General Manager.
*Description:* Mix of films and syndicated programs. Local AM show and news.

**KGO-TV (ABC)**    (415) 863-0077
277 Golden Gate Park
San Francisco, CA 94102
*Contact:* Robert Edens, Personnel.
*Description:* Channel 7; three local programs daily plus documentaries.

**KICU-TV**    (408) 298-3636
1536 Kerley Dr.
San Jose, CA 95109
*Contact:* Jim Evers, Operations Manager
*Description:* Offers mix of films and syndicated programs. Produces news.

**KPIX (Westinghouse) (CBS)**    (415) 362-5550
855 Battery St.
San Francisco, CA 94111
*Contact:* Anne Godfrey, Human Resources
*Description:* Produces five local shows and three news shows plus documentaries.

**KQED, KQEC-TV**    (415) 864-2000
500 8th St.
San Francisco, CA 94103
*Contact:* Robert Liscano, Personnel.
*Description:* Public service stations.

**KRON (NBC)**    (415) 441-4444
1001 Van Ness Ave.
San Francisco, CA 94119
*Contact:* Lori Fava, Personnel Director
*Description:* Channel 4, features extensive news coverage.

**KTSF**    (415) 495-4995
185 Berry St.
San Francisco, CA 94107
*Contact:* Zoila Bruhns, Personnel
*Description:* Channel 26, independent.

**KTVU**    (415) 834-1212
2 Jack London Sq.
Oakland, CA 94607
*Contact:* Bill Castellanos, Personnel
*Description:* San Francisco–Oakland independent station.

**Viacom Cablevision**    (415) 828-8510
6640 Sierra Lane
Dublin, CA 94568
*Contact:* Bruce Gillman, Human Resources
    John Goddard, President
*Description:* Cable network part of "Bay Area Interconnect."


## News Bureaus

**ABC News**    (415) 626-0320
277 Golden Gate Ave.
San Francisco, CA 94102
*Contact:* Bill Knowles, Bureau Chief in Los Angeles, (213) 557-5261, where all
    hiring is done.
*Description:* Network's San Francisco affiliate for local news.

**Cable News Network**    (415) 434-1661
50 California St.
San Francisco, CA 94111
*Contact:* Claudia Schatz, Bureau Chief
*Description:* San Francisco Bureau of Cable News Network, covering San
    Francisco for the network.

## Radio Stations

**KABL**   (415) 788-5225
632 Commercial St.
San Francisco, CA 94111
*Contact:* Dorthea McKinsey, Office Manager.
*Description:* AM and FM station featuring beautiful music.

**KBAY/KEEN**   (408) 370-7377
PO Box 6616
San Jose, CA 95150
*Contact:* Steve Snell, General Manager.
*Description:* FM station playing beautiful music.

**KCBS/KRQR**   (415) 982-7000
1 Embarcadero Center
San Francisco, CA 94111
*Contact:* Theresa Timpson, Personnel.
*Description:* KCBS is all news; KRQR is rock station.

**KFOG**   (415) 885-1045
900 Northpoint
San Francisco, CA 94109
*Contact:* John Gaston, General Manager.
*Description:* General Electric station featuring album-oriented rock.

**KFRC**   (415) 986-6100
415 Bush St.
San Francisco, CA 94108
*Contact:* Patrick Norman, Vice-President, General Manager.
*Description:* Top 40 contemporary music station.

**KGO**   (415) 863-0077
277 Golden Gate Ave.
San Francisco, CA 94102
*Contact:* Bob Edens, Personnel
*Description:* Network radio station; ABC.

**K101**   (415) 956-5101
700 Montgomery St.
San Francisco, CA 94111
*Contact:* Fritz Beesemyer, Vice-President, General Manager.
*Description:* Contemporary music.

**KMEL**   (415) 391-9400
2300 Station St.
San Francisco, CA 94133
*Contact:* Rick Lee, General Manager.
*Description:* Contemporary album-oriented rock.

**KNBR**   (415) 951-7000
1700 Montgomery St.
San Francisco, CA 94111
*Contact:* William Dwyer, General Manager.
*Description:* NBC radio affiliate.

**KNEW/KSAN**   (415) 836-0910
66 Jack London Sq.
Oakland, CA 94607
*Contact:* Steve Edwards, General Manager.
*Description:* Modern country music.

**KOIT**   (415) 434-0965
77 Maiden Lane
San Francisco, CA 94108
*Contact:* Jack Adamson, General Manager.
*Description:* FM station featuring beautiful music.

**KSFO**   (415) 398-5600
950 California St.
San Francisco, CA 94108
*Contact:* Greg Reed, VP, General Manager.
*Description:* Middle of the road, contemporary.

**KYUU**   (415) 951-7200
530 Bush St.
San Francisco, CA 94108
*Contact:* John Hayes, General Manager.
*Description:* Soft rock FM station.

## Broadcast Production and Film Making

Broadcast production companies provide the production expertise and facilities needed to produce films, national and local commercials, corporate films (called "Industrials"), and presentations and programming for cable television and magazine broadcast shows.

It is not necessary to have a degree in communications or broadcasting in order to get a nontechnical job at a production company. Backgrounds in business, psychology, journalism, and English are common; most learning takes place on the job.

### FILM RESOURCES

- *On Location*, 6777 Hollywood Blvd., Hollywood, CA 90028; (213) 467-1268.

- *Film Makers*, PO Box 607, Andover, MA 01810; (617) 475-4760.

- *American Cinematographer*, 172 North Orange Dr., Hollywood, CA 90028; (213) 576-5080.

- *Videography*, 475 Park Avenue South, New York, NY 10017; (213) 725-2300.

- *Lighting Dimensions*, 3900 South Wadsworth Blvd., Denver, CO 80235; (303) 988-4670.

The market for production jobs in the Bay Area is extremely competitive. Most production work for Bay Area companies is still done in Los Angeles or New York City, where most of the nation's film, video, and sound production facilities are located.

Bay Area production job opportunities may occasionally be found through the Bay Area Video Coalition (415) 861-3282, or through the Reel Directory (707) 795-9367. Both of these organizations are described earlier in the broadcast media section of this book.

## BROADCAST PRODUCTION JOB TITLES AND SALARIES

Most broadcast production companies in the Bay Area are fairly small and the owner is frequently the president and general manager. The *operations manager* runs the day-to-day business and makes sure the necessary equipment is available for the scheduled jobs. The *operations supervisor* or *scheduler* takes bookings for the facilities and services and schedules the crew. *Production managers* handle field work, hire the crew (most are union members who work day or job contract rates.) The crew usually includes *cameraman, gaffers,* and *grips.* *Engineers* are the technical people who set up and run the field and post production equipment. *Sales managers* are the marketing people who represent the firm to ad agencies and corporations who need production services. *Production assistant* is the entry level job; it is essentially a learning and coordinating position where initiative, good attitude and high energy are needed. The *director* may work for the production company or be hired for his/her expertise on a contract free-lance basis.

These are the Bay Area production salary estimates. They vary by size of firm and individual experience and reputation.

- President; General Manager: $50,000–$100,000
- Operations Manager: $40,000–$50,000
- Operations Supervisor: $18,000–$24,000
- Production Manager: $20,000–$25,000
- Engineer: $30,000–$40,000
- Sales Representative: $28,000–$38,000 (salary and commission)
- Production Assistant: $12,000–$15,000

- Director: $30,000–$100,000
- Crew (Day Rates):
     Cameraman: $200–$500
     Entry Level Gaffer (Lighting): $150–$250
     Grip (equipment moving and set up): $100–$150

## INSIDERS' ADVICE

Experienced broadcast production professionals advise that really the only ways to start a broadcast career here are to:

- work as a video equipment assistant or technician, literally setting up and running projectors—for example, at meetings at ad agencies;
- work as a "gofer" at a production company;
- start as a secretary at a production company or ad agency production department and work up to production assistant;
- start at a sales promotion or multi-media company (see sales promotion chapter), working on corporate slide or video presentations.

## BROADCAST PRODUCTION AND FILM MAKING DIRECTORY

**Chronicle Productions**    (415) 561-8663
1001 Van Ness Avenue
San Francisco, CA 94119
*Contact:* Stephen Smith, Director of Production
*Description:* Produce commercials, industrial films and post-production
     services.

**Lucas Films**    (415) 457-5282
PO Box 2009
San Rafael, CA 94912
*Contact:* Lauren Romano, Personnel
*Description:* George Lucas' film production company.

**McCune Studios**    (415) 777-2700
951 Howard St.
San Francisco, CA 94103
*Contact:* Mort Feld, General Manager
*Description:* Equipment rental and industrial film producer.

**One Pass Video**    (415) 777-5777
1 China Basin Building
San Francisco, CA 94107
*Contact:* Buena Reutita, Personnel
*Description:* Produces commercials, industrial films, post-production services.

**Snazalle Film/Tape Inc.**    (415) 431-5490
155 Fell Street
San Francisco, CA 94103
*Contact:* Greg Snazelle, President
*Description:* Produces commercials and rents studio and post-production
    facilities and services.

**Varitel Productions**    (415) 495-0910
350 Townsend
San Francisco, CA 94107
*Contact:* Jack Schaeffer, General Manager
*Description:* On-site shoots, editing services.

**Versatile Video Inc. (VVI)**    (408) 734-5550
151 Gibraltar Court
Sunnyvale, CA 94086
*Contact:* Personnel Department
*Description:* On-site production, specializes in multi-camera or remote shoots
    (e.g., concerts).

## *Publishing*

Publishing careers are to be found not only in magazine, newspaper, and book publishing but also in universities, big corporations, the government, and nonprofit organizations. Generally publishing jobs fall into the following categories.

*Writing:* The jobs may include those of editor, writer, researcher, and proofreader.

*Art:* The job titles generally include those of art director, photographer, illustrator, layout artist, and designer.

*Sales:* Circulation sales focuses on sales to subscribers or sales to newsstands. Advertising sales focuses on selling ad space to ad agencies and their client companies.

*Production:* These jobs require knowledge of typography, printing, binding, paper, and film.

This section will list the Bay Area publishers of books, magazines, and newspapers. But keep in mind that your publishing job may actually turn out to be that of writer for an in-house magazine or newsletter for a Bay Area corporation. These jobs are usually part of corporate communications or public relations, so refer to the sections on public relations and consumer products and manufacturing in other chapters.

The Bay Area is not the nation's publishing headquarters. New York City has that status followed by Boston, Philadelphia, Chicago, and then San Francisco, so it is not surprising that jobs in publishing in the Bay

Area are in high demand. However, the publishing business here is varied and vital.

It helps to have a journalism degree, though this is not necessary. It is far more helpful to have some experience (especially in writing or sales) and to be able to communicate clearly what it is specifically that you want to do in publishing.

For example, if you are in search of a job as a writer, be clear about what kind of writing it is you want to do (e.g., technical, consumer, promotional, textbook, etc.). It also helps to have developed some areas of expertise. These may be fields in which you have an interest such as aviation, architecture, interior design, computers, or whatever. This will help distinguish you from all the English major generalists that employers meet and will help you target your job search.

By all means, try to use your experience to demonstrate the benefits of hiring you. For example, perhaps your years as a teacher gave you certain insights into how textbooks could be organized better to help teachers and students alike.

If you don't yet have any experience, look for ways to get some via free-lancing or by volunteering on nonprofit publishing projects such as for local organizations' newsletters.

## PUBLISHING RESOURCES

To get a job in publishing you will probably have to establish some contacts who will let you know when job openings occur. You may get some help through the Media Alliance mentioned earlier [Bldg. D, at Fort Mason Center, San Francisco, CA 94123; (415) 441-2557]. This is an organization of 2,000 media people that sponsors seminars and keeps a job file. Also contact the International Association of Business Communicators, mentioned in Chapter 7 [870 Market St., San Francisco, CA 94102; (415) 433-3400]. This organization also welcomes non-members and keeps a job file.

Be sure to read *Publishers Weekly* [1180 Ave. of the Americas, New York, NY 10036; (212) 764-5153] for job listings and information about publishing firms.

Other publishing resources include:

**California Press Association**    (415) 392-2353
657 Mission St.
San Francisco, CA 94105
*Contact:* Phil McCaubs

**California Newspaper Publishers Association**    (415) 392-9259
657 Mission St.
San Francisco, CA 94105

**California Press Women**    (415) 751-3839
114 21st Ave.
San Francisco, CA 94121

**Pacific Coast Women's Press Association**    (415) 474-4643
900 Bay St. #3
San Francisco, CA 94109
*Contact:* Mrs. Cecil Cooley

**San Francisco Press Club**    (415) 755-7800
555 Post St.
San Francisco, CA 94102

**Women in Communications, Inc.**    (415) 849-4768
4861 Geranium Place
Oakland, CA 94619
*Contact:* Joyce Smith

## PUBLISHING JOB TITLES AND SALARY RANGES

### Newspapers

Bay Area job titles and salary ranges depend on the circulation and size of the newspaper.

Starting level newsroom pay averages $11,000–$13,000. The average experienced *reporter* may earn $14,000–$23,000. *Senior reporters* could earn $50,000.

*Copy editors* or *photographers* with experience could earn $24,000–$28,000. The *editor* or *executive editor* could earn $50,000. *Top executives* of large newspaper chains may earn as much as $600,000.

### Magazines

Most of the magazine jobs in the Bay Area are sales jobs such as that of *sales representative* ($20,000–$30,000) or that of *regional sales manager* ($40,000–$60,000). Occasionally a *regional sales manager* may earn as much as $100,000. Income is affected by bonuses, expense accounts for entertaining, and the availability of a company car.

Magazines here also employ researchers, writers, editors, and publicity managers at approximately the same salary ranges as in book publishing.

### Books

Most people start in entry level jobs such as those of *secretary, correspondent, reader, editorial assistant, design assistant, production assistant, publicity assistant,* and *assistant copy editor.*

These are the Bay Area salary ranges for the many publishing jobs:

- Reader: $9,000–$11,000
- Editorial Assistant: $9,000–$14,000
- Associate Editor: $14,000–$16,000
- Editor: $15,000–$22,000
- Publicity Manager: $18,000–$22,000
- Marketing Manager: $11,000–$24,000
- Marketing Director: $35,000–$60,000
- Sales Promotion Associate: $9,000–$11,000
- Promotion Director: $35,000–$40,000
- Top Sales Executive: $50,000–$80,000
- President/Editor-in-Chief: $40,000–$80,000

### INSIDERS' ADVICE

In general it seems that experience is a greater advantage than education. So Bay Area professionals urge you to get experience in any way you can. The best way seems to be through school publications and then free-lance work.

When approaching a publisher for a writing or editorial job it is preferable to send a well-written cover letter, your resume, and several short writing samples. State in your letter that you do not expect the writing samples to be returned and that you will follow up and request an informational interview. Very persistent but pleasant follow-up will work. Keep in mind that magazines, newspapers, and book publishers receive large amounts of resume correspondence because publishing remains a very popular field.

To get freelance work you must first build a portfolio; it is preferable to have a portfolio with published writing samples and clippings included. Non-profit newsletters and local community newspapers are good places to offer your writing services for free in order to be published and build your portfolio. You can offer to write a general interest article or review a book for the paper. Once you have any experience in publishing you are entitled to be listed in the *Literary Market Place* (1180 Avenue of the Americas, New York, NY 10036). This is a reference book usually available at local libraries that lists publishing companies and individuals along with their addresses and areas of expertise in the field.

Freelance copy editing, indexing, picture search, proofreading, rewriting, publicity and cataloging are all possiblitities in the Bay Area. By attending any of the meetings of the publishing organizations listed in this book you may stand a good chance of meeting other freelancers. Ask them to recommend you for an assignment whenever they are too busy to handle it on their own.

Sales is a very good foundation for all kinds of other publishing jobs since publishers frequently rely on the salespeople's judgment of what will sell. Former teachers have an advantage in getting sales jobs in the new educational publishing areas, which include publication of teaching aids in the form of computer and audiovisual materials.

## PUBLISHING DIRECTORY

### Newspapers

**Oakland Tribune**　(415) 645-2000
409 13th St.
Oakland, CA 94612
*Contact:* Robert Maynard, Editor
*Description:* Morning newspaper; one of the Gannett newspaper chain; circulation 173,000

**The Independent Journal**　(415) 234-6262
164 10th St.
Richmond, CA 94801
*Contact:* Chazy Dowaliby, Manager
*Description:* Marin County-/San Rafael evening newspaper; circulation 45,000

**Peninsula Times Tribune**　(415) 326-1200
245 Lytton Ave.
Box 300
Palo Alto, CA 94301
*Contact:* William Rowe, Publisher, CEO
*Description:* Daily evening newspaper; circulation 62,000

**San Francisco Bay Guardian**   (415) 824-7660
2700 19th St.
San Francisco, CA 94110
*Contact:* Bruce B. Brugmann, Editor and Publisher
*Description:* Free alternative lifestyle newsweekly.

**San Francisco Chronicle-Examiner**   (415) 777-1111 *Chronicle*
925 Mission St.                         (415) 777-2424 *Examiner*
San Francisco, CA 94103
*Contact:* William German, Managing Editor, *Chronicle*
    James Willse, Managing Editor, *Examiner*
*Description:* Largest morning and evening newspaper in the Bay Area;
    circulation 500,000

**San Jose Mercury News**   (408) 920-5000
750 Ridder Park Dr.
San Jose, CA 95190
*Contact:* Pat Dillon, City Editor
*Description:* Morning and evening newspapers; part of Knight-Ridder
    newspaper chain; circulation 202,000

**San Mateo Times & Daily Newsletter**   (415) 348-4321
1080 South Amphlett Blvd.
San Mateo, CA 94402
*Contact:* Jack Wilson, Personnel Director.
*Description:* Daily evening newspaper; circulation 48,000; part of the Golden
    Gate Suburban Newspaper Group, which includes *Hayward Daily Review,*
    *Livermore Tri-Valley Herald, Fremont Newark Argus, San Ramon Valley*
    *Herald, Pleasanton News,* for a total circulation of 162,000

## Magazines

**Art Beat**   (415) 641-4580
1020 Valencia St.
San Francisco, CA 94110
*Contact:* Susan Barnes, Publisher
*Description:* Community art magazine.

**BAM: The California Music Magazine**   (415) 652-3810
5951 Canning St.
Oakland, CA 94609
*Contact:* Dennis Erokan, Founder
*Description:* Free music magazine distributed in music and record stores.

**City Sports**   (415) 788-2611
Pier 5 S.
San Francisco, CA 94111
*Contact:* Maggie Cloherty, Managing Editor
*Employs:* 10.

*Description:* Monthly magazine specializing in participatory sports.

**East Bay Review**   (415) 841-5185
1800 Dwight Way
Berkeley, CA 94703
*Contact:* Nancy Banks, Publisher.
*Description:* Free alternative lifestyle magazine.

**Levin Publishing Co.**   (415) 931-0900
1528 Fillmore St.
San Francisco, CA 94115
*Contact:* Jeri Bell, Office Manager
*Employs:* 20.
*Description:* Publishes three tour magazines, featuring events of the week in San Francisco, Reno and Lake Tahoe.

**McGraw Hill Publications**   (415) 362-4600
625 Battery St.
San Francisco, CA 94111
*Contact:* Bud Schirmer, Regional Vice President
*Description:* Regional office of publications subsidiary of McGraw Hill, specializes in business and technical magazines such as *Business Week, International Management, Textiles, Architectural Record, Aviation Week.*
Positions in San Francisco: Editorial, sales representatives, clerical.

**Miller Freeman**   (415) 397-1881
500 Howard St.
San Francisco, CA 94105
*Contact:* Barbara Hampson, Personnel Director
*Employs:* 145.
*Description:* Magazine and book publisher for mining, forestry, pulp, and paper industries.

**Pacific Sun**   (415) 383-4500
21 Corte Madera
Mill Valley, CA 94941
*Contact:* Steve McNamara, Publisher
*Description:* Free alternative lifestyle magazine.

**San Francisco Bay Views Magazine**   (415) 472-3220
124 Paul Dr.
San Rafael, CA 94903
*Contact:* Betsy Foster, Editor
*Description:* Published monthly—features Bay Area events, entertainment, people, finance. Circulation 30,000.

**San Francisco Business Journal**   (415) 552-7690
745 Stevenson St.
San Francisco, CA 94103
*Contact:* Max Kvidera, Editor
*Employs:* 25.

*Description:* Scripps-Howard Cordovan publication. Published weekly, featuring articles on Bay Area business, including finance, real estate, manufacturing, retail, communications, marketing, agribusiness, and transportation. Circulation 8,000.

**San Francisco Focus**    (415) 864-2000
500 8th St.
San Francisco, CA 94103
*Contact:* Earl Adkins, Publisher
*Employs:* 16.
*Description:* Published monthly by KQED (public television); features arts, culture, and entertainment articles as well as TV program listing. Circulation 135,000.

**San Francisco Magazine**    (415) 777-5555
973 Market St.
San Francisco, CA 94103
*Contact:* Joane Lange, Publisher Editor-in-Chief
*Employs:* 20
*Description:* Published monthly—features investigative reporting, consumer services, food, fashion, travel, and regular columns. Circulation 43,000.

**Sunset Magazine**    (415) 321-3600
85 Willow Rd.
Menlo Park, CA 94025
*Contact:* Nancy Creames, Personnel
*Description:* West Coast lifestyle magazine.

## Magazine Advertising Sales Offices

These magazines are published elsewhere but maintain advertising sales offices in the Bay Area.

- *California Magazine:* 986-5196
- *Cosmopolitan:* 434-2675
- *Discover, Life, Time, Fortune, Money, People, Sports Illustrated* (all part of Time, Inc.): 982-5000
- *Newsweek:* 788-2651
- *New Yorker:* 434-3232
- *U.S. News & World Report:* 781-2832
- *Woman's Day:* 397-3441
- *Forbes:* 788-2366
- *Architectural Digest:* 781-1888

## Book Publishers

**Academic Press**    (415) 771-3500
101 Polk St.
San Francisco, CA 94109

*Contact:* Elizabeth Baker, Personnel Director.

*Employs:* 200.

*Description:* West Coast office of New York firm; specializes in textbook publishing for university, high school, and grammar school levels.

*Positions in San Francisco:* Editorial assistant, editor, sales agent, clerical.

**Addison-Wesley Publishing Co., Inc.**   (415) 854-0300
2725 Sand Hill Rd.
Menlo Park, CA 94025
*Contact:* Jenny Anderson, Personnel.
   Wayne Oler, Executive Vice-President, Director.
*Description:* West Coast office has school publishing division only.
*Positions in Bay Area:* Editorial assistant, assistant editor, senior editor, project manager, copy editor, proofreader.

**Bancroft-Whitney**   (415) 986-4410
301 Brannan St.
San Francisco, CA 94105
*Contact:* Thomas Levernier, Director of Personnel.
*Employs:* 286
*Description:* Subsidiary of Lawyers Cooperative Publishing Company of Rochester, New York; specializes in law books for libraries and legal clients.
*Positions in Bay Area:* Attorneys who do research, customer service representatives, accountants, marketing management, personnel, and management.

**Book People**   (415) 549-3030
2940 7th St.
Berkeley, CA 94710
*Contact:* Robert Sheldon, Marketing Director.
*Description:* Small local publisher and distributer for independent publishers.
*Positions in Bay Area:* Clerical, copy editor, proofreader.

**City Lights**   (415) 362-8193
261 Columbus Ave.
San Francisco, CA 94133
*Contact:* Lawrence Ferlinghetti, Editor and Poet.
*Employs:* Eight.
*Description:* Publishes poetry and modern literature and manages bookstore.
*Positions in Bay Area:* Bookstore staff, cashiers, bookkeeper, and editors.

**W H Freeman**   (415) 391-5870
660 Market St.
San Francisco, CA 94104
*Contact:* Y. Wada, Personnel Manager.
*Employs:* 85.
*Description:* Publisher of College Science textbooks.
*Positions in Bay Area:* Editing, product design, accounting, order processing, sales, marketing, and advertising jobs.

**Harcourt Brace Jovanovich, Inc.**   (415) 771-3600
1001 Polk St.
San Francisco, CA 94109
*Contact:* Beth Baker, Personnel Director.
*Description:* New York–based publisher that specializes in textbooks.
*Positions in San Francisco:* Editor, clerical.

**Holden Day, Inc.**   (415) 428-9400
4432 Telegraph Ave.
Oakland, CA 94609
*Contact:* Frederick Murphy, President.
*Employs:* 15.
*Description:* Publishes textbooks on physics, mathematics, business
    management, and computer sciences.
*Positions in Bay Area:* Editorial, production, customer service, and sales.

**Jossey-Bass, Inc.**   (415) 433-1740
433 California St.
San Francisco, CA 94104
*Contact:* Maralene Phipps, Personnel Director.
*Employs:* 30.
*Description:* Publishes professional books on behavioral sciences, psychology,
    health sciences.
*Positions in San Francisco:* Acquisitions, customer service, production,
    financial, and marketing jobs.

**Lane Publishing Co.**   (415) 321-3600
(Sunset Books, Magazines & Film)
85 Willow Rd.
Menlo Park, CA 94025
*Contact:* Nancy Creamer, Personnel.
    John F. Hennings, President.
    Paul Silinger, Film Division Director (495-4555).
*Description:* Best known for its Western lifestyles magazine, *Sunset;* also has
    book and film division.
*Positions in Bay Area:* Editorial assistant, editor, producer, production
    assistant.

**Macmillan Publishing**   (415) 254-8015
23 Orinda Way
Orinda, CA 94563
*Contact:* Personnel Department.
*Description:* National firm headquartered in New York; sales service office
    here in Bay Area.
*Positions in Bay Area:* Customer service, sales rep, consultant.

**McGraw-Hill Book Company**   (415) 897-5201
8171 Redwood Highway
Novato, CA 94947
*Contact:* Lillian McKernen, Personnel.

*Description:* Regional office for book company, publishes 70% educational books.
*Positions in Bay Area:* Editors, sales, clerical, film production, customer service.

**Northpoint Press**   (415) 527-6260
850 Talbot Ave.
Berkeley, CA 94706
*Contact:* Jack Shoemaker, Editor-in-Chief.
*Employs:* 10.
*Description:* Two-year-old publishing firm specializing in scholarly literature and old classics as well as some first novels.
*Positions in Bay Area:* Editor, publicist, production manager, designer, marketing director, and bookkeeper.

**Prentice-Hall**   (415) 421-2761
110 Sutter St.
San Francisco, CA 94104
*Contact:* Ed O'Connor, District Sales Manager.
*Description:* Publishing firm headquartered in New Jersey; San Francisco office specializes in tax materials; all writing is done in New Jersey.
*Positions in San Francisco:* Sales, clerical; need knowledge of taxes and experience in dealing with accountants and financial people.

**Stanford University Press**   (415) 497-9434
Stanford University
Stanford, CA 94305
*Contact:* Leon E. Seltzer, Director.
*Employs:* 34.
*Description:* Publisher of scholarly books in history, political science, economics, law, literature, and especially China, Japan, Latin America.
*Positions in Bay Area:* Editing, production, design, customer service, shipping, promotions, advertising, accounting, and computer service jobs. Uses freelance editors and proofreaders; ask to take test to qualify for freelance work.

**Ten Speed Press**   (415) 845-8414
900 Modoc
Berkeley, CA 94707
*Contact:* Peg Nakahara, Personnel Director.
*Description:* Small local publisher specializing in nonfiction how-to books.
*Positions in Bay Area:* Sales representative, clerical, free-lance writer, editor.

**University of California Press**   (415) 642-5393
2223 Fulton St.
Berkeley, CA 94720
*Contact:* Pam Wimberly, Personnel Manager.
*Employs:* 70.
*Description:* Scholarly academic publisher in Asian studies, literary criticism, musicology, science, anthropology, and sociology.

*Positions in Bay Area:* Editing, production, design, advertising, accounting jobs, etc.

**Wadsworth, Inc.**   (415) 595-2350
70 Davis Dr.
Belmont, CA 94002
*Contact:* Ed Key, Personnel Director.
*Description:* West Coast local publisher specializing in college textbooks.
*Positions in Bay Area:* Requires sales background for editorial staff. Free-lancers are hired regularly for artwork and proofreading.


## *Printing*

Printing is one of the largest industries in the United States made up of many small businesses specializing in design and layout, composition, paper manufacturing, printing, inks, and binding. Here in the Bay Area the printing industry is quite active and quite technically advanced, with approximately 1,000 printing companies of various sizes.

The business is a "demand response" industry, and print production is a service that companies perform for their clients, which include manufacturing companies, advertising agencies, packaging firms, and publishing houses. This means that employees are generally working to meet tight deadlines. As a result companies look for employees who are not only technically competent but who also are willing to work hard and have a "can do" attitude.

Bay Area printing companies are unanimous in recommending print production training at these California schools:

Graphic Communications Department
California Polytechnic State University
San Luis Obispo, CA 93407
(805) 546-1108

Technical Art/Graphic Department
College of San Mateo
1700 West Hillsdale Ave.
San Mateo, CA 94420
(415) 574-6124

Art Department
San Francisco State University
1600 Holloway Ave.
San Francisco, CA 94132
(415) 469-2176

Courses in computer graphics, packaging, and printing management are particularly recommended. Company training programs in the industry usually depend on the size of the firm. Most training is done on the job. The field has become quite technical and requires constant adaptation to the new breakthroughs in production techniques.

Positions in the industry include those involving art and design, layout, composition (typesetting), preparation (including camera work, stripping, platemaking), press work, binding and trimming, estimating, production planning, quality control, scheduling, sales, marketing, and management.

## PRINTING PUBLICATIONS

For more information, refer to these periodicals.

- *Printing Journal,* 2401 Charleston Rd., Mountain View, CA 94043; (415) 962-8972
- *Graphic Arts Monthly,* Technical Publishing Co., A Dun & Bradstreet Co., 666 5th Ave., New York, NY 10019.
- *Pacific Printer Pilot,* 583 Monterey Pass Rd., Monterey, CA 91754.
- *Pocket Pal,* published by International Paper Company, 77 W. 45th St., New York, NY 10036; (212) 431-5222

## PRINTING JOB TITLES AND SALARY RANGES

Printing is considered a trade and many of the jobs are unionized and hourly and weekly wages set. Here are some examples:

- Binder Operator: $23,000
- Typesetter/typographer: $15,000–$24,000
- Art and design: $15,000–$25,000
- Camera processor: $20,000–$24,000
- Press operator: $26,000–$34,000

Entry-level jobs require a B.S. degree in printing. A *management trainee* in production, scheduling, estimating, or marketing can start at $14,000–$18,000, depending on the size of the firm. The next step might be to *assistant production manager* ($18,000–$22,000), then to *production manager* ($22,000–$40,000), and then to *plant manager* (up to $70,000).

Sales jobs for printing firms are generally paid by commission.

## INSIDERS' ADVICE

Bay Area printers say to be sure to contact the Printing Industries of Northern California when you are job hunting in the printing field:

PINC
185 Berry St.
San Francisco, CA 94107
(415) 495-8242

This organization represents the printing companies, fosters communications, offers seminars and provides a personnel placement service. Contact Frank Drolet for information on how to be listed as a job applicant.

Rapid technical advances in printing make the language of printing difficult to understand. The field was once a craft and is now highly technical and computer-oriented. Those with a background in computer electronics, chemistry, or optics—as well as those with an art background—are needed.

Printers say it is very hard for them to find employees who want to work hard and put real care into their jobs. A skilled printer can make or break a business and employers are constantly looking for "skilled perfectionists."

In the Bay Area the lithography industry is the largest area of specialization but also the most difficult area in which to find work. Job prospects are considered better in the silk screen and flexography specialties.

## PRINTING DIRECTORY

**Balzer Shopes Litho Plate Co.**   (415) 781-8074
835 Howard St.
San Francisco, CA 94103
*Contact:* Paul Martin, Personnel Director.
*Employs:* 55.
*Description:* Prepares and makes film for offset printing.

**Pacific Lithographics Co.**   (415) 467-5200
2555 Bayshore Blvd.
San Francisco, CA 94104
*Contact:* Bob Miller.
*Employs:* 180.
*Description:* Printing plant that specializes in high-quality commercial printing.

**Pisani Carlisle Graphics**   (415) 583-0325
301 East Grand Ave.
South San Francisco, CA 94080
*Contact:* Bill O'Leary, General Manager.
*Employs:* 85.
*Description:* Specializes in multicolor processing, and printing for high-quality commercial point-of-sale signs and posters.

**H.S. Crocker Co., Inc.**   (415) 761-1555
1000 San Mateo Ave.
San Bruno, CA 94066
*Contact:* Dave Rogers, Personnel.
*Employs:* 1,000.
*Description:* Flexographers specializing in package and label printing.

**Walker Engraving Co.**   (415) 433-7900
333 Freemont St.
San Francisco, CA 94103
*Contact:* Gary Melrose, Personnel.
*Employs:* 115.
*Description:* Prepares camera-ready art for advertising and packaging printing.

**Gazette Press, Inc.**   (415) 540-8500
2920 7th St.
Berkeley, CA 94710
*Contact:* Melissa Ridlon, Human Resources.
*Employs:* 170.
*Description:* Specializes in web printing of advertising materials, posters, and signs.

# 9

# Technology and Applied Sciences

The image of technology has come a long way since 1968, when computers were portrayed in that year's hit movie, *2001: A Space Odyssey*, as malevolent murdering villains. In the film Hal, the computer, turned out to be a pretty bad guy/machine. Now that we've reached the '80s, however, technology companies have succeeded in making computers and technology in general seem a lot more friendly and helpful.

This chapter is about some of the companies that are responsible for the dramatic change in the public's attitude toward technology. It will give you an overview of the burgeoning applied science and high-tech industries in the Bay Area and some ideas about how to begin a job search in these fast-paced fields.

Since there are career opportunities of both a technical and a non-technical nature, the chapter is written so as to provide some help to the uninitiated as well as to interest some of the electronics mavens who may read this.

For the past 10 years the United States gradually has been losing its lead in the steel and auto industries and in many consumer product categories (e.g., television) to foreign competitors. At the same time, in the Bay Area there has been an explosion of technological breakthroughs and opportunities for American entrepreneurs to demonstrate their expertise. It isn't an overstatement to say that a big part of the future of our economy and the makeup of our society is dependent on these new technologies. High-tech is here to stay and will have as much, if not more, impact on our society as the invention of the automobile has had during the past three-quarters of the century.

## Bay Area Technology and Applied Science Fields

### KEY SEGMENTS

So many new companies and new technologies are still developing in the Silicon Valley that it's hard to make generalizations about all that the Bay Area technical and scientific field has to offer. But to draw a partial picture of what's meant by *high-tech* the field has been divided into some basic categories in this chapter. The following segments often overlap.

#### Government or Government-Supported Research

This category includes laboratories, weapons, and aerospace projects, including Lawrence Livermore labs, Lawrence Berkeley Labs, and Lockheed Missiles and Space Company.

#### University Research

This includes the science and engineering departments of the Universities of Stanford and California at Berkeley and Stanford's spin-off research institute, SRI.

#### Semiconductors

This industry manufactures the silicon chips that the computer revolution depends on and for which Silicon Valley is named. Fairchild, which really started the semiconductor industry, spawned Intel and National Semiconductor, which, in turn, bore Advanced Micro Devices, Apple, and LSI Logic. Currently the semiconductor industry is going through some dramatic shifts as foreign competition, price promotion, and new forms of semiconductor technology create rapid changes in the market. Companies that have invested heavily in research and development have seen it pay off in new product breakthroughs that have allowed them to fare relatively well.

The semiconductor industry employs electrical technicians, hardware and software engineers, and manufacturing personnel as well as corporate communications, sales, finance, industrial relations, strategic planning, quality control, data processing, and marketing people.

## Computers

The computer industry here includes IBM, Hewlett-Packard, Amdahl, Apple, Tandem, and Atari. IBM was in the Silicon Valley first, and Gene Amdahl worked for IBM. He started his own firm in 1970. Hewlett-Packard is one of the original Bay Area companies that began the high-tech industry. Its founders were two graduating students urged by a Stanford electrical engineering professor to stay in the Bay Area and found their company locally. All three—IBM, Hewlett-Packard, and Amdahl—are known for large, main-frame computer systems. High-tech analysts expect that the market for main-frame computers will be five times as large in 1985 as it was in 1975 and that the emphasis will be on development of new services and additional software packages to meet the specific needs of computer users. The shift away from new equipment and toward new software needed to use the equipment is likely to give the market leaders in large-scale computers a distinct advantage. It is they who can best afford to develop and market software that is compatible with their own machines.

One new large-scale computer company that is expected to grow in the next few years is Trilogy. Gene Amdahl and his son formed this new company, which is designing and manufacturing a new IBM-compatible, high-performance computer that will be easier and more reliable to use. Another growing company is Tandem, which builds non-stop "failure-proof" computers that continue the job even if parts fail somewhere in the system.

The other side of the computer business is that of the so-called personal or small computers. Apple, Tandy, Commodore, and Atari, along with IBM, are the leaders in these home and office computers. Wang and Xerox are also competing in the growing market. A little-known fact is that Apple is actually an offshoot of Atari. Apple founders had an idea that their Atari employer wasn't ready to invest in. So they designed the Apple, the first personal computer, on their own. As the market for personal computers continues to expand, Apple will likely hold its own in the face of competition. As in the main-frame side of the industry, the emphasis will be shifting to service and applications, and that means software. Apple has more software written for it than any other kind of computer to date. That alone is expected to make it continue to appeal to a widening audience.

Entry level jobs in the computer business may include system analysts, sales representative, mechanical and electrical engineers, drafters, mechanical designers, customer service personnel, systems engineers who work on hardware, and programmers who work on developing software. The companies advise that completion of crash courses (e.g., Control Data) are not really sufficient to meet most of their hiring needs. A BS in engineering or computer science is preferred for the technical jobs.

Computer companies also employ people in accounting, finance, training and development, sales, public relations, sales promotion, marketing, and advertising. For marketing or advertising jobs technical marketing experience is preferred but not absolutely necessary; an interest and growing fascination with the computer "revolution" *is* necessary.

### Robotics

The robotics companies are currently working to develop considerably smarter robots than ever before. Firms like United Technologies, Ford Motor Company, Fairchild, Lockheed, and Hewlett-Packard, and think tanks at Stanford and SRI International, all are taking robotics very seriously.

Some of the most exciting breakthroughs are coming from fairly young firms like Machine Intelligence and Microbot. Mathematical formulas, complex circuitry, and new programming are all being experimented with in order to make the next generation of robots truly helpful to people.

### Computer Support and Services

This field includes firms such as Raychem, which makes the wire, cable, and tubing for computers, and Visicorp Personal Software, which designs and markets the computer software that allows lay people with no programming knowledge to use the computer efficiently. Visicorp Personal Software is best known for its Visicalc software package, which allows managers to try out various budget options quickly and see the likely impacts on sales and profits.

The computer support and service industry hires engineers, testing technicians, quality assurance people, personnel workers, graphics designers, computer graphics specialists, marketing managers, and technical writers.

### Data Storage

Companies such as Ampex and Memorex develop the tapes and discs that make higher-density information storage possible. The latest breakthroughs are in the Alar discs, which are reusable discs with advanced technology film read/write heads.

Data storage companies employ primarily engineers and programmers, sales and customer representatives, and designers. They also have public relations, human resources, finance, training, sales promotion (especially exhibits and trade shows) advertising, and marketing people.

### Telecommunications and Microwaves

This field includes companies like Rolm and Avantek, which will likely benefit from the antitrust settlement between the Justice Department and American Telephone and Telegraph.

Fiber optics is the new technology in telecommunications. Laser-filled optical fibers transmit 10,000 times faster than copper cable, weigh less and are more reliable.

Telecommunications and microwave firms have design, manufacturing, microwave, mechanical, and electrical engineers, and programmers as well as public relations, advertising, planning, finance, and human resources people. Sales managers may often be promoted from within the engineers' ranks.

### Laser Technology

This industry may soon make possible the invention of three-dimensional semiconductors. These companies develop a variety of scientific and medical applications for laser use in manufacturing and medicine. Coherent Inc. and Spectra Physics are two of the well-known laser applications firms here.

### Video Entertainment

The industry that began with Atari's Pong game in 1972 has now passed the film industry in profits. The leading Bay Area firms are Atari, Activision, and Imagic. Others, like Magnavox's Odyssey, are headquartered elsewhere. The industry is currently estimated to be at about $3 billion in annual sales and is expected to increase to $5 billion by 1986. But some believe that interest in video games may cool, making it impossible to reach more than 20 percent of the population. Price wars on machines and cassettes have also begun to affect profit margins.

Jobs in the game companies include sales and marketing, hardware and software engineering, finance, administration (e.g., personnel, security, safety, etc.) and manufacturing operations management. The companies look for electronics backgrounds for the manufacturing jobs. Marketing and sales jobs, on the other hand, have gone to people with wine, apparel, or consumer products marketing backgrounds.

## Science and Applied Medical

This group includes genetic engineering, pharmaceutical, medical instrumentation, and research firms. This is a controversial field in that the scientists are at the forefront of human biology and drug research. Most of these products cannot be pretested on large samples of humans, and even after approval by the FDA the effects of the new drugs may remain unknown. Bay Area genetic engineering companies such as Genentech and Cetus have attracted attention recently with their breakthroughs in applications of recombinant DNA. Clinical trials with Interferon provided to cancer patients began in 1982.

The pharmaceutical and applied medical research companies employ pharmacologists, physicists, and biologists, along with designers, draftsmen, packaging engineers, lab technicians, chemical and electrical engineers, computer scientists, geneticists, technical writers, marketing and sales managers, finance, personnel, and administrative services people. Some of the firms (e.g., Collagen Corporation) have rather traditional marketing career paths, beginning with assistant product managers.

## GETTING A JOB IN A TECHNOLOGICAL OR APPLIED SCIENCE FIRM

Although the technology and science fields described here are highly diverse, there are some fundamental features that are common to most of the fields and companies represented. If you understand these, you will be far better prepared to launch your job search in that you will know which aspects of your background and abilities to emphasize.

1. *High-tech is a field populated with entrepreneurs.* Your ability to take risks and be competitive will likely be viewed as highly important since this is the fundamental culture of the Silicon Valley. Employers will be looking for creativity and imagination as well as good analytical skills.
2. *Marketing know-how and leadership are needed.* Recently there has been a shift in the high-tech fields from product technology breakthroughs to service- and user-oriented breakthroughs. Most high-tech people are oriented towards the former rather than the latter. Your ability to demonstrate marketing knowledge that can be applied to problem solving will be impressive. But make sure you can move fast.

These people get impatient with packaged-goods rules of thumb and risk-averse lengthy research on every aspect of a marketing decision. They are looking for people who can use their background experience to make decisions and judgments quickly in this fast-paced world.

3. *Communication with lay people is becoming more important.* If the technical fields are to expand to an ever greater portion of the public, they require the ability to make the benefits of science and technology understandable to a wider audience (hence the concept of "user-friendly" computers.) This means that there will be a demand for more software programs to make computers usable; more technical and PR writers to make products comprehensible; more customer service people, system analysts, and repair experts to repair and adapt equipment to meet customer needs; and more marketing people and salespeople to create more product demand.

4. *The workstyle and lifestyle in the valley is casual, incestuous, egalitarian, and competitive.* Results, not outward accoutrements of success, seem to matter more than anything in these technical fields. Dress is casual, work spaces are rather egalitarian (e.g., everyone in cubicles), and everyone seems to know everyone else sooner or later.

Competition among companies for experienced personnel is fierce, so companies are constantly recruiting for experienced managers. There is a lot of job hopping, so this adds to the fertilization process between firms.

## TECHNICAL PUBLICATIONS

- *Information Systems in the 80's: Products, Markets and Vendors,* by Ulric Weil, who is Morgan Stanley's computer industry analyst.
- *Innovative Work Places of San Francisco Bay Area,* Association of Bay Area Governments, Claremont Hotel, Berkeley, CA 94523; (415) 841-9730.
- *Genetic Prophecy: Beyond the Double Helix,* by Dr. Zsolt Itarsanyi and Richard Hutton.
- *The Soul of a New Machine,* by Tracey Kidder.
- *Who's Who in Technology Today.*
  This four-volume reference series includes biographies of 27,000 professionals in all areas of high technology. If your library does not yet have a copy it can be ordered from J. Dick & Co., at 500 Hyacinth Place, Highland Park, IL 60035; (312) 433-0824.

There are also numerous periodicals to read, including:

- *Word Processing World*
- *Byte* (microcomputers)
- *Output* (data processing)

## TECHNICAL ORGANIZATIONS

Some organizations through which to make contacts include the following.

American Electronics Association
2680 Hanover St.
Palo Alto, CA 94306
(415) 857-9300

Society of Women Engineers
160 Sansome St.
San Francisco, CA 94114
(415) 421-3184

California Society of Professional Engineers
1005 12th St.
Sacramento, CA 95814
(916) 442-1041

Another way to work in the technology and science fields is to contact the venture capital firms who finance the new companies in exchange for partial ownership and future profits. These companies hire experienced investment and financial analysts as well as some new MBA's. Keep in mind that talking to venture capitalists can be an excellent way to gain insight into some of the high-tech businesses you have an interest in. It is their business to stay informed about the new trends in these fields and they provide investment advice (which can sometimes be helpful career research information too) to interested potential investors. It is estimated that 30 percent of all United States venture capital goes to Silicon Valley start-up firms.

Some of the venture capital firms in the Bay Area are:

Asset Management Associates
1417 Edgewood Drive
Palo Alto, CA 94301
(415) 321-3133
*Contact:* Franklin Johnson, Partner.

Capital Management Services
2200 Sand Hill Road
Menlo Park, CA 94025
(415) 854-3927
*Contact:* Don Valentine, President.

Early Stages
244 California St.
San Francisco, CA 94111
(415) 986-5700
*Contact:* Michael Berolzheimer, Partner.

Hambrecht Quist
235 Montgomery St.
San Francisco, CA 94104
(415) 986-5500
*Contact:* William Hambrecht, Partner.

Institutional Venture Associates
3000 Sand Hill Rd.
Menlo Park, CA 94025
(415) 854-0132
*Contact:* John Poitras, Partner.

Kilner, Perkins, Caulfied & Byers
4 Embarcadero Center
San Francisco, CA 94111
(415) 421-3110
*Contact:* Tom Perkins, Partner.

For more information on venture capital firms read *Venture Capital Journal,* P.O. Box 348, Wellesley, MA 02181; (617) 235-5405, or contact Western Association of Venture Capitalists, 3000 Sand Hill Rd., Menlo Park, CA 94024; (415) 854-1322.

There are also career/job fairs at many of the big Bay Area hotels. Check with the San Francisco Convention and Visitors Bureau, 201 Convention Plaza, San Francisco, CA 94102; (415) 974-6900, for information on dates.

## RECRUITERS

Headhunters who specialize in technical companies include these:

Abdo Associates
1310 Hollenbeck Ave.
Sunnyvale, CA 94087
(408) 736-0650
*Contact:* Ron Abdo, Manager.
*Description:* Specializes in engineering recruiting.

Chase Executive Personnel
226 W. Brokaw Rd, Ste. 645
San Jose, CA 95410
(408) 998-0600
*Contact:* Todd Perry, General Manager.

Colehower Associates
375 Distel Circle
Los Altos, CA 94022
(415) 968-3060
*Contact:* Howard Colehower, President.
*Description:* Technical recruitment of all kinds.

Dunhill
150 N. Wiget
Walnut Creek, CA 94598
(415) 543-0308
*Contact:* Dave Doyle, President.
*Description:* Specializes in data processing, systems analysis, and engineering recruitment.

Mandles Information Services
44 Montgomery St., Ste. 2424
San Francisco, CA 94104
(415) 781-0241
*Contact:* Clifford Roseman, Partner.
*Description:* Specializes in data processing search.

Source EDP
50 California St.
San Francisco, CA 94111
(415) 434-2410
*Contact:* Don Hackett, Associate Director.
*Description:* Specializes in professional recruitment for computing field.

## TECHNOLOGY-RELATED JOB TITLES AND SALARY RANGES

The technological fields employ a wide variety of professionals at all levels. Status and salaries tend to increase with the amount of education far more than is generally the case. Of course, experience and reputation also affect job titles and income.

Most technology-related fields offer job opportunities related to computers, the sciences, engineering, and business management. Each of these categories is discussed below, with Bay Area salary ranges provided.

## Computers

One good example of a career path in the computer field is that leading from *programmer* to *management information systems (MIS) director*. The career starts with a *programmer* who may perform design, coding, and testing of information systems. The next step could be to *systems analyst* (or *senior programmer analyst*), a person who guides programmers, modifies and creates new software, and ensures system reliability. Next is the *project manager* job, which involves supervision and communication of outcomes of computer projects or studies. The next level is management, where the title is *programming supervisor* or *systems manager*, and responsibilities include achievement of company objectives for programming (e.g., compatibility with finance or marketing administration). Eventually the next promotion may be to *MIS director*, the person who has responsibility for the profitable application of computer resources to company problems.

The ranges provided here for Bay Area salaries in the computer field assume at least a BS degree.

- Programmer Trainee: $15,000–$22,000
- Junior Programmer: $16,000–$27,000
- Senior Programmer: $23,000–$38,000
- Systems Programmer (Analyst): $18,000–$48,000
- Project Manager: $20,000–$54,000
- Programming Supervisor: $25,000–$60,000
- MIS Director: $29,000–$87,000
- EDP Auditor: $19,000–$44,000
- Marketing Representative (sales): $26,000–$33,000
- Marketing Manager: $35,000–$97,000

## Sciences

Science job titles and income levels are affected by your educational degree, and in some career fields advancement requires a PhD.

- Chemistry: $17,500–$27,000 (with PhD)
- Computer Science: $18,700–$24,000 (with PhD)
- Physics: $21,000–$28,000 (with PhD)
- Geology: $23,000–$26,000
- Biology: $15,000–$18,000
- Math: $18,000–$24,000

Usually the career paths start with *researcher* ($20,000–$29,000), then move to *research scientist* ($23,000–$35,000), and next to *senior research scientist* ($27,000–$42,000). *Project director* follows, and then *chief scientist* or *laboratory head* ($36,000–$56,000) or a transition to general management.

## Engineering

West Coast engineers draw the highest engineering salaries in the United States. And engineering job offers continue to lead most other fields in providing job offers for college graduates.

Engineering career paths generally start with the title of *junior engineer* ($18,000–$26,000), then go to *associate engineer* ($19,000–$29,000), then to *senior engineer* ($23,000–$38,000). Next is *engineering supervisor* ($29,000–$43,000), followed by *chief engineer* ($32,000–$47,000).

Different engineering specialties vary in salary potential, with petroleum engineering usually paying the highest starting salary of those hiring at the bachelor's degree level. Here are typical ranges for starting salaries in the Bay Area:

|  | *Bachelor's Degree* | *Advanced Degree (PhD)* |
|---|---|---|
| Nuclear | $22,000 | $25,000 |
| Mechanical | $22,000 | $25,000 |
| Industrial | $16,000 | $24,000 |
| Electrical | $15,000 | $30,000 |
| Civil | $14,000 | $30,000 |
| Chemical | $23,000 | $31,000 |
| Aeronautical | $21,000 | $32,000 |
| Petroleum | $26,000 | $36,000 |

## General Management

Other job titles in technical firms tend to be similar to those in other fields except that in many of the new technical businesses in the Silicon Valley salaries are higher than in the more traditional industrial firms. This seems to be because many of these companies are growing so fast that they are anxious to hire the best managers they can possibly find and pay them generously to perform well. Also, since many of these companies have been extremely profitable they can afford to pay top dollar.

## INSIDERS' ADVICE

Silicon Valley experts agree that there are several things you can do to land the job you want:

1. *Identify specifically what job you want,* by name and by division, and clearly describe your requirements (salary, four-day work week, flextime, etc.).
2. *Contact the head of the firm.* Many of these companies are really personality cults following a strong entrepreneurial personality. This person (almost always a man) is usually the founder and is still apt to be the real decision maker for the firm. Try contacting him at 7:30 A.M. when he gets to work.
3. *Find ways to demonstrate your genuine interest and potential long-term loyalty to the company.* Because many of these companies are somebody's "baby," this approach will have a real impact. Many of the firms, such as Activision, actively encourage a family feeling among their staff by vacationing all together in Europe or Hawaii. See if this is true for your target firm and then start acting like a new member of the family.

## TECHNOLOGY DIRECTORY

Listings are organized within the general scientific and technical categories discussed in the chapter. Because of the overlapping nature of the technological field, some companies may actually belong in several categories. Companies are grouped according to their primary reputation.

### Government Contracted or Supported

**Applied Technology, Division of Itek**    (408) 732-2710
645 Almanor Ave.
Sunnyvale, CA 94086
*Contact:* Dr. John Grigsby, Vice-President
   Bernie Dolling, Employment Manager.
*Employs:* 1,800
*Description:* State-of-the-art technology design and manufacture of early warning threat systems.

**Ford Aerospace & Communications**    (415) 494-7400
Western Development Lab
3939 Fabian Way
Palo Alto, CA 94303
*Contact:* Dr. Kenneth Rose, General Manager
   Bill Jones, Employment Manager
*Employs:* 5,000

*Description:* Division of Ford Motor Company that manufactures and tests aerospace equipment such as satellites. Approximately 50 percent of contracts are private. Communications satellites.

**Kaiser Electronics** (408) 946-3000
2701 Orchard Parkway
San Jose, CA 95134
*Contact:* Joe Smead, President.
   Sharon McCarthy, Employment.
*Employs:* 1,400
*Description:* Design and development of CRT display systems for military aviation.

**Lawrence Berkeley Laboratory** (415) 486-4000
University of California
1 Cyclatron Rd.
Berkeley, CA 94720
*Contact:* Jim Coleman, Chief of Staff.
*Employs:* 2,500
*Description:* Operated by Berkeley under contract to U.S. Department of Energy. Research in nuclear science, biology, medicine, high energy, physics, molecular and materials science. This is the so-called "Rad Lab."

**Lawrence Livermore Labs** (415) 422-1100
PO Box 808
Livermore, CA 94550
*Contact:* James McCullom, Personnel Director.
*Employs:* 7,200.
*Description:* Part of University of California under contract to Department of Energy. Research and development of weapons, energy, medicine, etc.

**Lockheed Missiles and Space** (408) 742-4321
1111 Lockheed Way
PO Box 504
Sunnyvale, CA 94086
*Contact:* George Burton, Employment Development Manager.
*Employs:* 18,000.
*Description:* Missile and space systems for NASA, DOD, etc. The laboratories employ scientists, computer scientists, mathematicians, and engineers as well as purchasing, transportation, and personnel specialists, technical editors, buyers, artists, film makers, photographers, architects, and business administrators.

**Sandia Laboratories** (415) 422-7011
East Ave.
PO Box 969
Livermore, CA 94550
*Contact:* Don Wagner, Personnel Director
*Employs:* 1,100.
*Description:* Under contract to Department of Defense. Research and development of nuclear weapons and alternate energy sources.

**Westinghouse Electric (Marine Division)**    (408) 735-2475
401 E. Hendy Ave.
Sunnyvale, CA 94088
*Contact:* Margaret Gurley, Communications and Employment.
*Employs:* 2,500.
*Description:* Large-scale manufacturing of equipment such as ship propulsion, submarine missile tubes, radiation shields.

## Energy Research

**Electrical Power Research Institute (EPRI)**    (415) 855-2000
3412 Hillview Ave.
Palo Alto, CA 94303
*Contact:* Floyd Culler, Administrative Director.
*Employs:* 700.
*Description:* The research institute for the nation's electrical power utility companies. The utilities fund EPRI to manage and conduct research on ways to maximize and develop electrical energy. Employs technical research people, including nuclear, coal, environmental engineers; scientists; systems analysts; and operations research specialists. Publishes *EPRI Journal.*

## Semiconductor Industry

**Advanced Micro Devices**    (408) 732-2400
901 Thompson Pl.
Sunnyvale, CA 94086
*Contact:* W.J. Sanders, President.
*Employs:* 4,200.
*Description:* Supplies consumer market (Atari video games such as Pac Man and E.T.) with integrated chips and makes large-scale chips for commercial and military.

**American Micro Systems Inc.**    (408) 246-0330
3800 Homestead Rd.
Santa Clara, CA 95051
*Contact:* Robert Penn, President.
*Employs:* 3,600.
*Description:* Manufactures semiconductors and microprocessors.

**Fairchild**    (415) 962-5011
464 Ellis St.
Mountain View, CA 94042
*Contact:* Bill Strickland, Vice-President, Personnel
*Employs:* 20,000 worldwide.
*Description:* Started the semiconductor industry and manufactures devices in every area of semiconductors; also develops and manufactures automatic test equipment.

*Positions and Training:* One of the only companies in the field to hire BAs, especially with business major, for sales jobs; training program for new engineer recruits.

**Intel** (408) 987-8080
3065 Bowers Ave.
Santa Clara, CA 95051
*Contact:* A.S. Grove, President.
*Employs:* 17,000.
*Description:* Inventors of microprocessors and market leader in sales and the new technology, microcontroller, destined to replace microprocessors (contains five times the transistors and works 10 times as fast, holding more than three times the data storage).

**National Semiconductor** (408) 721-5000
2900 Semiconductor Dr.
Santa Clara, CA 95051
*Contact:* Ellen Mickelfelder, Corporate Director of Staff and Placement.
*Employs:* 8,500 in Bay Area.
*Description:* Large semiconductor firm; experienced slowdown in '82 as a result of changing technology and increased price competition.

**Raytheon Semiconductor** (415) 968-9211
350 Ellis St.
Mountain View, CA 94040
*Contact:* Lance Barnard, Recruitment.
*Employs:* 850.
*Description:* Specializes in MSI, LSI, VLSI monolith circuits and bipolar memory products.

**Signetics** (408) 739-7700
811 East Arques Ave.
PO Box 409
Sunnyvale, CA 94086
*Contact:* Bonnie Nunke, Corporate Director of Employment.
*Employs:* 4,000.
*Description:* Integrated solid-state circuitry and semiconductors; experienced slowdown in '82 due to changing technology.

## Computer Industry

**Amdahl Corporation** (408) 746-6000
1237 E. Arques Ave.
Sunnyvale, CA 94086
*Contact:* Jack Lewis, President.
  Sam Osaki, Technical Recruiter.
*Employs:* 4,000.
*Description:* Large-frame data processing computers.

**Apple Computers**   (408) 996-1010
20525 Mariani Ave.
Cupertino, CA 95014
*Contact:* Jay Elliot, Human Resources Manager.
*Employs:* 1,661.
*Description:* Designed and introduced personal computers.

**Commodore Business Machines**   (408) 727-1130
3330 Scott Blvd.
Santa Clara, CA 95054
*Contact:* Jack Tramiel, Vice-Chairman.
*Employs:* 300.
*Description:* Known for the Vic-20, the under-$300 home computer you attach
    to your television.

**Digital Equipment Corporation**   (408) 727-0200
2525 Augustine Dr.
Santa Clara, CA 95051
*Contact:* Nancy Moser, Personnel Director.
    Ken Olsen, President.
*Employs:* 1,000 in Bay Area.
*Description:* A leading manufacturer of minicomputers.

**Four Phase Systems**   (408) 255-0900
10700 N. De Anza Blvd.
Cupertino, CA 95014
*Contact:* Ted Sorenson, Staffing Manager.
*Employs:* 2,800.
*Description:* Manufactures minicomputers, word processors, office automation.

**Hewlett-Packard**   (415) 857-1501
3000 Hanover St.
Palo Alto, CA 94304
*Contact:* William Kravens, Personnel Director.
*Employs:* 66,000.
*Description:* Manufactures computers, electronic measuring instruments,
    calculators, solid-state components, medical and chemical instrumentation.

**IBM**   (415) 545-2000
425 Market St.
San Francisco, CA 94105
*Contact:* Howard Siegel, Employment Representative.
*Employs:* 3,000 in the Bay Area.
*Description:* Manufactures large-scale computers, personal computers, word
    processors, office equipment.

**Sperry Univac**   (415) 986-6070
3 Embarcadero Center
San Francisco, CA 94111

*Contact:* James Parker, Personnel Manager.
*Employs:* 2,250.
*Description:* Manufactures large-scale main-frame computers.

**Trilogy Systems Corporation**    (408) 973-9333
5150 Great American Parkway
Santa Clara, CA 95050
*Contact:* Brian Duff, Personnel Specialist.
*Description:* Manufactures high-performance computers.

**Wang**    (415) 956-7077
30 Grant Ave.
San Francisco, CA 94108
*Contact:* Stephen Glenn, Personnel Manager.
*Employs:* 150 in Bay Area.
*Description:* One of the leaders in word processing systems and minicomputers.

## ROBOTICS

**Androbot**    (408) 745-1084
1287 Lawrence Station Rd.
Sunnyvale, CA 94086
*Contact:* Thomas Frisina, President.
*Employs:* 35.
*Description:* A new Nolan Bushnell (founder of Atari) company that manufactures robot servants for the home.

**Machine Intelligence**    (408) 737-7960
330 Potrero Ave.
Sunnyvale, CA 94086
*Contact:* Barry Rapozzo, Vice-President.
*Employs:* 90.
*Description:* Manufactures robots with eyes especially for work in plants manufacturing auto parts and toxic chemicals.

**Microbot**    (415) 968-8888
453 H Ravendale Dr.
Mountain View, CA 94043
*Contact:* G. W. Rhodes, President.
*Employs:* 30.
*Description:* Manufactures robotic arms for computerized construction and assembly.

**Superior Robotics of America**    (707) 763-9625
Petaluma, CA 94952
*Contact:* Bill Bakaleinikoff, President.
*Employs:* 10.
*Description:* Manufactures robot security guards and industrial robots, known

for "Robot Redford," a robot that makes appearances at trade shows.

**Syn-Optics**    (408) 734-8563
1240 Birchwood Drive
Sunnyvale, CA 94086
*Contact:* Bob Magill, Sales Manager.
*Employs:* 50.
*Description:* Division of Tele-Syn-Optics, Inc.; manufactures mechanical eyes
and vision systems for medical and industrial use.

## Computer Support and Services

**Applied Materials**    (408) 727-5555
3050 Bowers Ave.
Santa Clara, CA 95051
*Contact:* Scott Lingen, Personnel.
James Morgan, President.
*Employs:* 900.
*Description:* Manufactures capital equipment that manufactures silicon
wafers.

**Calma Company (Subsidiary of GE)**    (408) 744-1950
212 Gibraltar Dr.
Sunnyvale, CA 94086
*Contact:* Tim Outman, Recruitment.
*Employs:* 1,100.
*Description:* Makes graphic data systems, computer-aided design (CAD)
equipment, automated insertion software.

**Cullinane Database Systems**    (415) 856-0100
2471 E. Bayshore Blvd.
Palo Alto, CA 94303
*Contact:* Jim Zimmerman, President.
*Employs:* 13 in this sales office.
*Description:* Leader in software package industry.

**Raychem**    (415) 361-3333
300 Constitution Dr.
Menlo Park, CA 94025
*Contact:* Claudia Lingquist, Corporate Selection Manager.
Paul Cook, President.
*Employs:* 5,000.
*Description:* Manufactures coaxial cable, termination device, and hookup wires
for the electronics and computer industries.

**Visicorp Personal Software**    (408) 946-9000
2895 Zanker Rd.
San Jose, CA 95134

*Contact:* Jack Hart, Personnel Manager.
   Terry Opdendyk, President.
*Employs:* 175.
*Description:* Software developers for IBM and Apple, best known for
   "Visicalc."


## Data Storage

**Ampex Corporation**   (415) 367-2011
401 Broadway
Redwood City, CA 94063
*Contact:* Judy Puckett, Employment Manager.
   Arthur Hausman, President, CEO.
*Employs:* 1,700 in the Bay Area.
*Description:* Disc drives for computers, video and audio tape recording
   equipment, instruction recorders for satellites.

**Datapoint**   (408) 732-7330
686 W. Maude Ave.
Sunnyvale, CA 94086
*Contact:* Elaine Goldberg, Professional Hiring.
*Employs:* 500.
*Description:* Design and manufacture of magnetic tape drives and discs.

**Memorex Corporation**   (408) 987-1563
San Thomas at Central Expressway
Santa Clara, CA 95052
*Contact:* Alan Hunt, Employment Manager.
*Employs:* 5,600.
*Description:* Design and manufacture of tapes and discs that can store ever-
   increasing amounts of information per square inch.

**Shugart**   (408) 733-0100
475 Oakmead Parkway
Sunnyvale, CA 94086
*Contact:* Stan Jones, Employment Manager.
   Jim Campbell, President.
*Employs:* 2,400.
*Description:* First brought out the "floppy disc," known primarily for OEM
   and disc manufacturing.


## Telecommunications and Microwave

**Addington Laboratories**   (408) 245-6810
785 Palomar Ave.
Sunnyvale, CA 94086

*Contact:* Cindy Boucher, Personnel Analyst.
*Employs:* 500.
*Description:* Does microwave component manufacture.

**Aertech Industries**    (408) 732-0880
825 Stewart Dr.
Sunnyvale, CA 94086
*Contact:* Kathy Cotton, Recruiter.
    Kenneth Thompson, President.
*Employs:* 700.
*Description:* Components for microwave systems for defense and space
    applications.

**Avantek**    (408) 727-0700
3175 Bowers Ave.
Santa Clara, CA 95051
*Contact:* Robert Bush, Vice President, Personnel
*Employs:* 1,500.
*Description:* Makes telecommunications and semiconductor components.

**California Microwave**    (408) 732-4000
990 Almanor Ave.
Sunnyvale, CA 94086
*Contact:* Ginger Washburn, Personnel.
    David Leeson, President, CEO.
*Employs:* 900.
*Description:* Design, develop, and manufacture communication equipment for
    telecommunications and defense applications.

**GTE Lenkurt**    (415) 595-3000
1105 County Rd.
San Carlos, CA 94070
*Contact:* Betty Pole, Recruiter.
    Herbert Krengel, President.
*Employs:* 2,500.
*Description:* Manufactures transmission equipment for telecommunications.

**ICOT**    (415) 964-4635
830 Maude Ave.
Mountain View, CA 94043
*Contact:* Gloria Flores, Recruiter.
*Employs:* 300.
*Description:* Manufactures data and telecommunication network equipment
    (modems, multiplexers).

**Paradyne**    (408) 559-4000
1901 South Bascom Ave.
Campbell, CA 95008
*Contact:* Bill Hofing, Regional Manager.
*Employs:* 30.

*Description:* Modem manufacturer that has developed a system for remote data processing equipment to function as centralized computer.

**Rolm Corporation**   (408) 988-2900
4900 Old Ironsides Dr.
Santa Clara, CA 95050
*Contact:* Ed Smith, Recruitment.
  Ken Oshman, President.
*Employs:* 3,500.
*Description:* Manufactures communications systems; best known for "Milspec" computer.

**Varian Associates**   (415) 493-4000
611 Hansen Way
Palo Alto, CA 94303
*Contact:* Bob Holtcamp, Personnel Director.
  Tom Sege, President.
*Employs:* 8,000.
*Description:* Invented the first microwave device; known for linear accelerators, nuclear magnetic resonance, vacuum pumps, analytic instruments, and klystron tubes for VHR television transmitters.

## Laser Technology

**Coherent Inc.**   (415) 493-2111
3210 Porter Dr.
Palo Alto, CA 94304
*Contact:* James L. Hobart, President.
*Employs:* 650 in the Bay Area.
*Description:* Makes a wide range of applied laser technology products for medical and industrial uses.

**Spectra Physics**   (408) 946-6080
3333 N. 1st St.
San Jose, CA 95134
*Contact:* Judy Herboer, Corporate Manager of Employee Relations.
  Sam Collela, CEO.
*Employs:* 2,500.
*Description:* Laser applications, including medical (microsurgery, spectroscopy) and construction and manufacturing.

## Video Games

**Activision**   (415) 960-0410
2350 Bayshore Frontage Rd.
Mountain View, CA 94042

*Contact:* Mary Costa, Employment Manager.
   Jim Levy, President.
*Employs:* 150.
*Description:* Makes video cartridges for home video games.

**Atari Inc.**   (408) 734-5310
1349 Moffett Parkway
Sunnyvale, CA 94086
*Contact:* Corporate Recruiting and Placement Manager (or call to check
   manager's name for appropriate division, e.g., Coin Op, Home Computer,
   Electronics Division).
*Employs:* 10,000.
*Description:* Fastest growing consumer electronics marketing company;
   invented video games; also markets home computers. $1 billion in sales.

**Imagic Corporation**   (408) 399-2200
981 University Ave.
Los Gatos, CA 95030
*Contact:* Kirsten Smith, Manager, Recruiting and Staffing
*Employs:* 200
*Description:* Game company; three plants in Bay Area; known for "Wordstar."

## Science and Applied Medical

**ADAC Laboratories**   (408) 736-1101
255 San Geronimo Way
Sunnyvale, CA 94086
*Contact:* Renda Blacker, Director of Personnel
*Employs:* 250
*Description:* Nuclear medicine and radiation diagnostic equipment systems.

**Alza Corporation**   (415) 494-5000
950 Page Mill Rd.
Palo Alto, CA 94304
*Contact:* Darlene Mankovich, Employment.
   Martin Gerstel, President.
*Employs:* 330.
*Description:* Pharmaceutical research company.

**Bio-Rad Laboratories**   (415) 234-4130
2200 Wright Ave.
Richmond, CA 94804
*Contact:* David Schwartz, President.
*Employs:* 400.
*Description:* Develops and markets hemoglobin kits, chromatographs, and
   other analytic instruments.

**Barnes-Hind Pharmaceuticals Inc.**   (408) 736-5462
895 Kifer Rd.
Sunnyvale, CA 94086
*Contact:* Kevin Regan, President.
*Employs:* 350.
*Description:* Manufactures ophthalmological products, especially for contact
  lenses.

**Cetus Corporation**   (415) 549-3300
600 Bancroft Rd.
Berkeley, CA 94700
*Contact:* Elaine Montaine, Personnel.
  Dr. Peter Farley, President.
*Description:* Does genetic engineering, immunology, microbiology; produces
  interferon (recombinant DNA).

**Collagen Corporation**   (415) 856-0200
2455 Saber Pl.
Palo Alto, CA 94304
*Contact:* Susan Hoppa, Personnel.
  Harold Palefsky, President.
*Employs:* 200.
*Description:* Biomedical research and marketing company, focuses on collagen
  products (skin protein) for use by plastic surgeons and dermatologists.

**Cooper Laboratories, Inc.**   (415) 856-5000
3145 Porter Dr.
Palo Alto, CA 94304
*Contact:* Norm Mason, Personnel Administrator
*Employs:* 4,000 in the Bay Area.
*Description:* Includes Cooper Labs, Cooper Vision, and Cooper Care;
  manufactures and markets pharmaceuticals associated with contact lenses,
  ophthalmic surgery, and dental care.

**Cutter Laboratories**   (415) 420-4000
2200 Powell St.
Emeryville, CA 94662
*Contact:* Heidi Lawton, Personnel.
  Theodore Heinricks, President.
*Employs:* 4,000.
*Description:* Manufactures pharmaceuticals, including medical, dental,
  biological, and nutritional products. Recently developed a human plasma
  protein, effective in treating emphysema.

**Finnigan Corporation**   (408) 946-4848
355 River Oaks Parkway
San Jose, CA 95134

*Contact:* Chris Crotzinger, Recruitment.
  T.Z. Chu, President.
*Employs:* 450.
*Description:* Pharmaceutical, medical research, forensic study; manufactures
  computer-based chromatograph spectrometers.

**Genentech Inc.**   (415) 952-1000
460 Point San Bruno Blvd.
South San Francisco, CA 94680
*Contact:* Bill Higgins, Human Resources.
  Robert Swanson, President.
*Employs:* 420.
*Description:* Does genetic engineering; manufactures human pharmaceuticals,
  including human insulin, interferon (recombinant DNA), animal health care
  products, and enzyme production for food processing industry.

**Smith-Kline Instruments**   (408) 732-6000
485 Potrero Ave.
Sunnyvale, CA 94086
*Contact:* Dr. Glenn Bartlett, Vice President, Research and Development
*Employs:* 300.
*Description:* Does research and development of chemistry diagnostic products.

**Syntex Corporation**   (415) 855-5050
3401 Hillview Ave.
Palo Alto, CA 94304
*Contact:* Larry Kane, Personnel.
  Richard Rogers, President.
*Employs:* 2,000.
*Description:* Inventors of the first birth control pill; develops and markets
  pharmaceuticals, including arthritis medicine (Naproxen).

# 10

# Real Estate

Government employment estimates show that approximately 10–15 percent of employment opportunities in the United States are found in real estate or real estate–related businesses. In addition to real estate agents and brokers, there are escrow and title officers, appraisers, property managers, and leasing and property consultation managers.

## *Real Estate Opportunities in the Bay Area*

This chapter will discuss commercial and residential real estate and title insurance. But if you are interested in real estate as a career, you should also consider the real estate departments of savings and loan associations, insurance companies, banks, the government, businesses (especially retail or food chains), and franchising operations.

You probably know that California leads the nation in home real estate prices. What you may not know is that the state is also the leader in real estate education and research. In California, in order to get a real estate broker's license, you must have two years of full-time sales experience working for a broker plus six college level courses: (1) legal aspects of real estate, (2) real estate practice, (3) real estate finance, (4) real estate appraisal, (5) real estate economics or accounting; and (6) principles, law, property management, administration, escrows, advanced finance, advanced law, or advanced appraisal.

Applications, information, and forms for exams for agents' and brokers' licenses are available from the Department of Real Estate, 185 Berry St., San Francisco, CA 94107; (415) 557-3953.

Real estate courses are available at many Bay Area private and public colleges and universities. Local realtors are unanimous in their recommendation of The Anthony Schools. Contact the San Francisco branch at 2145 19th Ave., San Francisco, CA 94116, (415) 564-2970, for information on courses throughout the Bay Area.

Most real estate work involves selling on commission and is a lot like going into business for yourself. There are real estate offices in every town in practically every neighborhood, so you can be rather flexible in terms of location. Bay Area realtors say that the best background for real estate is sales experience and a business education. They mention that the sales training one gets at Xerox or IBM is particularly good background for real estate selling.

There are two broad areas of real estate: commercial real estate and residential real estate. Currently in the Bay Area they are being affected quite differently by the economy. Commercial real estate sales in San Francisco have been very good because of the new buildings that have gone up and the diversified local economy, which has kept businesses fairly stable. The residential picture has been totally different, with sales down about 35 percent due to the dramatic effects of high interest rates and uncertainty about the economy.

If you are trying to decide which kind of real estate market to enter, you should definitely arrange for informational interviews with a few of the many friendly brokers in the area. One important point to consider is that there is far more money to be made in commercial real estate than in residential real estate, and commercial real estate tends to be more business-oriented and less emotional than residential.

If you like real estate but would prefer a more secure salary than what you may earn selling on commission, you may want to consider property management or title insurance.

As a property manager you take care of investment property for the owner and handle upkeep, rent collection, tenant relations, etc. In exchange for these services your company receives a percentage (usually 30–40 percent) of the income on the property and pays you a steady salary.

Title insurance is a West Coast phenomenon that is an outgrowth of the pioneer and Gold Rush history of the area. Title insurance protects the title or deed to your property by first searching the public records for any obscure liens or claims to the property and then insuring you, the new owner, against any litigation that may arise. Title insurance companies have escrow and title officers. Escrow officers handle the close of a contract. This is a somewhat stressful job in that you must deal with the client buyer, broker, and lawyer at an emotional point in the buying-selling process and involves handling all the contract documents and financial details of the close.

The title department researches the history of the property and determines the risk of claims against the deed.

## REAL ESTATE PUBLICATIONS

For more information on Bay Area real estate, write for *California Real Estate Reference Book,*California Department of Real Estate, 185 Berry St., San Francisco, CA 94107.

Or read these periodicals:

- *Real Estate Today*
- *Real Estate Investors*
- *Fortune*
- *Commercial Remodeling* from QR Publishing in Chicago
- *San Francisco Progress* Real Estate Section

A good book to read on the overall real estate field is *The Real Estate Career Guide* by William Pivar, 1981.

Overall the trend in real estate is toward increasing professionalism and a more sophisticated understanding of the economic implications of property investments.

## REAL ESTATE JOB TITLES AND SALARY RANGES

### Real Estate

There are really only two jobs in real estate: the agent (or associate) and the broker. When you work as an agent you are almost always working on 100 percent commission with a contract specifying the commission split between you and the company.

In the Bay Area it is likely that you will start with a 50-50 split, and you often can produce about $40,000 in commissions. The split may change in your favor to 55-45 or 60-40 and so on.

The company pays no Social Security and provides no benefits. What you earn depends entirely on how hard you work and the clientele you can build up.

In residential real estate a good average agent earns $20,000–$40,000 per year.

In commercial real estate you may take longer to build your business, and you may have fewer sales (one per year), but you can probably make more money. The good average commercial agent could start at $10,000 per year, reach $25,000 in the second year, $50,000 in year three, and then $75,000 after that. For those who are really good $150,000–$200,000 a year is possible. Of course, real estate has good and bad years and, as is true of other commission sales work, you don't know what you'll make in any given year.

Some Bay Area commercial firms (Coldwell Banker and Cushman Wakefield, for example) may provide a "draw" for new agents just starting out. In these cases, the entry level person then begins by "going through the wheel," which means learning the ropes by serving as a helpful underling to more senior agents.

## Title Insurance

Title insurance has two major career paths: title search and escrow.

In title search the career path may start with the job of *title policy typist* (or preliminary typist) or *searcher*, who searches property title records to establish the "chain of records" or ownership history of a given property. Next is the *examiner*, who decides if any liens or claims currently exist on a property, and then the *title officer*, who determines risk levels for existing claims and puts the deal together for title insurance working with the escrow officer. The senior title officer is called an *advisory title officer* and may have several *title officers* to manage. Often title employees work "at the plant," where the county records of ownership on property are kept.

In escrow the career path may begin with the job of *title secretary* or *junior escrow officer* at entry level. At the next level is *senior escrow officer,* who is the key customer contact person and works with the real estate agents and consumer clients to finalize the sale of the property. *Advisory escrow officers* perform a coordinating administrative function and have less direct client contact.

Below are the typical Bay Area salary ranges for these careers.

ESCROW

- Title Secretary: $13,000–$17,000
- Junior Escrow: $20,000–$28,000
- Senior Escrow: $30,000–$55,000
- Advisory Escrow Officer: $30,000–$45,000

TITLE SEARCH

- Typist: $12,000–$16,000
- Searcher: $13,000–$18,000
- Examiner: $18,000–$22,000
- Title Officer: $24,000–$26,000

- Advisory Title Officer: $28,000–$32,000

## INSIDERS' ADVICE

Bay Area insiders advise you to have a nest egg of about six to eight months of living expenses to support yourself when you enter the real estate field. This is because real estate is a commission business and can be very difficult at the beginning, before you have learned a geographic area and built up a clientele.

To get a residential real estate job Bay Area realtors advise you to select the real estate office where you'd like to work and contact the people there directly. New agents begin by "taking floor time," which involves greeting and interviewing walk-in clients and handling new client calls.

For commercial real estate the approach is similar. Write to or call the manager of the target office and demonstrate your selling skills by selling your abilities.

If a real estate office has an empty desk, and you can convince the owners of your eagerness to learn, your hard-working orientation, and your sales abilities, they may be willing to give you a chance. Since there is no salary to be paid, the investment they make in trying you out is one of time (to show you the ropes) and $10,000–$15,000 per year for the secretarial and telephone support you'll need.

Insiders say that real estate is one field in which your traditional educational credentials are not a key factor in landing a job. Who you are and your family's social status are also unimportant. It will help to have attended the Anthony school real estate courses and to have your license in hand, though this also is not absolutely necessary.

California realtors recommend that you read *California Real Estate* to become more familiar with real estate trends here. You can order this magazine by writing or calling their office at 505 Shatto Place, Los Angeles, CA 90020; (213) 380-7190.

## REAL ESTATE DIRECTORY

### Commercial and Residential

**Cushman & Wakefield**   (415) 397-1700
Bank of America Center
San Francisco, CA 94104
*Contact:* B. J. Connell, Vice-President and Manager.
*Training:* Offers on-the-job program in building leasing (three months).
*Description:* Subsidiary of Rockefeller Center, headquarters in New York; 40 offices, nine in Bay Area.

**Coldwell Banker**   (415) 772-0291
1 Embarcadero Center
Ste. 2300
San Francisco, CA 94111
*Contact:* John C. Moss, Regional Personnel Manager.
*Training:* Offers six-month to one-year training program and will pay a salary
  to carry you until commissions take over.
*Description:* Second-largest commercial real estate firm in the United States.
  Also sizable residential real estate business. Subsidiary of Sears, and Co.

**Grubb & Ellis**   (415) 444-7500
1333 Broadway
Oakland, CA 94612
*Contact:* John Guillory, District Manager.
  Peggy Stinnett, Personnel.
*Description:* Third-largest commercial real estate firm in United States
  (largest headquartered here). Also large residential business.

**Hanford Freund & Co.**   (415) 981-5780
47 Kearney St.
Ste. 300
San Francisco, CA 94608
*Contact:* Andrew Stone, Vice-President, Sales.
  Glenn Matsui, Vice-President, Property Management.
*Description:* Investment and commercial real estate and property management.


## Residential Only

**Century 21**   (415) 932-2021
1777 North California Blvd.
Walnut Creek, CA 94596
*Contact:* This is a franchising office only; contact the office you want to work
  with (e.g., Century 21 - Brown & Brown Realty, 1936 Ocean Avenue, San
  Francisco, CA 94127)
*Description:* National franchised chain of real estate brokers.

**Hill & Co.**   (415) 921-6000
2107 Union St.
San Francisco, CA 94123
*Contact:* Barbara Sherer, Administration.
  John Levinsohn, Partner.
*Description:* Broker for medium to higher priced homes in San Francisco, no
  commercial real estate.

**Saxe Realty**   (415) 665-3800
1390 Noriega
San Francisco, CA 94122
*Contact:* Each branch manager hires own staff.
*Description:* Residential real estate and property management.

## Title Insurance

**Founders Title Co.**    (415) 421-9770
265 Montgomery St.
San Francisco, CA 94104
*Contact:* Robin Gurland, Personnel Manager.
*Description:* 10 offices in San Francisco.

**First American Title Co.**    (415) 989-1300
300 Pine St.
San Francisco, CA 94104
*Contact:* County manager at each office (listed in telephone book).
*Description:* Five offices in San Francisco.

**Safeco Title Insurance Company**    (415) 362-1871
417 Montgomery St.
San Francisco, CA 94104
*Contact:* Tom Kellogg, County Manager.
*Description:* One of the top five national title insurance companies.

**Title Insurance and Trust**    (415) 781-3500
160 Pine St.
San Francisco, CA 94111
*Contact:* Call San Francisco office for county managers' names, who decide
    hiring.
*Description:* Three offices in San Francisco.

**Transamerica Title Insurance Co.**    (415) 983-4400
600 Montgomery St.
San Francisco, CA 94104
*Contact:* David Porter, President.
*Description:* Subsidiary of Transamerica Corp. One of the leading title
    insurance companies, operating in 100 counties primarily in western states.

# 11

# Tourism, Hospitality, Arts, and Recreation

Tourism is a major part of the Bay Area's economy. This chapter presents some of the important segments of the industry: convention hospitality (especially hotels and restaurants), recreation, art, and science museums. The sights and cultural activities that attract visitors are enjoyed and supported by Bay Area residents and are an important contribution to the lifestyle.

Every year the Bay Area is visited by about 3 million tourists and conventioneers. They bring more than $1 billion in revenue, which supports some 60,000 full-time and part-time jobs for Bay Area residents. Around San Francisco there is some concern that the temporary shutdown (two years, from September 1982 to 1984) for repair of the cable car system will be a deterrent to travel to the Bay Area. However, the Moscone Convention Center, which opened in 1982, is expected to contribute to San Francisco's continuing position as one of the nation's most desirable sites for business and association meetings.

There are myriad ways to work in tourist-related business here. Many of the jobs are seasonal or in small restaurants, hotels, or retail shops located in high-traffic areas. This chapter covers only the major employers. Each segment is discussed, and then key businesses and organizations are noted.

## *Conventions and Tourism*

For national or large conventions the Bay Area has the new Moscone Convention Center in San Francisco. Other smaller convention sites include centers in San Mateo, Oakland, San Jose, and resort hotels such as Silverado Country Club in Napa and The Claremont Resort Hotel and Tennis Club in the East Bay.

The San Francisco Convention and Visitors Bureau is the city's tourist promotion agency. It is funded through San Francisco's hotel tax and through dues from member businesses. The objective of the organization is to increase the flow of visitors to San Francisco and thus maintain important tourism jobs and revenues. The bureau has three divisions: conventions, tourism, and administration. Expertise in sales, marketing, advertising, and hospitality is represented on the staff.

Convention exposition companies such as Greyhound Exposition Services operate primarily as trade show or convention contractors and arrange the logistics and set up presentations for meetings.

Convention contracting companies prefer people who are good at planning and problem solving and who are willing to work long hours.

The large tour companies such as Grayline contract with conventions to provide group-chartered sightseeing tours of the Bay Area.

## CONVENTIONS AND TOURISM JOB TITLES AND SALARY RANGES

Some of the jobs in tourism and at a convention center or bureau include:

- The *PR Director* who is in charge of marketing the city or facility to convention prospects, usually by familiarizing travel agents with the local attractions and amenities.
- The *Media Services Manager* who issues calendars of events and works with the media to gain publicity and enhance the facility's image.
- The *Convention Services Manager* who services the needs of the sponsoring organization and works to make its convention a success.
- The *Director* who oversees the organization, prepares the budget, and is responsible for operating within a budget.

Country club or convention center directors may earn $25,000 to $40,000 for a small club or center, and $40,000 to $70,000 for a large club or convention bureau. PR Directors can earn $20,000 to $35,000.

Experienced tour guides may earn $16,000 to $18,000, while tour managers may earn $30,000.

## INSIDERS' ADVICE

Since convention centers are organized to provide services and expert advice to the organizations and companies that are sponsoring the convention, there are very few entry level jobs. Insiders say that they generally hire experienced people from related areas such as travel agencies, large hotels or other convention facilities. Experts advise that experience as a desk clerk at a large hotel or as sales meeting coordinator at a large manufacturing firm is a good background for moving into a job with a convention facility.

## CONVENTIONS AND TOURISM DIRECTORY

**Claremont Resort Hotel and Tennis Club**    (415) 843-3000
41 Tunnel Rd.
Berkeley, CA 94623
*Contact:* Karen Antonucci, Personnel Manager
*Employs:* 35.
*Description:* First-class resort; 20 minutes from downtown San Francisco.

**Convention Cultural Facility**    (408) 277-5277
291 S. Market St.
San Jose, CA 95113
*Contact:* John Popovich, Director, or San Jose City Hall.
*Employs:* 34.
*Description:* Promotes and operates multipurpose performing arts center.

**Grayline Tours**    (415) 885-8500
420 Taylor St.
San Francisco, CA 94102
*Contact:* David Caldwell, Senior Vice-President.
*Employs:* 200.
*Description:* Sightseeing tour company.

**Greyhound Exposition Services**    (415) 761-0333
100 Utah Ave.
South San Francisco, CA 94080
*Contact:* Donna Randle.
*Description:* Convention and meeting presentation and logistics.

**International Visitors Center**    (415) 986-1388
312 Sutter St.
San Francisco, CA 94115
*Contact:* Virginia Farr, Director.
*Employs:* Three full-time plus volunteers.
*Description:* Nonprofit organization that promotes international understanding
    and profit by hosting and guiding foreign visitors on tours to the Bay Area.

**Oakland Convention and Visitors Bureau**   (415) 839-9000
1330 Broadway
Ste. 1105
Oakland, CA 94612
*Contact:* Chris Davis, Executive Director.
*Description:* Marketing agency for hotel industry and other local attractions.

**Oakland Convention Center**
450 10th St.
Oakland, CA 94607
*Contact:* John Conway, General Manager
*Description:* Under construction as of this publication date. Scheduled to open
   in spring 1983.

**Red and White Fleet—San Francisco Bay Cruise**   (415) 546-2810
Pier 41
San Francisco, CA 94133
*Contact:* David Pense, General Manager.
*Employs:* 200.
*Description:* San Francisco Bay Cruise and tourist ferry operates a fleet of
   seven boats.

**San Francisco Convention & Visitors Bureau**   (415) 974-6900
201 Convention Plaza
San Francisco, CA 94103
*Contact:* George Kirkland, Director.
   Charles Ahlers, Convention Sales Director.
   James Brokema, Vice President, Marketing
*Employs:* 50.
*Description:* City's promotion agency and liaison between visitors and business.

**Silverado Country Club & Resort**   (707) 255-2970
1600 Atlas Peak Rd.
Napa, CA 94558
*Contact:* Susan Williams, Personnel Director.
*Employs:* 450.
*Description:* Private country club and conference resort for groups of up to
   500.

## Hotel Management

   Career jobs in hotels include those in marketing, personnel, public
relations, food/beverage, catering, banquet, reservations, housekeeping
management. There are also controllers and general managers. Most of
the hotels prefer to train and promote from within. You may start in
sales management, as assistant duty manager at the front desk, or as
assistant restaurant manager. Many of the big hotels prefer a degree in
hotel/restaurant management or business. However, since they offer on-
the-job training, business degrees are not absolutely necessary.

## HOTEL MANAGEMENT RESOURCES

For more information check the following sources.

- Review the *Hotel and Motel Red Book,* which lists major hotels and manager contacts geographically.
- Contact the Hotel Sales Management Association, North California Chapter, (415) 921-1562.
- The University of San Francisco is offering a new business major called Hospitality Management. The studies include food and beverage, lodging and entertainment, travel and tourism. Contact the McLaren College of Business, 2130 Fulton St., San Francisco, CA 94117; (415) 666-6771; Dr. Joe Koppel, Director.
- By reading *Lodging Hospitality,* a monthly magazine serving the business, you will familiarize yourself with the concerns and trends in this field.

## HOTEL JOB TITLES AND SALARY RANGES

Hotel salary ranges vary by the size of the hotel. For the job titles below hotel sizes are defined by number of rooms:

- Small: 150–400 rooms
- Medium: 400–700 rooms
- Large: 700–1,000 rooms

| | *Small* | *Medium* | *Large* |
|---|---|---|---|
| Front Office Manager | $14,000–$16,000 | $16,000–$22,000 | $23,000–$32,000 |
| Assistant Housekeeper | $13,000–$15,000 | $15,000–$19,000 | $18,000–$26,000 |
| Executive Housekeeper | $14,000–$17,000 | $18,000–$23,000 | $25,000–$32,000 |
| Controller | $17,000–$25,000 | $24,000–$34,000 | $30,000–$42,000 |
| Sales Manager | $14,000–$18,000 | $18,000–$24,000 | $25,000–$34,000 |
| Director of Sales | $18,000–$23,000 | $24,000–$31,000 | $27,000–$39,000 |
| Director of Purchasing | $16,000–$22,000 | $23,000–$30,000 | $32,000–$41,000 |
| Director of Catering | $17,000–$22,000 | $21,000–$29,000 | $30,000–$40,000 |
| Kitchen Manager | $14,000–$16,000 | $17,000–$22,000 | $22,000–$25,000 |
| Maitre D' | $13,000–$16,000 | $17,000–$22,000 | $22,000–$25,000 |
| Chef | $16,000–$27,000 | $24,000–$31,000 | $32,000–$50,000 |
| Executive Chef | $20,000–$28,000 | $28,000–$45,000 | $47,000–$90,000 |
| Restaurant Manager | $15,000–$18,000 | $18,000–$24,000 | $25,000–$34,000 |
| Director of Marketing | $22,000–$27,000 | $29,000–$43,000 | $46,000–$90,000 |
| Director of Personnel | $18,000–$26,000 | $26,000–$43,000 | $46,000–$68,000 |
| Asst. General Manager | $16,000–$22,000 | $17,000–$24,000 | $25,000–$34,000 |
| General Manager | $18,000–$33,000 | $24,000–$44,000 | $35,000–$90,000 |

## INSIDERS' ADVICE

If you are willing to relocate, one way to get a job in the hotel business is to contact vice-presidents of franchise operations at the major hotel chains. These managers know about new hotels or motels that are opening or expanding and they may be more helpful than the personnel department can be. Vice-presidents of franchise operations can generally be found at the hotel chain's headquarters office. Many of the large chains have west coast branch offices in San Francisco or Los Angeles and may have a franchise manager in these locations as well.

## HOTEL DIRECTORY

**Campton Place Hotel**   (415) 956-3773
Ayala Hotels Corporation
340 Stockton St.
San Francisco, CA 94108
*Contact:* William Wilkinson, President.
*Employs:* 135.
*Description:* New hotel management corporation and new hotel scheduled to
  open July 1983. Hotel located on Stockton one block from Union Square,
  site of Old Drake Wilshire Hotel.

**Cantebury Hotel**   (415) 474-6464
750 Sutter St.
San Francisco, CA 94109
*Contact:* Scott Astle, Assistant Manager
*Employs:* 95
*Description:* Full service hotel.

**Dunfey San Mateo Hotel**   (415) 573-7661
1770 South Amphlett Blvd.
San Mateo, CA 94402
*Contact:* Eileen Harris, Employment.
*Description:* Full service hotel.

**Fairmont Hotels**   (415) 772-5000
950 Mason St.
San Francisco, CA 94106
*Contact:* Noel Lopez, Personnel.
  Richard Swig, President.
*Employs:* 75 professionals.
*Description:* Corporate headquarters for Fairmont Hotels.

**Holiday Inn**   (415) 626-6103
50 Eighth St.
San Francisco, CA 94103
*Contact:* Adelyn Ung, Personnel.

*Description:* Full service hotel and convention center; nine Bay Area hotels.

**Hyatt Hotel Corporation**    (415) 398-1234
345 Stockton St.
San Francisco, CA 94108
*Contact:* Henry Diaz, Personnel (this location).
   Craig Keller, Personnel (Embarcadero Center).
*Employs:* 6,500 in these two hotels.
*Description:* Large hotel chain. Headquarters in Chicago. Five Bay Area
   hotels.

**Le Baron Hotel**    (408) 288-9200
1350 North First St.
San Jose, CA 95113
*Contact:* Phyllis Deauler, Personnel.
*Description:* Full service hotel and convention facility.

**Mark Hopkins Hotel**    (415) 392-3434
999 California St.
San Francisco, CA 94106
*Contact:* Louise Bittner, Personnel Manager.
*Employs:* 420.
*Description:* Luxury hotel; one of San Francisco's most prestigious and
   historical.

**Ramada Inn**    (415) 885-4700
590 Bay St.
San Francisco, CA 94133
*Contact:* Dale Bennett, Personnel.
*Description:* Full service hotel near Fisherman's Wharf.

**San Francisco Airport Hilton**    (415) 589-0770
San Francisco International Airport
San Francisco, CA 94128
*Contact:* Dale Black, Personnel.
*Description:* Full service hotel with meeting facilities.

**San Francisco Hilton Hotel and Tower**    (415) 771-1400
Mason & O'Farrell Streets
San Francisco, CA 94102
*Contact:* James Donlin, Personnel.
*Employs:* 950.
*Description:* Large hotel chain offers Corporate Training Program, requires
   relocation.

**Sheraton Hotel**    (415) 362-5500
2500 Mason St.
San Francisco, CA 94133
*Contact:* Russ Melagrini, Personnel Manager
*Description:* Full service hotel near Fisherman's Wharf; second San Francisco
   location on 639 Market Street.

**Stanford Court Hotel**    (415) 989-3500
905 California Hotel
San Francisco, CA 94105
*Contact:* Robert Berger, Director of Personnel.
*Employs:* 350.
*Description:* European service hotel rebuilt within building that survived San
   Francisco earthquake.

**Westin–St. Francis**    (415) 397-7000
335 Powell St.
San Francisco, CA 94102
*Contact:* Jerry Evans, Personnel Manager.
*Employs:* 1,100.
*Description:* Luxury hotel. Part of Western International chain, which was
   renamed Westin.


## *Restaurant Management*

The increase in the number of working women has had a positive
impact on the restaurant business. Affluent singles and two-income families choose to go out to eat regularly, and thus a demand for new restaurants is expected in the Bay Area.

The forecasted growth in the tourism business also will positively
affect restaurants. The Moscone Convention Center will contribute by
bringing 4,000 new jobs to the area, and many of these will be in restaurant operations and management.

There are three very different kinds of restaurant/food service businesses: traditional; fast food; and institutional food service.

In traditional restaurants the market is fairly tight and the business is
becoming more competitive and sophisticated. Sole-owner restaurants
are starting marketing departments and hiring ad agencies to help them
compete. General business background and skills are important here.
The training you can get at big hotels or corporations is frequently mentioned as a positive benefit. Individuals who have a background or experience in kitchen management are hard to find and so have an advantage
in job hunting.

There is a growing trend toward ethnic and cafe-style restaurants,
which are less expensive to run and can offer lower prices. If you have
experience in this kind of restaurant operation, that will be an advantage.

In fast food restaurant chains the focus is on concept, menu, and geographic location. Fast food concepts tend to be somewhat faddish, and
thus companies must change to keep consumers interested or risk new
competition. Recently the trend is to combine food with entertainment
(e.g., Chuck E. Cheese Pizza Time Theatre) and make going out to eat

an entertainment experience. Menus usually have a core item (hamburgers, chicken, pizza), but increasingly the fast food chains have had to go to a full range of food items in order to compete. Most large urban and suburban areas have thriving fast food franchises. Currently the trend is toward smaller communities where, when an outlet opens, it is possible to see an immediate impact on sales.

Professional level jobs in fast food include those of store manager, operations manager, and group store manager, as well as marketing and real estate positions.

Institutional food service is growing rapidly and there are excellent opportunities to learn institutional or traditional restaurant business basics with Bay Area companies (e.g., Saga). These firms offer excellent training at all levels, with a focus on the business and service aspects of the food industry.

## RESTAURANT MANAGEMENT RESOURCES

For information on Bay Area restaurant opportunities, contact:

- *Alice Statler Library for Motel and Restaurant,* 50 Phelan St., City College of San Francisco, San Francisco, CA; (415) 239-3460
- *University of San Francisco Hospitality Management School,* 2130 Fulton St., San Francisco, CA 94117; (415) 666-6771

For reading on the subject, ask your librarian for these periodicals:

- *National Restaurant News*
- *Western Real Estate News*
- *Pacific Food Service Magazine*
- *Cornell Motel and Restaurant Administration Quarterly*
- *California Inn Touch*
- *Wines and Vines*

A professional level employment service that specializes in restaurant work is:

Roth Young Personnel Service
44 Montgomery St.
San Francisco, CA 94111
(415) 391-3865
*Contact:* Jill Appenzeller, Hospitality Manager.

## RESTAURANT JOB TITLES AND SALARY RANGES

The restaurant field is divided into fast food restaurants, traditional restaurants, and institutional or food service firms. Here are approximate salary ranges for the Bay Area.

## Fast Food

- Trainee: $14,000–$18,000
- Assistant Manager: $16,000–$28,000
- Manager: $20,000–$42,000
- Multiunit Manager: $26,000–$42,000
- Real Estate Field Rep: $22,000–$30,000
- Real Estate, Regional: $34,000–$45,000
- Director of Real Estate: $45,000–$60,000
- VP Real Estate: $60,000–$90,000
- Ad Manager: $25,000–$55,000

## Traditional Restaurants

Restaurants that include wine and liquor on their menu generally pay high salaries and expect more experience and responsibility than those that do not.

- Trainee: $14,000–$24,000
- Assistant Manager: $16,000–$28,000
- Manager: $20,000–$50,000
- Chef: $20,000–$55,000
- Sous-Chef: $18,000–$32,000
- Cook: $13,000–$19,000
- Pastry Chef: $18,000–$30,000
- Purchasing: $20,000–$35,000
- Controller: $19,000–$45,000
- Personnel: $18,000–$34,000
- Advertising: $25,000–$44,000

## Food Service

- Cafeteria: $19,000–$32,000
- Vending Manager; $17,000–$32,000
- Unit Manager: $16,000–$29,000
- Chef Manager: $17,000–$31,000
- Dietician: $16,000–$33,000
- Personnel: $19,000–$42,000
- Purchasing: $19,000–$40,000
- District Manager: $23,000–$40,000
- Food Service Director: $17,000–$36,000
- Regional Manager: $26,000–$56,000

## INSIDERS' ADVICE

Experienced restaurateurs point out that two key decisions for someone interested in the (non-institutional) restaurant business are:

- fine dining vs. high volume/fast food
- front or back room management

In the Bay Area there is a trend toward fine dining and a demand for kitchen (back room) management. If you are just starting out and are interested in these aspects of the business you should contact the restaurant owner or manager directly. Try to find a way to apprentice or perhaps volunteer in order to get experience.

Experts warn that you should keep in mind that 95% of restaurants fail in their first year. Therefore your job will be more secure if you start with an established restaurant.

Insiders also advise that to gain more perspective on the business you read the magazine *Restaurant Business,* 633 3rd Avenue, New York, NY 10017; (212) 986-4800. They also recommend the books *The Practice of Hospitality Management,* by Pizam, Lewis and Manning, and *Creative Marketing For The Food Service Industry,* by William P. Fisher.

## RESTAURANT AND INSTITUTIONAL FOOD SERVICE DIRECTORY

**Calny**   (415) 574-2455
1650 Borel Pl.
San Mateo, CA 94402
*Contact:* Marie Crouch, Employee Benefits
*Employs:* 25 at headquarters
*Description:* Franchiser of Taco Bell restaurants.

**Distribuco Inc.**   (415) 887-8400
25954 Eden Landing Road
Suite 201
Hayward, CA 94545
*Contact:* Richard Kraber, Vice President Personnel
*Description:* Headquarters of institutional food service.

**Farrell's Ice Cream Parlour Restaurants, Inc.**   (415) 362-8100
425 California St.
San Francisco, CA 94114
*Contact:* Personnel Department
*Description:* Corporate headquarters; ice cream parlor chain; five Bay Area locations.

**Host International, Inc.**   (415) 761-1177
San Francisco International Airport
San Francisco, CA 94128
*Contact:* Personnel Manager
*Description:* Institutional food and hospitality service; specialty restaurants
    and gift shops.

**Lyons Restaurants**   (415) 783-3200
1165 Triton Dr.
Foster City, CA 94404
*Contact:* Barbara Wallace, Personnel Manager.
*Employs:* 40.
*Description:* Chain of 40 informal dinner restaurants owned by Consolidated
    Foods.

**The Magic Pan Restaurants**   (415) 421-9750
50 Francisco St.
San Francisco, CA 94111
*Contact:* Tim Ryan, Vice President, Marketing
*Description:* Headquarters and western regional office for restaurant chain.

**McDonald's**   (408) 287-4377
2025 Gateway Place
San Jose, CA 95110
*Contact:* Elaine Hansen, Personnel
    Ed Biever, Senior Regional Manager
*Description:* Regional office. Oversees McDonald stores and franchises; also
    does real estate, construction, and local advertising work.

**Perry's**   (415) 922-9008
1944 Union St.
San Francisco, CA 94123
*Contact:* Perry Butler, Owner
*Employs:* 150.
*Description:* Best known for Union Street singles bar and restaurant. Now has
    restaurants in Bay Area.

**Pizza Time Theatre**   (408) 744-7300
1213 Innsbruck
Sunnyvale, CA 94086
*Contact:* Ramona Carrington, Corporate Recruiter
*Employs:* 250 in corporate headquarters
*Description:* Nolan Bushnell, inventor of Atari's first video game, founded this
    entertainment/restaurant company, known as Chuck E. Cheese Pizza Time
    Theatre. There are 150 restaurants nationwide.

**PYA Monarch Food Service**   (415) 467-2500
240 Valley Dr.
Brisbane, CA 94005

*Contact:* Mel Sims, Personnel
*Description:* Distributor and institutional food service.

**Round Table Franchise Corporation**    (415) 392-7500
601 Montgomery St.
San Francisco, CA 94111
*Contact:* Norman Dean, President
*Employs:* 50 at headquarters; others employed at franchise locations.
*Description:* Pizza chain with six Bay Area locations.

**SAGA Corporation**    (415) 854-5150
1 Saga Lane
Menlo Park, CA 94025
*Contact:* Sharon Bue, Personnel Director
*Employs:* 500
*Description:* Restaurant chains including Velvet Turtle, Strawhat Pizza, and
   Black Angus; also restaurant institutional food service for businesses and
   colleges.

**Spectrum Foods**    (415) 398-5704
617 Front St.
San Francisco, CA 94111
*Contact:* Larry Mindel, President.
*Employs:* 300 in Bay Area.
*Description:* Restaurant management company that owns Ciao, Prego,
   MacArthur Park Restaurants in San Francisco and on the Peninsula.

**Victoria Station**    (415) 461-4550
Wood Island
Larkspur, CA 94939
*Contact:* Ron Neach, Vice-President, Human Resources.
*Employs:* 50 at headquarters.
*Description:* Steak restaurant chain with seven Bay Area locations, including
   The Royal Exchange and Quinn's Lighthouse.

**Zim's Restaurants**    (415) 921-7505
2218 Lombard St.
San Francisco, CA 94105
*Contact:* Personnel Manager
*Description:* General offices for restaurant chain with 12 Bay Area locations.


## Recreation

There are two large Bay Area amusement parks, which employ marketing, sales, and public relations people; biologists; and special events
specialists.
Marine World/Africa USA has recently been refurbished and

enlarged, with more animals and rides and shopping facilities than ever before.

Great America is owned by the Marriott Corporation, and there is some chance that a job at Great America could lead to advancement within that corporation, especially for marketing people and salespeople.

The Bay Area is also home to several professional sports clubs including baseball, soccer, football, and basketball. These companies may employ 30-50 people full-time, and usually increase their sales and support staffs during the respective sports season.

Sports clubs are generally organized into sales, marketing, public relations, tickets, finance, operations and publication functions.

## RECREATION JOB TITLES AND SALARY RANGES

Job titles and salary ranges for recreational parks run the gamut from scientist/animal keepers to marketing professionals. The job titles, with salary ranges, follow.

- Personnel Manager: $15,000–$40,000
- Purchaser: $25,000–$45,000
- Ad Manager: $22,000–35,000
- Marketing Director: $35,000–$55,000
- Sales Promotion Special Events Manager: $28,000–$45,000
- Biologist: $15,000–$24,000
- Engineer: $14,000–$35,000
- Animal Trainers/Managers: $24,000-$28,000

At professional sports clubs the job titles and salary levels are:

- Director of Ticket Sales: $20,000–$30,000
- Director of Marketing: $35,000–$50,000
- Public Relations Manager: $20,000–$30,000
- Director of Operations: $35,000–$60,000
- Finance Manager: $28,000–$38,000
- Sales Representative: Commission sales usually 8–12%

## INSIDERS' ADVICE

Insiders note that volunteers do get noticed and are considered seriously for full or part-time positions as they become available. But the best way to get a start in sales or marketing is to join the sales organization and demonstrate your aggressiveness and creativity in selling (especially season or group tickets).

## RECREATION DIRECTORY

**California Jockey Club**    (415) 574-7223
PO Box 5050
San Mateo, CA 94402
*Contact:* General Manager.
*Description:* Headquarters for race track, recreational company (golf, tennis facilities).

**Golden Bay Earthquakes**    (408) 946-5020
800 Charcot Avenue
San Jose, CA 95131
*Contact:* Steve DesGeorges, Personnel.
*Employs:* 50.
*Description:* Professional soccer team, member of North American Soccer League.

**Golden State Warriors**    (415) 638-6300
Oakland Coliseum
Oakland, CA 94621
*Contact:* Eric Chapman, Public Relations.
*Employs:* 40.
*Description:* Professional basketball team that has been in Bay Area for more than 20 years.

**Marine World/Africa USA**    (415) 591-7676
101 Marine World Parkway
Redwood City, CA 94065
*Contact:* Carla Igoe, Personnel.
   Michael Demetrios, President.
*Employs:* 500 full-time, more during summer season.
*Description:* 68-acre park featuring land, sea, and air animals.

**Marriott's Great America**    (408) 496-0141
PO Box 1776
Santa Clara, CA 95052
*Contact:* Anita Wagner, Employment.
   Jim Morron, General Manager.
*Employs:* 170 full-time, 2,500 during summer season.
*Description:* Amusement park featuring roller coasters and water slides, theater, and music events.

**Oakland Athletics Baseball Co.**    (415) 430-8020
Oakland/Alameda County Coliseum
Oakland, CA 94621
*Contact:* Andy Dolich, Vice-President Business Operations.
*Employs:* 30 full-time, 50 during season.
*Description:* Baseball club; publishes three publications.

**Oakland Invaders** (415) 638-7800
7850 Edgewater Drive
Oakland, CA 94621
*Contact:* Howard Friedman, Vice-President, Administration.
*Employs:* 40.
*Description:* Member of new U.S. Football League.

**San Francisco Forty-Niners** (415) 593-9710
711 Nevada St.
Redwood City, CA 94061
*Contact:* George Heddleston, Director of Public Relations.
   Keith Simon, Business Manager.
*Description:* National Football League team.

**San Francisco Giants** (415) 468-3700
Candlestick Park
San Francisco, CA 94124
*Contact:* Pat Gallagher, Vice President Business Operations.
*Employs:* 200 full-time, 1,000 during season.
*Description:* National League baseball team.

## *Art and Science (Museums and Galleries)*

Salaried jobs in arts and in museums are scarce. The best way to get one seems to be to volunteer long enough to make yourself invaluable.

### ART

The Bay Area has a large number of art museums and art galleries; however, there are many highly educated and experienced people who have chosen to live here. Thus the jobs are few and far between.

There are approximately 250 art galleries in the Bay Area. Most are small and employ 3 to 6 people. A degree in art history or business is generally needed. Herbert Hoover of the Hoover Gallery is the local authority on Bay Area art galleries and is a good person to try to get to know. He has written a book that lists and describes the Bay Area galleries: *Hoover's Guide to Galleries in San Francisco.* The book includes names of a contact person at each of the various galleries.

One good source for art-related jobs of all kinds is Art Jobs Agency, 622 Washington Street, San Francisco, CA 94111; (415) 392-2186. Dora Williams helps to place photographers, art teachers, art history majors who are just starting out, drafts people, art directors, lecturers, museum curators, etc.

Finding employment in art museums is very difficult and requires patience and perseverence because the competition is fierce and most applicants are over-qualified for the available jobs. An art history or fine arts background is preferred and advanced degrees are common among museum secretaries and bookstore clerks. Job openings may be in the publicity, membership, conservation or preparation of exhibits departments. Other positions include development (fund raising), researcher, librarian, and museum curator.

Art-related job salary ranges begin at $21,000 for *art* or *historian curators* with a PhD. Other full-time jobs begin at approximately $11,000 and progress to $20,000.

A local publication called *Artweek* occasionally publishes jobs, and a national publication called AVISO lists jobs throughout the United States. Also read *Museum News,* published by American Association of Museums, 1055 Thomas Jefferson Street NW, Washington, DC 20007; (202) 338-5300.

The following are three New York publications which may help to keep you current with some of the latest trends in the art world.

- *Art News*, 122 East 42nd St., New York, NY 10168
- *Art in America*, 850 3rd Ave., New York, NY 10022
- *Art Forum*, 667 Madison Ave., New York, NY 10021

## INSIDERS' ADVICE

The best way to get a job in an art-related position is to be willing to start by doing just about anything. This may include hanging shows, working odd hours, performing secretarial tasks, etc.

Hiring managers indicate an interest in job-seekers who have experience with Christie's or Sotheby's, or who are experienced in selling corporate art programs to businesses. Individuals with excellent writing skills or knowledge of how to adapt a personal computer to museum or gallery use would also have an advantage.

If you are a recent art graduate with no experience it is imperative that you volunteer in order to get some experience. One way to get a good idea of trends in Bay Area art would be to volunteer for work in the rental gallery of the Museum of Modern Art.

## ART MUSEUM DIRECTORY

**Asian Art Museum**    (415) 558-2993
Golden Gate Park
San Francisco, CA 94118
*Contact:* Rene Yuon D'Argence, Director.

**The Fine Arts Museum of San Francisco** (415) 558-2881
**The DeYoung Museum**
Golden Gate Park
San Francisco, CA 94118
*Contact:* Stephen Dukes, Deputy Director for Administration.

**Oakland Museum** (415) 273-3515
1000 Oak St.
Oakland, CA 94607
*Contact:* Julian Euell, Director.

**Richmond Arts Center** (415) 231-2163
25th and Barnett Avenue
Civic Center Plaza
Richmond, CA 94804
*Contact:* Lynda Gutherie, Director.

**San Francisco Museum of Modern Art** (415) 863-8800
Van Ness and McAllister
San Francisco, CA 94102
*Contact:* Michael McCone, Associate Director of Administration.

**San Jose Museum of Art** (408) 294-2787
110 South Market St.
San Jose, CA 95113
*Contact:* Martha Manson, Director.

**San Mateo Historical Association** (415) 574-6441
1700 West Hillsdale Blvd.
San Mateo, CA 94402
*Contact:* Herbert E. Garcia, Director.

**Stanford Museum of Art** (415) 497-4177
Stanford University
Stanford, CA 94305
*Contact:* Doctor Lorenz Eitner, Director.


## ART GALLERY DIRECTORY

**Braunstein Gallery** (415) 392-5532
254 Sutter St.
San Francisco, CA 94102
*Contact:* Ruth Braunstein, Owner/Director
*Employs:* 3-5
*Description:* Avant-garde painting and sculpture.

**Carol Covington Gallery** (415) 974-1930
564 Fourth St.
San Francisco, CA 94107

*Contact:* Carol Covington, Owner/Director
*Employs:* 3
*Description:* Cartoons and covers by artists from *The New Yorker.*

**Fuller-Goldeen Gallery**   (415) 982-6177
228 Grant St.
San Francisco, CA 94108
*Contact:* Diana Fuller or Dorothy Goldeen, Owner/Directors
*Employs:* 4
*Description:* One of the oldest galleries in San Francisco. Primarily sculpture
and paintings of 20th century.

**Gallery Paule Anglin**   (415) 433-2710
14 Geary St.
San Francisco, CA 94108
*Contact:* Jane Trotter Oleson, Director
*Employs:* 3 full-time, 2 part-time
*Description:* Gallery specializing primarily in contemporary Bay Area and
American artists.

**Grapestake Gallery**   (415) 931-0779
2876 California St.
San Francisco, CA 94115
*Contact:* Ursula Gropper or Tom Meyer, Director
*Employs:* 5-6
*Description:* Contemporary painting, photography and sculpture.

**Hoover Gallery**   (415) 558-8944
1681 Folsom St.
San Francisco, CA 94103
*Contact:* F. Herbert Hoover, Director/Owner
*Employs:* 4
*Description:* Features abstract expressionists, sculpture, American
impressionists, contemporary art.

**William Sawyer Gallery**   (415) 921-1600
3045 Clay St.
San Francisco, CA 94115
*Contact:* Dr. William Sawyer, Owner/Director
*Employs:* 5
*Description:* Contemporary painting, publishes Gallery Guide, a bi-monthly
newsletter listing current exhibits.

**Triangle Gallery**   (415) 777-2710
95 Minna St.
San Francisco, CA 94105
*Contact:* Jack Van Hiele, Owner/Director
*Employs:* 2
*Description:* One of the oldest galleries in San Francisco, featuring
contemporary painting, sculpture and ceramics.

**Vorpal Gallery**    (415) 397-9200
393 Grove St.
San Francisco, CA 94102
*Contact:* Frank Downing, Director
*Employs:* 8
*Description:* Specializes in works of M.C. Escher, Jesse Allen and Gary Smith.

## SCIENCE

Most of the jobs at science museums or associations require advanced degrees at the master's or PhD level. In Bay Area museums the job titles include those of researcher, curator, physicist, and biologist. Other jobs, not requiring advanced degrees, include those of graphic artist, designer, and photographer. Salaries start at $21,000 with a Ph.D. Other jobs pay $12,000 and up.

The few openings that become available generally go to longtime museum volunteers who have demonstrated their ability and commitment.

## SCIENCE MUSEUM DIRECTORY

**Exploratorium**    (415) 563-7337
3601 Lyon St.
San Francisco, CA 94123
*Contact:* Gloria Graff, Manager
*Description:* Experiential participatory science museum.

**California Academy of Sciences**    (415) 221-4214
Golden Gate Pk.
San Francisco, CA 94118
*Contact:* Nancy Dykes, Director of Administration
*Description:* General science, natural history, space and anthropology.

**Coyote Point Museum**    (415) 342-7755
Coyote Pt.
San Mateo, CA 94401
*Contact:* Linda Liebes, Director
*Description:* Environmental science and education.

**Lawrence Hall of Science**    (415) 642-5132
University of California at Berkeley
Berkeley, CA 94720
*Contact:* Dr. Glenn Seaborg, Acting Director
*Description:* Astronomy, computer and biology museum.

**Lowie Museum of Anthropology**   (415) 642-3681
103 Kroeber Mall
Berkeley, CA 94720
*Contact:* James Deetz, Director
*Description:* Natural history, anthropological science.

## Music

The Bay Area is an active and vital music center with a broad range of types of music, from The San Francisco Opera—considered the best opera company in the United States—to Bill Graham, a rock concert impresario who is considered the nation's best rock producer, having managed concerts for leading groups including the Beatles, the Rolling Stones, Willie Nelson, and Santana.

The Bay Area has its own contemporary music magazine, *BAM, the California Music Magazine,* 5951 Canning Street, Oakland, CA 94609; (415) 652-3810. This is a good publication to read to develop a real understanding of the popular music opportunities in this area.

Two other publications may be of help to job seekers in all aspects of the music field; both list employment opportunities.

* *Billboard,* 9000 Sunset Blvd., Los Angeles, CA 90067; (213) 273-7040
* *Performing Arts Magazine,* 651 Brannan St., San Francisco, CA 94107; (415) 558-8040

For information on the recording end of the music business, you should consider subscribing to:

* *Mix,* 2608 9th St., Berkeley, CA 94710; (415) 843-7901
* *Recording Engineer/Producer,* 1850 Whitley Blvd., Hollywood, CA 90028; (213) 467-1111

And look for these books:

* *The Recording Studio Handbook,* by John Worans
* *Sound Recording Practice,* by John Borwick
* *The Technique of the Sound Studio,* by Alec Nisbett

*The Reel Directory,* P.O. Box 866, Cotati, CA 94928; (707) 795-9367, is a media production directory for Northern California which lists musicians and recording studios of all kinds.

Music production and recording training can be arranged at the College for Recording Arts, 665 Harrison Street, San Francisco, CA 94107; (415) 781-6306. This school offers a one-year technical course for recording engineers.

The musicians' union, the American Federation of Musicians, 230 Jones Street, San Francisco, CA 94102; (415) 775-8118, is a good place to make contacts in the local music field. Music by the Bay, Fort Mason, Building C, Room 200, San Francisco, CA 94123; (415) 474-5600, a network organization of 500 musicians, is also an avenue for meeting fellow musicians of all music styles and disciplines.

## MUSIC-RELATED JOB TITLES AND SALARY RANGES

On the classical side, job titles generally include *operations director,* who handles concert production and management; *director of development,* who manages fund-raising; and *shows manager,* who works with musicians. Full-time business staff is generally fewer than 10 people.

The salary for a performer with a major symphony orchestra begins at about $14,000 and may reach $33,000 per year. Strictly regional or local orchestra performers salaries are lower, ranging from $8,000 to $20,000.

Symphony orchestras generally have up to 100 musicians; chamber orchestras are much smaller and the number of musicians varies according to the program.

In the contemporary music field, there are commercial as well as onstage opportunities. If you are a musician, you may find free-lance work through local recording studios, or through composers who are working on commercial music for advertising or films. You will be paid by "the session" in which you perform. If you have a technical background, you may find work in recording or post-production studios. Some of these jobs include *maintenance engineer,* who keeps the equipment functioning; *second engineer,* who sets up and later breaks down equipment for the actual recording sessions; and *first engineer,* who does the actual recording in the session.

*Composers* and *arrangers* often hire musicians as well as "chart people" or "copyists" who transform the original composition into a music score.

Here are commercial music and production salary ranges for the job titles just discussed:

- Recording Studio Assistant: $12,000–$16,000
- Chart Person: $8,000–$16,000
- Maintenance Engineer; $10,000–$22,000
- Second Engineer: $18,000–$26,000
- First Engineer: $20,000–$35,000
- Studio Manager: $22,000–$35,000

## INSIDERS' ADVICE

There is enough work in the Bay Area music business to keep a small number of musicians and music recording experts employed. But to earn a steady income, you have to develop new contacts and stay in touch with existing contacts.

To get a job as a commercial musician or arranger, you should develop tapes of your work and take them around to ad agencies, recording studios, and arrangers. If you offer to work the first time for free or to help them out on a rush job, you stand a better chance of getting hired.

Musicians associated with orchestras are most often hired by reputation and the competition is intense. Insiders contend that your best bet is to get to know others already with the orchestra, so that you learn early about openings or are available as a back-up or understudy in an emergency.

## MUSIC DIRECTORY

### Opera And Orchestras

**The Oakland Symphony Orchestra**    (415) 444-3531
2025 Broadway
Oakland, CA 94604
*Contact:* Sarah Chambers, Director of Education and Personnel.
*Employs:* 110 musicians.

**San Francisco Chamber Orchestra**    (415) 788-1240
840 Battery St.
San Francisco, CA 94111
*Contact:* (Run by volunteers.)
*Employs:* 35 musicians.

**San Francisco Concert Orchestra**    (415) 751-3955
520 A Clement St.
San Francisco, CA 94118
*Contact:* Saul Feldman, General Manager.
*Employs:* 60-80 musicians depending on program.
*Description:* For musicians under 30.

**San Francisco Opera Association**    (415) 861-4008
War Memorial Opera House
301 Van Ness Avenue
San Francisco, CA 94102

*Contact:* Terrance A. McEwen, General Director
*Employs:* Seventy full-time; orchestra hired separately for each "gig".

**San Francisco Symphony**    (415) 552-8000
Davies Symphony Hall
San Francisco, CA 94102
*Contact:* Betty Fingold, Manager.
*Employs:* 104 musicians.


## Music Recording Studios

**The Automatt**    (415) 777-4111
829 Folsom St.
San Francisco, CA 94107
*Contact:* Dave Rubenston, President

**Bear West**    (415) 543-2125
915 Howard
San Francisco, CA 94103
*Contact:* Larry Kronan, Office Manager.

**Coast Recorders Inc.**    (415) 864-5200
1340 Mission St.
San Francisco, CA 94103
*Contact:* Steve Atkins, Studio Manager

**Cora Sound**    (415) 472-3745
122 East Paul Dr.
San Rafael, CA
*Contact:* Steve Hart, Principal

**Different Fur**    (415) 864-1967
3470 19th St.
San Francisco, CA 94114
*Contact:* Patrick Green, Owner

**Kaleido Sound**    (415) 543-0531
185 Berry St., Suite 6801
San Francisco, CA 94107
*Contact:* Forrest Patton, Owner

**Russian Hill Recording**    (415) 474-4520
1520 Pacific Ave.
San Francisco, CA 94109
*Contact:* Bob Shotland or Jack Leaky, Owners

**Tres Virgos**    (415) 456-7666
1925 Francisco Blvd.
San Rafael, CA 94901
*Contact:* Jerry Jacob, Principal

# MUSIC PROMOTIONS AND CONCERTS

**Concord Pavillion**    (415) 798-3315
PO Box 6166
Concord, CA 94524
*Contact:* City of Concord Personnel
  1950 Parkside Drive
  Concord, CA 94519 (415) 671-3308
*Description:* Performing arts pavillion for rock, jazz, classical, opera, ballet
  and big band music.

**Bill Graham Enterprises**    (415) 864-0815
201 11th St.
San Francisco, CA 94103
*Contact:* Nick Clainos, Personnel Manager
*Description:* Concert tour and entertainment company with six divisions: 1)
  concert tours and staging 2) artist management 3) music merchandising 4)
  night clubs 5) technical production service, and 6) food concessions.

**Great American Music Hall**    (415) 885-0750
859 O'Farrell
San Francisco, CA 94140
*Contact:* Tom Bradshaw, Owner
*Description:* 450 seat concert hall.

**Keystone**    (415) 781-0697
750 Vallejo
San Francisco, CA 94140
*Contact:* Bob Corona, Personnel Manager
*Description:* Night club chain in Berkeley, Palo Alto and San Francisco.

## Music Composers And Arrangers

**Bogus Productions**    (415) 673-2532
680 Beach St., Ste. #495
San Francisco, CA 94109
*Contact:* Ed Bogus.

**Bernie Krause & Gary Remal**    (415) 673-4544
Parasound Inc.
680 Beach St. Suite 414
San Francisco, CA 94109
*Contact:* Betsy Zeger, Personnel Manager

**Rick Nowels**    (415) 751-0214
1442 Waller St.
San Francisco, CA 94117
*Contact:* Tim McDaniel, Manager
  Rick Nowels, Principal

**Art Twain**   (415) 531-2267
329 Rischell Dr.
Oakland, CA 94619
*Contact:* Art Twain, Principal


## Theater and Dance

Theater and dance job opportunities generally include acting, dancing, directing, stage management, production, costuming, public relations, advertising, graphics, ticket sales and fund raising.


## THEATER

The Bay Area has one of the most exciting and active theater communities in the country, However, as is often true of other artistic job categories, the opportunities for full-time employment are few. Most people in this field support themselves with less glamorous work as waiters, waitresses, secretaries, etc.

The largest theater company in San Francisco is the American Conservatory Theatre (see listing). During its season, it may employ as many as 60 people, and it has a small theater internship program with apprenticeships in stage management, public relations, sound, and administration.


## DANCE

The Bay Area is also a very active dance community with approximately 160 dance companies located here.

The *Dance Coalition* at Fort Mason (see listing) has a complete listing of all the dance companies in the Bay Area and can help you with your job search. Also, the California Alliance of Health, Physical Education, Recreation, and Dance can sometimes provide advice on how to find work in dance. Write to them at 401 South Hartz Avenue, Suite 203, Danville, CA 94526.

You may wish to teach dance. There are approximately 300 dancing schools in the Bay Area. San Francisco alone has 100 schools teaching a wide range of dance from ballet to aerobic dancing.

Because Bay Area theaters and dance companies are experiencing cutbacks in government funds for the arts they are in need of experienced fund-raisers. If you have fund-raising skills and are willing or able to volunteer your services you may be able eventually to turn this into a paid part-time or full-time job in the performing arts.

## Theatre and Dance Publications

Publications which may be helpful to job-seekers include:

- *Footnotes,* 1300 Arch St., Philadelphia, PA 19107
- *In Performance,* 950 Battery St., San Francisco, CA 94111
- *Back Stage,* 165 West 46th St., New York, NY 10036
- *Daily Variety,* 1400 North Cahuenga Blvd., Hollywood, CA 90028

## THEATER AND DANCE JOB TITLES AND SALARY RANGES

Job titles and salaries at theater and dance companies fluctuate with the fluctuations in economic support of the company.

In general, medium size theaters or dance companies (defined as those with a budget of $2-4 million) have two to three paid management level employees. These are likely to be the *development director* who does fund-raising ($15,000 to $20,000), and the *general manager* ($16,000 to $22,000). Other full-time employees may include *publicity coordinator,* or the *box office manager.*

Players or dancers may receive a weekly salary or be paid per performance.

### Title/Experience And Average Salary

- Entry level Performer: $17,500
- Corp de Ballet or Group Performer: $20,700
- Solo Performer: $23,140
- Principal Performer: $25,000

Single performance rate average $125 per performance plus ten hours guaranteed paid rehearsal and per diem for travel expenses.

### INSIDERS' ADVICE

Theater and dance jobs may be found through the Theatre Communications Center of the Bay Area, a clearing house for job-seekers. It publishes a monthly job and performance listing called *Callboard* and has a library for job research. Contact Jane Benson at (415) 621-0427, or visit 2940 16th Street, San Francisco, CA 94121.

Bay Area insiders report that The Theater Communications Group of New York publishes a national newsletter, *Art Search,* which is often helpful to job-seekers. You can contact this organization at 355 Lexington Avenue, New York, NY 10017; (212) 697-5230. *The National Arts Job Bank* is published by the Western States Art Foundation. This publication comes out twice a month and lists jobs including opportunities in theater and dance. Write or call them at 141 East Palace Avenue, Santa Fe, New Mexico 87501; (505) 988-1166.

Bay Area experts urge job-seekers to volunteer at the theater or dance company you are most interested in. Offer to work on advertising, as an usher, or on scenery, and generally do what you can to get to know the group and make contacts.

Also, keep in mind that performers may find dance or acting jobs in films or commercials through a talent agency. The largest in the Bay Area is Brebner Talent Agency, 161 Berry Street, San Francisco, CA 94107; (415) 495-6700.

## THEATER DIRECTORY

**American Conservatory Theatre**    (415) 771-3880
450 Geary St.
San Francisco, CA 94102
*Contact:* John Wilk, Casting.
   John Brown, Stage Management.
*Employs:* 60.
*Description:* Large company, offers internship program.

**Berkeley Repertory Theatre**    (415) 841-6108
2025 Addison Ave.
Berkeley, CA 94704
*Contact:* Mitzi Sales, Managing Director.
*Employs:* 35 including full time actors.
*Description:* Innovative theatre company.

**One Act**    (415) 421-5355
430 Mason St.
San Francisco, CA 94102
*Contact:* Steve Siegel, General Manager.
*Description:* Small company; offers internship program for college students.

**One Act II—Playwrights Theater**    (415) 843-3405
430 Mason St.
San Francisco, CA 94102
*Contact:* J.D. Trow, Director.
*Employs:* 30 per show, 2 permanently.
*Description:* Specializes in Bay Area playwrights with emphasis on women and
   third world writers.

**Magic Theatre**    (415) 441-8001
Fort Mason Center, Building D
San Francisco, CA 94123

*Contact:* Marcia O'Dea, General Manager.
*Employs:* 10 full-time.
*Description:* Playwright's theater, 8 new plays per season.

**San Francisco Repertory**    (415) 864-3305
4147 19th St.
San Francisco, CA 94114
*Contact:* Charlotte Selligman, Manager.
*Employs:* 2 full-time, plus volunteers.
*Description:* Focuses on lesser-known plays from around the world.

**San Jose Repertory Company**    (408) 294-7572
32 South 16th St.
Box 9584
San Jose, CA 95157
*Contact:* Kathryn Davies, Production Manager.
*Employs:* 25.
*Description:* Non-musical dramas and comedies, 5 plays per season.


## DANCE DIRECTORY

**Margaret Jenkins Dance Company (415) 863-9830**
**The Oberlin Dance Collective**
The New Performance Gallery of San Francisco
3153 17th St.
San Francisco, CA 94110
*Contact:* Sarah Wilson, Director of Programs.
*Description:* Two dance companies, which share facilities and staff, including
   artistic director, publicist, lighting directors, technicians, and management.

**San Francisco Ballet**    (415) 751-2141
378 18th Ave.
San Francisco, CA 94121
*Contact:* Meg Madden, Personnel and Community Relations Manager.
*Employs:* 30.
*Description:* Ballet company employs PR, marketing, development, research,
   accounting, and management staff.

**San Francisco Bay Area Dance Coalition**    (415) 673-8172
Fort Mason Center
Bldg. C
San Francisco, CA 94123
*Contact:* Ann Azevedo, Resource Center Director.
*Description:* Publishes newsletter and has dance job board.

# 12

# Travel and Transportation

The travel and transportation industries are two of the largest businesses in the United States.

In the past few years both industries have experienced major restructuring of competitive forces in their industries. These changes are the result of government deregulation of the industries, intense price wars that in some cases resulted in price promotions offering services below cost, the devastating effects of striking workers, high fuel prices, and the economic recession. Neither of the industries could be said to be growth industries, but the long-term effects of deregulation may yet prove positive. Many travel industry experts expect travel to be a growth industry.

Travel, as discussed here, will focus on "luxury" passenger travel, while transportation will cover the movement of cargo and shipping. Many of the companies that transport passengers (e.g., airlines) also have large shipping and transportation functions. In spite of these overlaps, companies are discussed here in terms of their primary roles.

Public transportation, or "everyday travel," is covered in the next chapter, along with the local utilities companies.

## Travel

The travel business in the Bay Area includes the luxury cruise lines, the airlines, and the many independent and associated travel agencies.

## LUXURY CRUISES

The luxury cruise business is perhaps best represented by Royal Viking Lines, a Norwegian registered line, headquartered here in San Francisco. The cruise company employs sales, entertainment, public relations, market research, finance and marketing specialists. The crew is hired through Oslo, Norway. Most other cruise lines have sales offices here, though they are headquartered elsewhere.

## AIRLINES

Naturally, all the major airlines have reservation offices at the Bay Area international airports. However, not all hire a great many Bay Area personnel. The largest airline employers here include United, TransAmerica (charter company), World Airways, Pan Am, and TWA.

The profitability of airline businesses has decreased dramatically in the past few years. Fierce competitive price promoting between airlines has raised the cost of doing business and cut into airline profit margins, even though the cheaper fares have made travel more accessible to more people. Airlines with strong cargo business divisions fared better than those with primarily passenger business.

## TRAVEL JOB TITLES AND SALARY RANGES

### Cruise Lines

Many of the jobs on cruise lines are similar to those in hospitality and hotel management. Here are some examples.

- Sales Manager: $20,000–$40,000
- Vice President Passenger Services: $25,000–$40,000
- Reservationist: $14,000–$20,000
- Vice President Hotel Operations: $40,000–$55,000
- Market Research Manager: $28,000–$33,000
- Public Relations Manager: $19,000–$28,000
- Vice President Marketing: $40,000–$65,000

### Airlines

Travel privileges are liberal, so you should consider this as part of your annual income.

- Flight Attendant/Supervisor: $18,000–$33,000
- Ticket Agent: $15,000–$30,000
- Cargo Agent: $16,000–$32,000
- Manager (e,g., agents or dispatchers): $35,000–$50,000
- Marketing Manager: $30,000–$50,000
- Vice President Marketing: $60,000–$70,000
- Accountant: $20,000–$35,000
- Director of Accounting: $40,000–$45,000
- Tour Manager: $25,000–$35,000
- District Sales Manager: $33,000–$42,000

## TRAVEL DIRECTORY

### Luxury Cruise Lines

**American Hawaiian Cruises**   (415) 392-9400
3 Embarcadero Center
San Francisco, CA 94111
*Contact:* Gail McCabe, Personnel.
*Employs:* 60.
*Description:* U.S. registered cruise line offering week long cruises to four
  Hawaiian islands.

**Royal Viking Line**   (415) 398-8000
1 Embarcadero Center
San Francisco, CA 94111
*Contact:* Warren Titus, Chairman
*Employs:* 135.
*Description:* Three world-class cruise ships.

## AIRLINES

**American Airlines, Inc.**   (415) 877-6395
PO Box 8277
Airport Station
San Francisco, CA 94128
*Contact:* J.W. Cance, Jr., General Manager
*Employs:* 1,400
*Description:* Hires ticket agents, pilots, flight attendants, sales reps, and
  marketing personnel in Bay Area. Western Division Personnel Office is in
  Los Angeles at PO Box 92246, World Way Postal Center, Los Angeles, CA
  90009; (213) 932-2326.

**Delta**  (415) 626-2991
San Francisco International Airport
San Francisco, CA 94128
*Contact:* Gene Hyde, District Marketing Director
*Employs:* 350 in Bay Area
*Description:* Although headquartered in Atlanta, the airline has three Bay
  Area reservations, marketing and air cargo sales operations, and
  maintenance personnel.

**Japan Airlines Co.**  (415) 982-8141
150 Powell St.
San Francisco, CA 94102
*Contact:* T. Hashizume, Vice President
*Employs:* 250 in Bay Area
*Description:* Headquartered in Tokyo. Bay Area employs sales, marketing,
  ticket, and passenger agents.

**PSA**  (714) 574-2116
San Francisco International Airport
San Francisco, CA 94128
*Contact:* Employment Office
  3225 North Harbour Dr.
  San Diego, CA 92101
*Employs:* 100
*Description:* Four ticket offices in Bay Area—reservations, ticket agents,
  passenger services.

**Pacific Express**  (916) 362-0676
1103 Fortress Street
Chico, CA 95926
*Employs:* 50
*Description:* New airline begun in 1982. Flies to Los Angeles, Palm Springs,
  Oregon, Idaho.

**Pan Am**  (415) 877-2350
San Francisco International Airport
San Francisco, CA 94128
*Contact:* Manager, Employment Services
*Employs:* 2,300 in Bay Area
*Description:* Five ticket offices in Bay Area—passenger services, cargo,
  maintenance, and ramp operations.

**Qantas Airways**  (415) 877-0694
360 Post St.
San Francisco, CA 94108
*Contact:* Richard Schumacher, Personnel Officer
*Employs:* 350
*Description:* Headquartered in Sydney, Australia. Bay Area has
  reservationists, sales reps, passenger sales, and air transport personnel.

**Republic Airlines**  (415) 877-5034
San Francisco International Airport
San Francisco, CA 94128
*Contact:* Sylvania Hutchinson, Regional Sales Manager
*Description:* Firm is headquartered in Minneapolis. It is known in Bay Area
   for acquiring Hughes Air West, and serves three Bay Area airports: San
   Francisco, Oakland, and San Jose.

**Transamerica Airlines**  (415) 577-6151
7901 Oakport St.
Oakland, CA 94621
*Contact:* Personnel Department or Henry Huff, President
*Employs:* 1,000
*Description:* Subsidiary of Transamerica Corporation. Charter flight airline in
   passenger and cargo markets; specializes in outsized equipment
   transportation service.

**Transworld Airways (TWA)**  (415) 864-5731
San Francisco International Airport
San Francisco, CA 94128
*Contact:* TWA Central Employment
   PO Box 20007
   Kansas City, MO 64195
*Description:* Bay Area employs ticket agents and flight attendants.

**United Airlines**  (415) 876-5432
San Francisco International Airport
San Francisco, CA 94128
*Contact:* Jean Casey, Senior Employment Representative
*Employs:* 5,000
*Description:* Headquartered in Chicago but has large reservation and
   maintenance centers here plus multiple ticket offices.

**Western Airlines**  (213) 646-4354
San Francisco International Airport
San Francisco, CA 94128
*Contact:* Employment Office
   6060 Avion Dr.
   Los Angeles, CA 90045
*Description:* Four ticket offices in Bay Area—reservations, cargo, ticket
   agents.

**World Airways**  (415) 577-2000
1100 Airport Rd.
Oakland, CA 94614
*Contact:* Elza Minor, Personnel
*Employs:* 400
*Description:* Bay Area is headquarters for this airline, which has suffered
   losses for two years. World is best known for its $69 transcontinental flights,
   begun in 1978 when airlines deregulated.

## TRAVEL AGENCIES

Bay Area travel agencies run the gamut from large travel chains such as American Express and Thomas Cook, to small entrepreneurial travel offices. The large firms may have a manager who handles personnel, while at the small companies hiring is usually done by the owner/manager.

Travel agents arrange transportation, prepare itineraries, make reservations, and act as travel consultants. The majority of Bay Area travel agents work for travel agencies (vs. airlines or cruise lines, etc.) and derive their income from sales commissions earned on the reservations they place with airlines, cruises, hotels, tours, rental cars and the like. Commissions generally range from 8 to 10 percent of the purchase price. The largest number of commissions are earned on airline reservations, followed by cruises, and then hotels.

There has been tremendous growth and change in the travel business in the past few years; this has created a demand for better trained travel agents. Deregulation, increases in foreign tourists visiting the U.S., and the fierce competition for the travel dollar among airlines and tour companies has resulted in a deluge of promotions, deals, and complex fare rates that agents must decipher and with which they must stay current. This has led three-quarters of the travel agencies in the U.S. to turn by necessity to computer information services to enable their staff to make accurate travel decisions and arrangements for clients.

Therefore, nowadays, in the travel business a love for travel and a mind for logistics and detail are not enough. Excellent analytic and numerical skills, and computer experience are necessary.

There are two travel associations that can provide complete member agency lists and some guidance to job seekers. These are their local listings.

American Society of Travel Agents
291 Geary St.
San Francisco, CA 94105
(415) 391-5159

Pacific Area Travel Association
228 Grant Ave.
San Francisco, CA 94108
(415) 986-4646

### Travel Publications

To further your education about the travel business you may want to read the two comprehensive travel industry books: *The Tourist Business,* by Lundberg, Barnet, and Crompton, and *Tourism Principles, Practices, Philosophies,* by McIntosh.

Reading travel periodicals will give you a feel for the competing travel packages and fares now being offered, and will familiarize you with travel agent "lingo".

- *Travel Weekly,* One Park Ave., New York, NY 10016
- *Travel Trade,* 605 Fifth Ave., New York, NY 10017
- *Travel Agent,* 2 West 46th St., New York, NY 10036

### Travel Agent Job Titles And Salaries

Bay Area travel agents' yearly average income ranges from $10,500 to $22,000. As a *manager of tour operations* or *department head* at a large travel agency you may earn $25,000 or more. Many travel agency managers start their own firms and then manage them on a full time basis.

Some of the departments and job functions within large travel agencies include *interstate, intrastate, international, sales, customer service,* as well as *travel agents.*

### INSIDERS' ADVICE

Bay Area travel business experts advise that it is easier to get a job in travel if you have a travel degree from an accredited travel school, computer knowledge, or are willing to start at a cruise line company and then make the transition to a general travel agency once you have some experience.

Bay Area experts believe this is a competitive field, but agree that those travel firms and applicants who know how to apply up-to-date business skills will do very well.

The local branch of the Echols International Travel Training School is frequently mentioned as a good way to increase your chances of being hired for a Bay Area travel job: Echols International, 218 FDX Plaza, 1390 Market St., San Francisco, CA 94102; (415) 861-1922. The school offers courses for beginning travel agents as well as courses for experienced agents to learn to use computers. The basic course costs about $2,000 and includes 46 sessions. Both day and evening sessions are offered. The school has a placement service and works closely with local travel agencies and travel firms to place graduates throughout their careers.

Insiders advise that any courses or experience you have in accounting or marketing will be a plus, so be sure to mention them on your resume and in interviews. Business and group travel is a very profitable and growing segment of the travel business, and so any business or sales experience can be presented as a real advantage for hiring you. Language skills are also an advantage (especially German or Spanish) in dealing with foreign travelers.

One local placement service that specializes in travel jobs is Pratt Personnel. Contact Colette Pratt, 703 Market Street, San Francisco, CA 94103; (415) 777-9722.

## TRAVEL AGENCY DIRECTORY

**Bryan International Travel, Inc.**    (415) 986-0967
57 Post St.
San Francisco, CA 94104
*Contact:* Christian Spirendelli, CEO
*Employs:* 17
*Description:* Specializes in group custom trips (e.g., music-oriented, study-oriented). Includes corporate travel department.

**Cardillo Travel Systems**    (415) 433-4180
1 Maritime Plaza
San Francisco, CA 94111
*Contact:* Colleen MacNamara, Vice President, Regional Operations
*Employs:* 100
*Description:* Largest corporate travel agency in California; five Bay Area offices. Offers training program but requires travel school or experience to start.

**Gelco Travel Service**    (415) 321-2890
550 Hamilton Ave.
Palo Alto, CA 94302
*Contact:* Mary Cardoza, Manager
*Employs:* 48 in Bay Area
*Description:* Full service travel agency with emphasis on commercial travel; provides training program.
*Second Bay Area location*    (415) 398-6789
500 Sansome St.
San Francisco, CA 94111
*Contact:* Ray Douglas, Director of Development.

**Haley Travel/American Express**    (415) 981-1880
111 Pine St.
San Francisco, CA 94111
*Contact:* Bangie Lopez at American Express: (415) 981-4103
*Employs:* 130
*Description:* Corporate travel agency.

**Siemer & Hand Travel**   (415) 434-1960
465 California St.
San Francisco, CA
*Contact:* Marvin Hand, President
*Employs:* 50
*Description:* Five San Francisco offices; one in Marin (Larkspur). General
   travel agency, personal and commercial.

**Thomas Cook Travel**   (415) 546-9113 or 392-2378
425 Market St.
San Francisco, CA 94105
*Contact:* John Mathew, Manager
*Description:* Largest travel agency in the world, specializes in commercial and
   group travel.
*Second Bay Area office:*
527 Lawrence Expressway
Sunnyvale, CA 94086
*Contact:* Michaela Popoff, Manager.

## *Transportation*

### TRUCKING AND RAILROAD SHIPPING

Back in 1980, when the transportation industry was still regulated,
solicitation of customers by transportation companies was not as important as it is now, as there was much less price competition. Since deregulation, price cutting and other competitive pressures have forced the
transportation businesses to demonstrate expertise not only in the logistics and operations disciplines, but also in marketing.

Profits are down because of deregulation, the recession, rising fuel
costs, and new forms of competition. Transportation experts do expect
the situation to improve as the U.S. economy strengthens, however, and
in spite of profit pressures, the changes in the industry are bringing some
positive elements. For example, there are new opportunities for contracts
with railroads, inter-modal transportation, etc.

If you are considering a career in transportation, it would be a good
idea to investigate the large Bay Area manufacturing firms which have
their own traffic departments and may operate their own corporate
truck fleets (you may wish to contact Del Monte, Bechtel, Crown Zellerbach, Shaklee, and Levi Strauss & Co.).

## Trucking Publications

To learn more about the trends in the transportation field, read these periodicals:

- *Pacific Traffic,* 2230 Big Ranch Rd., Napa, CA 94558. Magazine of western transportation and distribution.
- *Traffic Manager,* 108 N.W. 9th St., Portland, OR 97209; (503) 222-9794. All types of freight transportation.
- *Distribution Manager,* Chestnut and 56th St., Philadelphia, PA 19139; (215) 748-2000. Magazine of physical distribution.
- *Traffic Management,* 221 Columbus Ave., Boston, MA 02116; (617) 536-7780. Issues in management of distribution and transportation.
- *Container News,* 390 5th Ave., New York, NY 10018; (212) 613-9728. Magazine for container shipping industry.
- *Handling/Shipping Management,* 111 Chester Ave., Cleveland, OH 44114; (216) 696-7000. Distribution management trends.

There are also two directories used in the transportation business that are full of helpful educational information.

- *Traffic World,* 1435 "G" St. N.W., Washington, D.C. 20005; (202) 626-4500
- *Chilton's Distribution,* Chilton's Way, Radnor, PA 19089; (215) 964-4000

## Maritime Shipping

In addition to trucking and rail shipping, there is maritime trade. San Francisco Bay is one of the world's great deep water harbors. Since the first settlement of the area, freight and passenger shipping from and to ports around San Francisco Bay has been an important economic factor.

Today the ports on the Bay are among the largest in the U.S. in tonnage and in dollar value of cargo. The San Francisco port generates $10 million in revenue, and the Oakland port generates $30 million in revenue. Ocean going ships coming in through the Bay also ascend the rivers to nearby deep water ports at Sacramento and Stockton.

According to a 1982 study by Pacific Merchant Shipping Association, about $2.3 billion flowed into the nine-county Bay Area from the maritime industry. Forecasts for 1983 were $2.5 billion. Bay Area ports in 1981 handled $14.2 billion worth of foreign trade, 4% of U.S. foreign trade. About 32% of the overseas trade with the Bay Area was carried on U.S. flag vessels.

There were approximately 17,000 jobs in maritime industries in the Bay Area during 1981–82. While many of these were blue collar jobs, the headquarters management and support staffs and the sales and marketing activities encompass an interesting variety of well paid positions.

In addition to the shipping lines and the longshore activities, the associated businesses range widely; from consulting specialists in bulky loads to builders of containers; from propeller foundries to ship chandleries. Many foreign shipping lines have local offices for sales and traffic purposes.

Shipping business out of San Francisco fans out into the whole Pacific Basin, so that job seekers with multi-lingual skills will find the marine trade a particularly interesting area to canvass.

Also, as you try to pinpoint job locations and possibilities, be aware of an interesting shift that has occurred to the facilities specializing in handling of containerized cargo (up 140% since even 1970) and specialized shiploads of items like automobiles. Throughout the settlement of the Bay Area and, indeed, until the last 20 years—San Francisco proper has been the major port location on San Francisco Bay. The wharves along San Francisco's Embarcadero have been the chief location for loading and unloading general cargo ships.

Then in the 1950s and 1960s, two things happened. One was the crowding of general businesses and residences into the valuable and scenic waterfront strip in San Francisco. Drainage became more and more difficult on the Embarcadero, land more and more expensive. Secondly, and more importantly, containers and container ships began to take over the handling of general cargos. These ships forced the nature of the waterfront facilities to change. The cargos require huge open areas for storing containers and massive cranes and other equipment. The Port of Oakland had the space; the Port of San Francisco did not. Oakland made the huge necessary investments in handling equipment; San Francisco did not.

The result: Today the Port of Oakland is the dominant cargo transfer point. San Francisco's elegantly designed piers stand empty (in many cases) or are used for parking or shopping centers, although cruise ships still dock there. Thus, some of the supporting marine service businesses have shifted to Oakland or Alameda or Richmond. However, the port of San Francisco is making a comeback with three straight years of increased revenues, earnings and tonnage, and capacity for 25 percent of container cargo business in the Bay Area.

In spite of the dominance of the Port of Oakland, you will find steamship agencies and steamship lines listings in the Yellow Pages are mostly in San Francisco business district locations.

For more information on shipping, read the periodical *American Shipper*, P.O. Box 4728, Jacksonville, FL 32201; (904) 355-2601.

The port organizations themselves are part of city government and as such are subject to Civil Service System. You may contact the San Francisco office at 646 Van Ness Avenue, San Francisco, CA 94102; (415) 558-4495, and the Oakland Civil Service office at 1221 Oak Street, Oakland, CA 94612; (415) 874-7337.

## AIR TRANSPORT

In the air transport field, there are air freight companies that deliver cargo from one airport to another, and air courier companies that pick up and deliver door to door.

In the Bay Area, the air freight cargo business is done primarily by the airline companies that have large freight departments as part of their total transportation operations (see the airline listings in the travel section of this chapter). Courier freight companies, on the other hand, are formed for the exclusive purpose of shipping. They hire *pilots, traffic managers, customer service representatives, accountants,* and *sales representatives.*

A magazine to read to learn more about this field is *Air Cargo Magazine,* 2000 Clearwater Dr., Oak Brook, IL 60521; (212) 977-8314.

## OTHER TRANSPORTATION FIELDS

In addition to the truck, air, railroad, and maritime freight carriers, there are the leasing companies such as Itel and Brae that acquire equipment, capitalize it for tax write-off purposes, and then lease or sell it to other firms. These firms are covered in Chapter 6, *Banking and Diversified Finance.*

## TRANSPORTATION JOB TITLES AND SALARY RANGES

Job functions in transportation carrier companies include *sales, operations* and *terminal management, traffic and rate setting, safety, finance, personnel, marketing, labor relations, training, planning, communications,* and *carrier company management.*

Job titles in industry may be part of the distribution traffic departments and include *rates, customer service, planning,* and *operations.*

Here are some examples of job titles and salary ranges for the Bay Area transportation field:

### Carrier Companies
- Sales Manager: $25,000–$35,000

- Top Marketing/Sales Executive: $59,000–$89,000
- Finance Manager: $23,000–$55,000
- Top Financial Executive: $56,000–$125,000
- Operations Manager: $30,000–$45,000
- Traffic and Rate Setting: $30,000–$60,000
- Top Legal Executive: $59,000–$80,000
- Executive Vice-President: $75,000–$150,000
- Chief Operating Officer: $76,000–$196,000
- Chief Executive Officer: $100,000–$235,000

## Industrial Traffic

- Vice-President (e.g., rates or planning): $60,000–$80,000
- Director of Services: $50,000–$70,000
- Manager (e.g., planning or operation): $40,000–$70,000

## Airport and Port Job Titles and Salary Ranges

Here are a few of the job titles and salary ranges for the Bay Area ports.

### PORT COMMISSION

- Marine Patrol Officer: $7,000–$14,000
- Dredging Supervisor: $14,500–$38,000
- Engineering Aide: $8,500–$21,000
- Harbor Police: $10,000–$25,000

### AIRPORT

- Airport Police: $10,000–$26,000
- Airport Electrician: $15,000–$39,000
- Airport Operations Coordinator: $15,000–$39,000
- Business Administration Manager: $19,000–$50,000

## INSIDERS' ADVICE

Local universities, such as the School of Transportation and Distribution at Golden Gate University, have courses of study leading to a BS, MBA, or certification in transportation/distribution. You may make helpful Bay Area traffic and transportation contacts by taking an evening course or by arranging to meet with one of the course's professors. Golden Gate University is located at 536 Mission, San Francisco, 94105; (415) 442-7000. Monroe Sullivan is the Dean of the School of Transportation. San Francisco State University also has a transportation and distribution department. It is located at 1600 Holloway Avenue, San Francisco, 94132; (415) 469-2141. Don Wood, a San Francisco State professor, is one of the co-authors of *the* basic college textbook on the transportation field: *Contemporary Transportation,* by Don Wood and James C. Johnson.

Insiders in the transportation field here point out the new emphasis on innovation and financial management skills that is one of the major results of industry deregulation. There are new opportunities in the field for people with experience in sales forecasting, inventory control, customer service, computer programming, and contract negotiation.

There are entry level opportunities in the Bay Area for college graduates, especially for those with courses or degrees in finance or the transportation/distribution aspects of business.

## TRANSPORTATION ORGANIZATIONS

A good way to make contacts and learn of job openings is through the local transportation organizations.

American Society of Traffic and Transportation
*Contact:* Karen Barnes
c/o Santa Fe Railroad
114 Sansome St.
San Francisco, CA 94120
(415) 781-7600

Women's Traffic Club of San Francisco
*Contact:* Carol Leone
c/o General Steamship
400 California St.
San Francisco, CA 94104
(415) 772-9262

Delta Nu Alpha
*For Bay Area chapters, contact:*
Robert Stevens
c/o IBM
5600 Cottle Rd.
San Jose, CA 95153
(408) 256-1600

National Council of Physical Distribution Management
*For information about Bay Area round tables, contact:*
Charles P. Strickler
c/o The Clorox Company
PO Box 24305
Oakland, CA 94623
(415) 271-7071

*For Job Bank information, contact:*
Stephanie Rennie
c/o National Council of Physical Distribution Management
2803 Butterfield Rd.
Oak Brook, IL 60521
(312) 655-0985

These organizations hold regular meetings, present speakers, publish news bulletins, and provide job listings.

For experienced distribution or traffic/transportation managers, insiders recommend contacting the following local executive recruiter:

George Hunt
Hunt Executive Services
1791 Green St.
San Francisco, CA 94123
(415) 441-4170.

## TRANSPORTATION DIRECTORY

### Trucking

**Consolidated Freightways**   (415) 326-1700
175 Linfield Dr.
Menlo Park, CA 94025
*Contact:* Larry Scott, President.
*Employs:* 300 in Bay Area.
*Description:* Largest trucking company in the United States.

**Delta California Industry**   (415) 577-7000
333 Hegenberger Rd.
Oakland, CA 94604
*Contact:* Sheri Stewart, Personnel.
*Employs:* 3,000.
*Description:* Trucking and freight of all kinds.

**PIE**    (415) 944-7398
5 N. Via Monte
Walnut Creek, CA 94598
*Contact*  Tim McCoy, Manager of Human Resources.
*Employs:* 600 in Bay Area.
*Description:* Sixth-largest trucking firm in United States, known for excellent
    training programs for college recruits.


## Railroads

**Southern Pacific Co.**    (415) 541-2640
1 Market St.
San Francisco, CA 94105
*Contact:*  Ken Wood, Personnel Manager.
*Employs:* 4,500.
*Description:* Diversified transportation company primarily in freight trucking
    and pipelines (nation's only coal slurry pipeline).

**Western Pacific**    (415) 982-2100
526 Mission St.
San Francisco, CA 94105
*Contact:*  A.P. Schuetz, Manager, Personnel
*Employs:* 300.
*Description:* Transport freight railroad that is merging with Union Pacific
    Railroad.


## Ocean Carriers

**American Presidents Line**    (415) 271-8373
1950 Franklin
Oakland, CA 94612
*Contact:*  Reginald Ardrey, Staffing Manager.
*Employs:* 550.
*Description:* Shipping freight of all kinds with extensive Pacific Basin routes;
    specializes in combination ship, truck, rail freight movement.

**Lykes Bros. Steamship Co., Inc.**    (415) 433-7400
320 California St.
San Francisco, CA 94104
*Contact:*  Cheryl Clahr, Personnel Supervisor
*Employs:* 55.
*Description:* Steamship liner service between United States and Far East,
    Africa, Mediterranean.

**Matson Navigation Co.** (415) 957-4534
333 Market St.
San Francisco, CA 94105
*Contact:* Marge Dineen, Manager of Employment.
*Employs:* 450.
*Description:* Shipping and freight of all kinds.

**SeaLand** (415) 271-1456
1425 Maritime St.
Oakland, CA 94623
*Contact:* John Stone, Personnel.
*Employs:* 300.
*Description:* Shipping freight of all kinds.

**United States Lines** (415) 465-4010
1579 Middle Harbor Rd.
Oakland, CA 94607
*Contact:* Giselle Smith, Personnel.
*Employs:* 200.
*Description:* Freight and shipping of all kinds.

**Airports and Ports**

**Oakland International Airport** (415) 577-4000
1 Airport Dr.
PO Box 45
Oakland, CA 94621
*Contact:* George Watson, Airport Manager.

**Port of Oakland** (415) 452-2381
66 Jack London Sq.
Oakland, CA 94607
*Contact:* Walter Abernathy, Director.
*Employs:* 490.
*Description:* The organization that manages the port, the Oakland Airport, and
   Jack London Square.

**Port of San Francisco** (415) 391-8000
Ferry Bldg.
Rm. 2000
San Francisco, CA 94111
*Contact:* Edward David, Port Director.
*Employs:* 210.
*Description:* Landlord port; collects revenue for city from renting property
   wharfage and dockage.

**San Francisco International Airport**    (415) 761-0800
PO Box 8097
San Francisco, CA 94128
*Contact:* Louis Turpen, Director.
*Employs:* 1,000.
*Description:* Fifth-busiest airport in United States. Jobs include operations,
    business and finance, engineering, maintenance, and airport police.

**San Jose Municipal Airport**    (408) 277-4204
1661 Airport Blvd.
San Jose, CA 95110
*Contact:* Gavier Perez, Personnel.
*Employs:* 300.
*Description:* Second-largest Bay Area airport.

**Air Transport**

**Airborne Freight Corporation**    (408) 745-6140
1319 Moffett Park
Sunnyvale, CA 94086
*Contact:* Charles Weaver, Manager.
*Employs:* 75 people.
*Description:* General air freight and courier service.

**Continental Express Company**    (415) 864-5851
58 Seward St.
San Francisco, CA 94114
*Contact:* Peter Lupsa.
*Employs:* 10 people.
*Description:* Headquarters office of small air courier company.

**Emery Air Freight**    (415) 877-1830
501 South Airport Blvd.
South San Francisco, CA 94080
*Contact:* Paul Klepacz, Service Manager.
*Employs:* 138 people.
*Description:* Worldwide air freight and courier services.

**Flying Tigers**    (415) 877-3111
San Francisco International Airport
San Francisco, CA 94128
*Contact:* Personnel Manager.
*Employs:* 300 people.
*Description:* World's largest air cargo carrier.

**Sky Pak**   (415) 348-5391
778 Burlway Rd.
Burlingame, CA 94010
*Contact:* John Callan, President
*Employs:* 70 people.
*Description:* Headquarters of international air courier firm, transporting
   packages up to 70 pounds.


## Trade and Service Organizations

**California State Auto Association**   (415) 565-2012
150 Van Ness Ave.
San Francisco, CA 94102
*Contact:* Lyle Engeldinger, Personnel Manager
*Employs:* 4,000.
*Description:* Service organization for auto industry, including insurance and
   traffic safety. Publishes *Motorland* magazine.

**California Trucking Association**   (415) 579-3500
1240 Bayshore Highway
Burlingame, CA 94010
*Contact:* William Rozay, President
*Description:* Nonprofit full-service support organization, including group
   insurance, cost analysis, and industrial relations for trucking companies.

**Pacific Maritime Association**   (415) 362-7973
635 Sacramento St.
San Francisco, CA 94111
*Contact:* Glee Tuttle, Personnel.
*Description:* Labor relations bargaining agents for shipping companies.

# 13

# Utilities and Mass Transportation

This chapter includes telephone companies, water and energy utilities, and mass transportation companies.

For jobs with the companies that are owned and operated by the city or county you will have to take the civil service exams in order to be considered. See Chapter 21 on government, in order to learn how to proceed.

## *Utilities*

### TELEPHONE

The telecommunications industry is an exciting business to be in right now. The technology is changing and making new products and systems possible. The settlement in the seven-year antitrust case against American Telephone and Telegraph Co. has opened up myriad business possibilities to both AT&T and its spin-off companies.

Pacific Telephone is the largest of the Bell Systems companies. It will be separated from its parent company by early 1984. The break-up will create an increased emphasis on competition and marketing of phone services in the Bay Area.

It is expected that in the Bay Area AT&T longlines will expand and

Pacific Telephone will shrink. However, some Pacific Telephone personnel will move over to AT&T.

## WATER

Personnel in water management include civil engineers who plan and design water facilities, hydrologists, customer service people, purchasing people, operations and construction personnel. Also there are jobs in real estate, law, auto mechanics, programming, and public information.

Publicly owned utility companies hire through the Civil Service exam. You may find out what jobs are available by contacting them directly or by checking with city and state employment offices.

## ENERGY

The energy utilities employ both technical and nontechnical personnel. In technical the jobs include electrical, mechanical, civil, chemical, nuclear, and industrial engineers. The hottest job categories in technical seem to be in the computer departments, where computer service people, programmers, and systems analysts are needed.

On the nontechnical side there are jobs in accounting, economics, personnel, market research, and rates and valuation, plus that of controller. The market research and rates and valuation departments are currently very active departments. Researchers monitor public attitudes toward PG&E and recommend programs to improve the utilities' image or cut costs. Frequently the research that is collected is then disseminated to the public through educational newsletters in utility bills or via press releases to the media.

## UTILITIES JOB TITLES AND SALARY RANGES

There is a wide range of technical and professional jobs with utilities. Government hires through the Civil Service exam process. Below are sample job salary ranges.

- Manager, Water Pollution: $23,000–$61,000
- Sewage Treatment Manager: $17,000–$45,000
- Electrical Maintenance Technician: $13,000–$32,000
- Customer Service Representative: $14,000–$19,000
- Accountant: $15,000–$21,000
- Rates and Valuation Manager: $25,000–$50,000
- Personnel Manager: $17,000–$40,000
- Computer Programmers: $17,000–$40,000

- Data Processor: $14,000–$24,000
- Systems Programmer: $18,000–$45,000
- Operations Manager: $24,000–$60,000
- Nuclear Engineer: $24,000–$60,000
- Civil Engineer: $24,000–$60,000
- Environmental Engineer: $24,000–$60,000
- Mechanical Engineer: $24,000–$60,000
- Electrical Engineer: $24,000–$60,000
- Physicist: $21,000–$26,000
- Biologist: $16,000–$18,000
- Chemist: $18,000–$26,000
- Director of MIS: $30,000–$87,000
- Top Financial Executive: $58,000–$100,000
- Top Marketing Executive: $71,000–$75,000
- Top Manufacturing Executive: $55,000–$82,000
- Executive Vice President of Utility: $68,000–$120,000
- CEO of Utility: $94,000–$182,000

Entry level engineers at utilities generally work under the supervision of registered engineers and rotate through an "on the job" training program for up to two years until they advance to the level of *Assistant Engineer.*

## INSIDERS' ADVICE

Insiders advise that the phone companies and the utilities give strong consideration to employee referrals. Recommended applicants still go through the screening and interviewing process but the fact that you are referred by an existing employee is a plus. This implies that you should put your energy into making a contact with someone already employed in one of these companies, and asking them to refer you to the personnel department.

Insiders also say that job-seekers with past telephone experience with "Ma Bell" have a background that will be increasingly in demand as competition returns to the communications field as a result of the Justice Department's antitrust settlement with AT&T. There will be more telephone retail opportunities at stores such as:

Phones, Ltd.
1032 Irving St.
San Francisco, CA 94108
(415) 665-4817

The Phone Company
1669 Bayshore Highway
Burlingame, CA 94010
(415) 697-2800

Phone Depot
555 Mission St.
San Francisco, CA 94105
(415) 777-3077

There may be opportunities for you with long distance telephone service firms such as Sprint, with teleconferencing companies such as Netcomm International, or with manufacturing firms such as Plantronics Inc.

## UTILITIES DIRECTORY

### Telecommunications

**American Telephone and Telegraph**   (415) 442-2600
795 Folsom St.
San Francisco, CA 94107
*Contact:* Employment Department.
*Employs:* 15,000 in Bay Area.
*Description:* Long distance telecommunications service; as a result of AT&T court case it is expected to expand in 1983.

**General Telephone Co.**   (408) 354-9000
PO Box 68
Los Gatos, CA 95031
*Contact:* Bruce Campbell, Staffing Manager.
*Description:* Telephone services headquartered in Santa Monica.

**Pacific Telephone & Telegraph**   (415) 433-5430
140 New Montgomery St.
San Francisco, CA 94105
*Contact:* Management Employment Office
    44 Montgomery St.
    San Francisco, CA 94104
*Employs:* 112,000.
*Description:* Local and long distance phone services.

**Western Electric Company**   (415) 639-1000
1717 Doolittle Dr.
San Leandro, CA 94577
*Contact:* Personnel Department.
*Description:* Manufacturing and supplies for Bell.

**Western Union Telegraph Company**    (415) 763-6100
303 Hegenberger Rd.
Oakland, CA 94621
*Contact:* Personnel Department.
*Description:* Diversified telecommunications.


## Water

**California Water Service**    (408) 298-1414
1720 N. 1st St.
San Jose, CA 95112
*Contact:* Roberta Nelson, Personnel.
*Employs:* 500.
*Description:* Privately owned water service (regulated by PUC) supplies water
    to more than 50 communities.

**East Bay Municipal Utility District**    (415) 835-3000
2130 Adeline St.
PO Box 24055
Oakland, CA 94623
*Contact:* Artis Dawson, Personnel Manager
*Employs:* 1,100.
*Description:* Public agency, provides water for Alameda and Contra Costa
    counties; operates sewage treatment plants.

**San Jose Water Works**    (408) 279-7808
374 W. Santa Clara
San Jose, CA 95196
*Contact:* Personnel Department.
*Employs:* 250.
*Description:* Privately owned company; service water in homes.

**Santa Clara Valley Water District**    (408) 265-2600
5750 Almaden Expressway
San Jose, CA 95118
*Contact:* Andrew Flores, Personnel.
*Employs:* 280.
*Description:* Wholesale water to eight counties and small water companies.


## Energy

**CP National Corporation**    (415) 680-7700
1355 Willow Way
Concord, CA 94520
*Contact:* Karen Thompson, Personnel.
*Employs:* 200 at headquarters; 1,300 total.
*Description:* Supplies electricity, gas, water, and telephone services.

**Pacific Gas & Electric Company**    (415) 781-4211
77 Beale St.
San Francisco, CA 94106
*Contact:* Professional Employment Department
   215 Market St.
   Rm. 1300
   San Francisco, CA 94106; (415) 974-6676
*Employs:* 24,000.
*Description:* Supplies electricity and natural gas.

**Pacific Gas Transmission Co.**    (415) 781-0474
245 Market St.
San Francisco, CA 94104
*Contact:* Employment Department.
*Employs:* 185.
*Description:* Natural gas pipelines.

## *Mass Transportation*

Public transportation, particularly "Muni", does not have a particularly good outlook, since Muni had to absorb the cable car employees displaced during the two year shutdown of the cable cars for repairs.

Job opportunities in mass transportation include those in the areas of financial analysis, marketing, sales, human resources, research, accounting, engineering, systems analysis, advertising, community services, scheduling, risk and insurance, legal, and data processing.

Middle or senior level jobs require degrees in traffic or transportation and experience in private or public transportation departments. Most of the companies will keep resumes on file for up to six months and will contact you when openings are available.

## PUBLIC TRANSPORTATION JOB TITLES AND SALARY RANGES

These are some of the job titles and salaries ranges for Bay Area public transportation:

- Car Cleaners and Supervisors: $8,000–$24,000
- Fare Collectors and Supervisors: $8,000–$28,000
- Ride Share Coordinator: $16,000–$19,000
- Bus Driver: $12,000–$16,000
- Financial Analyst $20,000-$25,000
- Station Supervisor: $10,000–$25,000
- Planning Director: $20,000–$42,000
- Data Processing: $20,000–$42,000
- Operations Manager: $22,000–$56,000

- Systems Engineer: $17,000–$19,000
- Public Relations Manager: $18,000–$38,000
- Marketing Manager: $20,000–$42,000
- Financial Manager: $35,000–$50,000
- General Manager: $26,000–$69,000

## INSIDERS' ADVICE

Mass transportation insiders point out that a growing segment of mass transportation in the Bay Area is that of the ride-sharing or car-pooling services. They advise that an entry level job in this area, as a *ride coordinator,* is a good way to develop management skills. Another growth area is *route planning* in which, for example, you plan more efficient bus routes. A background in scheduling or planning is preferred for this area. *Equipment maintenance* is an area that is also getting increased attention.

Although transportation and business education are desirable, many Bay Area public transportation managers started as bus drivers. Starting as a bus driver is still considered the best way to get a clear understanding of how the public transportation systems really work.

## MASS TRANSPORTATION DIRECTORY

**Alameda–Contra Costa Transit District (AC Transit)**    (415) 891-4777
508 16th St.
Oakland, CA 94612
*Contact:*  Personnel Department.
*Description:*  Private bus service company contracted with government.

**Bay Area Rapid Transit (BART)**    (415) 465-4100
800 Madison St.
Oakland, CA 94607
*Contact:*  Rodney Williams, Recruitment Manager.
*Description:*  City-suburban underground train system, considered the most advanced transit system in United States.

**Golden Gate Bridge, Highway & Transportation District**    (415) 921-5858
PO Box 9000
Presidio Station
San Francisco, CA 94129
*Contact:*  Andrea Ferrell, Personnel.
*Employs:*  900.
*Description:*  Serves Marin County; operates ferry-boat service to Sausalito and Larkspur.

**Municipal Railway**    (415) 558-4843
949 Presidio Ave.
San Francisco, CA 94115

*Contact:* Personnel Department.
*Employs:* 4,000.
*Description:* City owned and operated public transportation, buses and cable cars. Cable cars are shut down for repairs until 1984.

**Southern Pacific Transportation Company**    (415) 541-1973
301 Mission St.
San Francisco, CA 94105
*Contact:* Employment Department.
*Description:* Railroad serving some of the San Francisco suburbs (Palo Alto, etc.); also operates oil and gas pipelines and telecommunications system.

# 14

# Consumer Products and Manufacturing

One of the biggest misconceptions about the San Francisco Bay Area is that since San Francisco is a well-known urban area there must be loads of consumer product firms ready and waiting to hire new MBAs or experienced marketing managers. This is simply not the case. In fact, there are very few such firms, and thus there are few *traditional* packaged goods jobs in the Bay Area.

This chapter will discuss the consumer marketing or manufacturing firms that *are* located here and will give you some ideas of the opportunities for applying the marketing, operations, or finance acumen you may have developed at Procter & Gamble, General Foods, General Mills, or elsewhere.

### Firms in the Bay Area

What follows is a short profile of each firm with information on how to contact them and some clues about how they are organized. It will help your job search if you use this information to identify the specific job titles or divisions you are interested in.

## MANUFACTURING JOB TITLES AND SALARY RANGES

Naturally Bay Area salary ranges for a particular field depend on the importance of that function to the specific industry. However, these ranges will provide a basis of comparison with other geographic areas and across functions.

- Accountant: $17,000–$29,000
- Auditor: $17,000–$24,000
- Controller: $22,000–$45,000
- Brand or Product Manager: $30,000–$36,000
- Senior Product Manager: $37,000–$50,000
- Group Brand Management: $50,000–$120,000
- Computer Programmer: $19,000–$23,000
- Quality Control Manager: $30,000–$38,000
- Production Manufacturing: $30,000–$61,000
- Publicity Specialist: $18,000–$28,000
- Public Relations Manager: $20,000–$40,000
- Corporate Communications Director: $27,000–$80,000
- Sales Trainee: $15,000–$20,000
- Sales Representative: $17,000–$24,000
- Senior Sales Representative: $25,000–$35,000
- Plant Manager: $30,000–$45,000
- Advertising Manager: $25,000–$50,000
- Marketing Manager: $50,000–$85,000
- Marketing Director: $60,000–$120,000
- Market Research: $30,000–$55,000
- Real Estate Representative: $24,000–$38,000
- Director of Operations: $38,000–$75,000
- Personnel Manager: $25,000–$50,000
- Personnel Director: $40,000–$70,000
- Assistant or Associate Attorney: $21,000–$37,000
- Senior Attorney: $36,000–$65,000
- Strategic Planning: $25,000–$70,000
- Finance Vice-President: $53,000–$110,000
- Executive Vice-President: $55,000–$150,000

## MANUFACTURING COMPANY PROFILES

**Amfac Inc.**    (415) 579-6750
111 Anza Blvd.
Burlingame, CA
*Contact:* Sandy Cowen, Director of Personnel.
*Employs:* 5,000 in Bay Area.
*Description:* A diversified company whose six operating divisions include retail, wholesale distribution, food processing, hotels and resorts, horticulture, and sugar and land. Its retail chain is Oakland-based Liberty House. It owns the Bay Area's Silverado Country Club in Napa. Its food products brands

include C & H Sugar. The headquarters is located in Honolulu, Hawaii, and 22 percent of the stock is owned by Gulf Western.

**Castle & Cooke**    (415) 986-3000
50 California St.
San Francisco, CA 94110
*Contact:* Linda Mabanglo, Corporate Director of Recruitment.
*Employs:* Approximately 400 in San Francisco.
*Description:* A food production, processing, and marketing company. Some of its familiar brands include Dole Pineapple and Bumble Bee Tuna. The Dole brand accounts for half the pineapple market and more than a third of the banana market in the United States. Other of their leadership categories in the United States include lettuce, celery, and cauliflower.

The corporation is headquartered in Hawaii, where it is reputed to be the fourth-largest landholder. However, the financial and marketing management of the company is located here in San Francisco.

There are five divisions: fresh products, processed products, new product development, financial administration, and real estate and diversified products.

Traditionally MBAs have entered the firm as market or financial analysts, and then advanced to assistant product manager, then to product manager and to director of marketing.

Of the 400 people employed here in San Francisco, about 225 are at the professional level. Castle & Cooke's advertising agencies include Foote, Cone & Belding & Honig, J. Walter Thompson, and Allan & Dorward.

**The Clorox Company**    (415) 271-7000
1221 Broadway
Oakland, CA 94612
*Contact:* Timothy Johnston, Employment.
*Employs:* Approximately 350 professionals at headquarters.
*Description:* The company is named after its original product, Clorox Bleach. Currently the Clorox Corporation is a diversified consumer products company with a reputation for research and marketing. Once part of Procter & Gamble (prior to 1973), Clorox prides itself on following P&G marketing guidelines. However, unlike P&G, acquisitions are currently an important part of Clorox's management strategy for diversifying the firm.

Clorox competes in the grocery products category with brands such as 409 Cleaner, Liquid Plumr, Twice as Fresh Air Freshener, and Kingsford Charcoal. It has recently diversified to include exterior paints (Olympic) and food service and restaurant operations.

Clorox hires about 50 BAs and MBAs per year as brand assistants. Most higher level positions go to internal people who are promoted. Clorox only rarely hires outside brand managers. The qualities it looks for in job candidates are strong analytical skills and excellent communication and interpersonal skills.

The Clorox divisions are household products, Kingsford, international, food service, and corporate. Traditionally there has been little cross-fertilizing between divisions, but this is now changing somewhat.

In Clorox's marketing departments there are three basic levels: brand assistant, assistant brand manager, and brand manager. Other departments include buying (where package or product ingredients are purchased), traffic (distribution), marketing research (research design and data analysis), manufacturing (processing and production), and research and development.

Clorox's ad agencies include Foote, Cone & Belding/Honig, Ketchum, and Young & Rubicam.

**Crown-Zellerbach**   (415) 951-5627
1 Bush St.
San Francisco, CA 94104
*Contact:* Thomas Shaw, Corporate Manager, Professional Employment.
*Employs:* 800 at headquarters
*Description:* A forest products manufacturer, specializing in timber and wood products, paper, corrugated containers, packaging and energy. It manufactures a few direct consumer products, including West Coast brands Chiffon and Marina toilet tissues, Tuf 'n Ready paper towels, and Linen Soft napkins.

Since housing construction has been among our country's most depressed industries, Crown-Zellerbach has been severely affected. Meanwhile, its specialty packaging business has been growing, and this is where the company is investing for the future.

Its divisions include pulp and paper (40 percent of company), lumber and wood products, specialty packaging and chemicals, the distribution group, and the container group.

One very bright spot in the hiring outlook at Crown-Zellerbach is data processing. Data processors are needed for support in all divisons. The headquarters office here in San Francisco has primarily staff groups such as employee relations, financial, controllers, and legal.

**Del Monte Corporation**   (415) 442-5171
1 Market Plaza
San Francisco, CA 94119
*Contact:* Don Sipes, Director of Employment.
*Employs:* 1,200 at headquarters.
*Description:* Largest fruit and vegetable canner in the United States. In most of the food categories in which it competes, Del Monte holds first or second place. In addition to the familiar Del Monte brand label, it also markets Chun King, Hawaiian Punch, and Granny Goose snack foods.

In 1979 R. J. Reynolds acquired Del Monte. As a result, the firm has become more consumer marketing–oriented than before. The new president, Robert Fox, came to Del Monte from R. J. Reynolds.

The company has four organizational units: dry grocery and beverage products, international grocery, fresh fruit and frozen foods, and the finance and staff group. It recruits approximately eight business administration graduates (BAs) per year for its 18-month training program, in which trainees are rotated through the various functional areas of the company, ending up in an analyst or assistant position. MBAs are recruited (two per year) for marketing positions at the assistant brand manager level. The marketing and advertising department employs a total of 30 people. Del Monte's ad agencies are McCann-Erickson, BBDO/West, and Young & Rubicam.

Worldwide the firm has 48,000 employees, a figure that increases to approximately 80,000 during peak harvest months.

**DiGiorgio Corporation**   (415) 765-0158
1 Maritime Plaza
San Francisco, CA 94111
*Contact:* Paul Berg, Manager Employee Relations.
*Employs:* 62.
*Description:* A diversified company in such broad areas as food processing, distribution, drugs, electronic appliances, building materials, land resources, and automotive accessories. Westerners are probably most familiar with DiGiorgio's Treesweet juice brand, while easterners may know the White Rose tea and canned good products. Treesweet is the number one brand of canned (nonfrozen) orange and grapefruit juice in the United States.

Half of the headquarters personnel are professional level. The office houses legal, finance and planning, real estate, audit, personnel benefits, and management departments. The operating division organizations are located elsewhere.

**Dreyer's Grand Ice Cream, Inc.**   (415) 652-8187
5929 College Ave.
Oakland, CA 94618
*Contact:* Paul Woodland, Vice-President, Administration.
*Employs:* 20 professionals at headquarters.
*Description:* Manufactures and distributes its premium brand of ice cream to retail and institutional outlets, and business is booming. Dreyer's is now the largest branded premium ice cream company in the western United States. Eighty-five percent of sales are to grocery stores.

Professionals employed at the Oakland headquarters include management, manufacturing, finance, marketing, and sales personnel. The marketing department focuses on promotions and new product development.

**Foremost-McKesson**   (415) 983-8316
One Post Street
San Francisco, CA 94104
*Contact:* Chuck Woods, Director of Employee Relations.
*Employs:* 2,000 in San Francisco.
*Description:* The nation's largest wholesaler of drugs and health care products, the leading supplier of bottled water, the largest distributor of alcoholic beverages, and one of the biggest producers of pasta in the United States. Products include Folonari wine, Chartreuse liqueur, Galliano liqueur, San

Miguel and St. Pauli Girl beer, and Mueller's pasta. Recently, Foremost sold its dairy and home-building operations in order to focus on higher margin distribution, drug and food businesses.

Sales and operations are the key career paths at Foremost. The combination of experience in these disciplines can lead to a regional vice-presidency. Foremost has marketing services, product managers, promotion services and market research managers, but these disciplines are somewhat secondary, due to the sales and operations orientation of the firm. Most of its packaged goods marketing activity has moved to the Mueller's subsidiary offices in New Jersey.

In San Francisco 500 of the employees are at the professional level. Foremost uses Ogilvy & Mather in New York for its wine and spirits advertising program.

**Hills Brothers Coffee Inc.**   (415) 546-4600
2 Harrison St.
San Francisco, CA 94105
*Contact:* Trudi Wesley, Corporate Personnel.
*Employs:* 90 professionals at headquarters.
*Description:* Primarily markets coffee, tea, and chocolate products. It has about a 6.5 percent share of the ground coffee category, behind Folgers and Maxwell House. However, ground coffee is a declining segment of the coffee market in that instant coffees have become an increasingly larger segment of the coffee market. Hills Brothers is not well represented in the instant segment; however, it does have an entry in flavored instant coffees (chocolate, almond, etc.) that competes with General Foods International Coffees. Since 1976 Hills Brothers has been owned by a Brazilian coffee grower, Copersucar.

MBAs and experienced marketing people are preferred for jobs in marketing, finance, distribution, commodity buying, and market research. The career path in marketing starts with assistant product manager, then moves to product manager, to group product manager, and then to vice-president, marketing. Other departments include quality assurance, sales management, data processing, purchasing, food service (vending machines), and retail food management.

Wells, Rich & Greene, Los Angeles, is the advertising agency for Hills Brothers.

**Kaiser Aluminum & Chemical Corporation**   (415) 271-3300
300 Lakeside Dr.
Oakland, CA 94643
*Contact:* Roger Dunn, Personnel.
*Employs:* 3,000 in Bay Area.
*Description:* The third-largest producer of aluminum in the world. Recently, with worldwide demand for aluminum down, the company has focused on its nonaluminum activities, including chemicals, real estate, and oil and gas. Domestically the firm has five divisions: aluminum products, agricultural

products, industrial chemicals, real estate development, and refractories. The company employs approximately 25,000 people worldwide. In addition to the Bay Area, large employment centers are in Spokane, New Orleans, and Ravenswood, West Virginia.

**Kaiser Cement Corp.**　(415) 271-2000
300 Lakeside Dr.
Oakland, CA 94612
*Contact:*　Connie Cavagnaro, Personnel Director.
*Employs:*　150 at headquarters.
*Description:*　One of the three companies that, before 1977, made up the Kaiser Industries empire, founded by Henry T. Kaiser. Kaiser Cement is the smallest of the three.

　　Half of the headquarters personnel are professionals. The departments include sales, accounting, legal, investor relations, public relations, computers, the international division, and company management. The decline in the nation's building industry has naturally had a negative impact on cement sales. Nonetheless, the corporation remains committed to the cement business long-term and is currently investing $300 million to modernize its five U.S. cement plants.

**Levi Strauss & Co.**　(415) 544-6000
Levi's Plaza
1155 Battery St.
San Francisco, CA 94111
*Contact:*　Dick Partida, Corporate Employment Manager.
*Employs:*　2,000 at headquarters.
*Description:*　This company's four domestic divisions and the international operation are headquartered here in San Francisco. The divisions include jeanswear, youthwear, menswear, and womenswear. The jeanswear division alone accounts for about $1 billion in sales. The other domestic divisons make up another billion, and international delivers a third.

　　Job categories include merchandising, sales, finance and planning, marketing services, manufacturing, distribution, operations, personnel, and corporate staff functions. Since job seekers frequently evidence some confusion about the distinctions between merchandising and marketing services here, these are described here in some detail.

　　*Merchandising* has bottom-line responsibility. Product managers and merchandisers determine what quantity of apparel styles, sizes, and fabrics will be made and how they will be priced.

　　*Marketing services,* on the other hand, is a division staff function. Consumer marketing directors and ad managers develop the division marketing plan and the advertising sales promotion and retail display programs. Market research managers design and implement consumer and product research studies for their division.

The marketing functions are split between these two departments. This is primarily because the job of designing and developing new (and continuing) apparel lines is so time consuming that it would not be possible for one brand manager to handle the entire job.

LS & Co. employs approximately 40,000 people worldwide. It actively recruits MBA students for its management training program and offers an open house walk-in interview service every Thursday, 3:00–5:30 P.M.

The company's ad agencies are Foote, Cone & Belding/Honig, McCann-Erickson, and Ketchum.

**MJB Company**    (415) 421-7311
665 3rd St.
San Francisco, CA 94107
*Contact:* Peggy Mitchell, Personnel Manager.
*Employs:* 70 in headquarters.
*Description:* A regional coffee company with sales concentrated in 11 western
   states. It also markets tea, stuffing, and rice under the MJB label. The
   headquarters in San Francisco employs people in accounting, data
   processing, general sales, institutional sales, military sales, commodity sales,
   credit, personnel, and treasury. The marketing department (five people)
   includes market research, new products, and marketing services.

   MJB's ad agency is Carlson, Lebowitz & Olsheuer in Los Angeles.

**Natomas**    (415) 981-5700
601 California St.
San Francisco, CA 94108
*Contact:* Personnel Department.
*Employs:* 300 in headquarters.
*Description:* A diversified energy manufacturer and holding company.
   Natomas operates through three subsidiaries: the Natomas Real Estate
   Company, which develops commercial and residential communities and
   operates Natomas' San Francisco world headquarters building; Natomas
   Energy Company, which conducts petroleum exploration and production and
   coal mining; and Natomas Transportation Company, which is the holding
   company for American President Lines. Most company employees are
   geologists and accountants. Most entry-level job openings are expected to be
   those of financial analysts.

**The North Face**    (415) 524-8432
1234 5th St.
Berkeley, CA 94710
*Contact:* Kevin Smith, Personnel.
*Employs:* 300 at headquarters.
*Description:* A privately owned outdoor equipment company. It manufactures
   and retails high-quality technical, hiking, mountaineering apparel,
   equipment, and tents. Among its many unique products are geodesic dome
   tents, which are based on the design concepts of Buckminster Fuller. The
   North Face has six retail stores in the Bay Area and wholesales its products
   to 700 stores nationwide. Forty of its headquarters personnel are

professionals in departments including merchandising, marketing, sales, accounting, engineering, sewing, and data processing.

**Potlatch Corporation**    (415) 981-5980
1 Maritime Plaza
San Francisco, CA 94111
*Contact:* Peggy Treadwell, Manager of Employee Relations.
*Employs:* 125 in San Francisco.
*Description:* A forest products company that grows and harvests lumber and manufactures wood, paper, and packaging products. The company has four operating units: (1) the consumer products division, which manufactures private label facial tissue; (2) the printing and business papers division, which specializes in coated papers; (3) the pulp, paperboard, and packaging division; and (4) the wood products division.

   The company is very decentralized. In San Francisco the staff includes vice-presidents of sales, marketing, controller, finance, and employee relations. Nationwide, the firm employs approximately 9,000 people. Because of the depressed housing market, the company is focusing on its printing and business papers markets.

**Shaklee**    (415) 954-3000
444 Market St.
San Francisco, CA 94111
*Contact:* Neil Barnhart, Corporate Personnel Manager.
*Employs:* 400 at headquarters.
*Description:* Markets household, personal care, beauty, and nutrition products. The company sells the products to a door-to-door sales force, which, in turn, markets them to neighbors and friends through parties and house-to-house visits. The nutritional products gave the company its start in 1956, and they still make up about 75 percent of the sales. Shaklee's primary products are vitamins and food supplements, but it also markets a line of cosmetics.

   There are 14 departments that make up the Shaklee headquarters organization. In marketing there are 30 people, including product and group managers. Shaklee prefers two years' experience for assistant product manager jobs and five years', experience for the product manager level. Then there are government relations, personnel, MIS, finance and accounting, distribution, customer service, sales administration, security administrative services, legal, and international. There is also a promotional department numbering 50 people who prepare flyers and selling tools for the sales force. And there is a fleet department that manages the bonus car reward program for the sales force.

   The company's overall strategy is to focus on the motivation and expansion of its sales force of independent contractors, who currently number about 2.2 million.

**Shasta Beverages Inc.**    (415) 783-3200
26901 Industrial Blvd.
Hayward, CA 94545

*Contact:* Donna Kern, Manager, Recruiting and Staffing.

*Employs:* 125 at headquarters.

*Description:* A subsidiary of Consolidated Foods of Chicago, Illinois, the company was acquired during the '70s and the new organization has transformed what was once a losing brand into a brand with a strong positioning niche and more than double its previous annual sales. It has embarked on an exciting new marketing program that has been planned for years that emphasizes the variety of flavors (18 regular and 17 diet) and the taste they deliver. Shasta accounts for approximately 2 percent of the regular soft drink market and 8 percent of the diet market.

The Bay Area Shasta headquarters employs 50 professionals in corporate finance, marketing, sales, engineering, purchasing, operations, finance, food service, technical development, data processing, and general management.

Shasta's advertising agency is Needham, Harper & Steers, Chicago. Other smaller subsidiaries of Consolidated Foods in the Bay Area include Lyons Restaurants, Gallo Salami, and Union Sugar.

**Sierra Designs**   (415) 835-4950
247 4th St.
Oakland, CA 94607

*Contact:* Arela Beary, Personnel.

*Employs:* 200.

*Description:* A privately owned specialty backpacking manufacturer and retailer. It has two Bay Area retail outlets for its products. The functional job titles include marketing, market research, advertising (10 marketing people in total), manufacturing, data processing, accounting, purchasing, and controller.

**Specialty Brands**   (415) 981-7600
633 Battery St.
San Francisco, CA, 94133

*Contact:* Peter Rosow, President

*Employs:* 45 at headquarters.

*Description:* A subsidiary of United Biscuit Company of England. The company is 12 years old and employs 25 professionals at the San Francisco headquarters. The company's brands include Marie's Salad Dressings; Spice Island Spices, Herbs, and Seasonings; Aunt Millie's Sauces; and Kosciusko Mustard. The firm primarily employs experienced professionals for its sales and marketing jobs.

**Spreckles Sugar**   (415) 362-5600
50 California St.
San Francisco, CA 94111

*Contact:* Ronald Friedman, Personnel.

*Employs:* 170 in San Francisco.

*Description:* A division of Amstar Corporation, which is the largest manufacturer and distributor of nutritive sweetners in the U.S. Spreckles supplies special grades of sugar to bakers and food and beverage manufacturers.

The Spreckles division headquarters here in San Francisco employs an estimated 35 professional or manager level people. Included are accounting, engineering, sales and marketing, legal, logistics, operations and personnel positions. Entry level positions may be as engineer, systems analyst, or legal assistant. The marketing department handles market research while advertising is done company-wide at Amstar headquarters in New York.

**Standard Oil Company of California**    (415) 894-7700
44 Montgomery St.
San Francisco, CA 94120
*Contact:*  Joseph E. Leitgeb, Manager Professional Employment.
*Employs:*  15,000 in Bay Area.
*Description:*  The nation's fourth-largest oil company and largest industrial firm west of the Mississippi. SoCal has seven domestic operating companies, and five of them are located in the Bay Area: Chevron USA Inc., San Francisco; Chevron Research Company, Richmond; Chevron Resources Company, San Francisco; Chevron Shipping Company, San Francisco; and Chevron Chemical Company, San Francisco. Headquarters and corporate staff departments are also headquartered in the Bay Area.

The company employs approximately 40,000 people worldwide; 85 percent of the professional level employees are technical. Most of the top officers of the firm are engineers or scientists by background. The firm is an active recruiter of business school students. Most start in financial or analyst positions. SoCal also offers a student co-op program that provides work opportunities for students still in college (your school must be a member of the program for you to enroll). SoCal publishes an excellent *Careers with Chevron* series. Request these from Professional Employment Department, Standard Oil Company, PO Box 3495, San Francisco, CA 94119.

J. Walter Thompson is SoCal's advertising agency.

**United Artists Communications Inc.**    (415) 928-3200
172 Golden Gate Ave.
San Francisco, CA 94102
*Contact:*  Jim Horning, Recruitment.
*Employs:*  150.
*Description:*  San Francisco is the corporate headquarters for United Artists Communications, which operates a chain of 350 theaters nationwide. Here in San Francisco its staff is employed in its computer center and in departments including operations, finance, data processing, and accounting. Entry level positions would be those of junior accountant or data processor.

## REGIONAL SALES OR MANUFACTURING OFFICES

The following companies are some of the major U.S. firms which have local manufacturing plants or regional sales offices in the Bay Area.

**American Home Foods**   (707) 448-8411
Vaca Valley
Vacaville, CA 95688
*Contact:* F.R. Schubert.
*Employs:* 250-500.
*Description:* Manufacturing plant for Chef Boy ar Dee and Dennison's canned
   products.

**Armour & Company**   (415) 588-7714
290 Utah Ave.
South San Francisco, CA 94080
*Contact:* Mario Raffaell, Personnel.
*Description:* Meat packing plant; headquarters is in Phoenix, AZ.

**Best Foods (CPC Northamerica)**   (415) 785-6381
21001 Cabot Boulevard
Hayward, CA 94545
*Contact:* James Pinkerton, Personnel.
*Description:* Regional sales office for Skippy Peanut Butter, Mazolla
   Mayonnaise, Niagara Spray Starch, Bosco. Headquarters is in Englewood
   Cliffs, NJ.

**Coca-Cola Bottling Company of California**   (408) 293-7812
1555 Old Bayshore Highway
San Jose, CA 95112
*Contact:* Personnel.
*Description:* Bottler and distributor; headquarters is in Atlanta, GA.

**Durkee Foods**   (415) 944-0530
33 Quail Ct.
Walnut Creek, CA 94596
*Contact:* Personnel.
*Description:* Regional sales office for Durkee Spices.

**Eastman Kodak Company**   (415) 928-1300
3250 Van Ness Ave.
San Francisco, CA 94109
*Contact:* Steve Gladwin, Personnel.
*Description:* Local sales and marketing facility; headquarters is in Rochester,
   NY.

**Frito-Lay Inc.**   (408) 251-8080
650 N. King Rd., Box 5536
San Jose, CA 95150
*Contact:* Personnel.
*Description:* Local sales office for chip manufacturer, subsidiary of Pepsico
   Inc. Headquarters is in Dallas, TX.

**Gallo Salame**   (415) 495-6000
250 Brannan St.
San Francisco, CA 94107

*Contact:* Leslie McLennan, Personnel.
*Description:* Headquarters for sausage company; subsidiary of Consolidated Foods Corporation.

**Gerber Products Company**    (415) 569-1100
9401 San Leandro St.
Oakland, CA 94603
*Contact:* Personnel.
*Description:* Baby food production plant; headquarters is in Fremont, MI.

**General Foods**    (415) 639-5000
100 Halcyon Dr.
San Leandro, CA 94578
*Contact:* Personnel.
*Description:* Two separate local operations: 1) Maxwell House Coffee processing plant and 2) regional sales office. Headquarters is in White Plains, NY.

**General Mills**    (415) 321-3900
730 Welch Ave.
Palo Alto, CA 94304
*Contact:* Don Latter, Regional Sales Manager.
*Description:* Regional sales office; headquarters is in Minneapolis, Minn.

**IBM**    (415) 545-2000
425 Market St.
San Francisco, CA 94105
*Contact:* Employment Office.
*Description:* Sales office for San Francisco, Oakland, San Mateo, Palo Alto; headquarters is in Armonk, NY.

**Kellogg**    (415) 944-1636
1990 North California Blvd.
Walnut Creek, CA 94596
*Contact:* Personnel.
*Description:* Regional sales office at this address. Cereal production plant at 2040 Williams Street, San Leandro, CA 94577; headquarters is in Battle Creek, MI.

**Libby McNeill of Libby, Inc.**    (408) 738-3450
444 W. California
Sunnyvale, CA 94086
*Contact:* Louis Johnson, Personnel.
*Description:* Canned fruit plant.

**Minnesota Mining & Manufacturing Company (3M)**    (415) 761-1155
320 Shaw Rd.
South San Francisco, CA 94080
*Contact:* Bruce Ryner, Operations Manager.
*Description:* Sales office and office equipment distribution center; headquarters in St. Paul, Minn.

**Otis Elevator Company**   (415) 421-7171
2300 Stockton St.
San Francisco, CA 94133
*Contact:* Elsie Gaspari, Personnel.
*Description:* Sales office for largest elevator firm; headquarters in Farmington, Conn.

**Pepsi-Cola Bottling Co.**   (408) 739-0521
960 Kifer Rd.
Sunnyvale, CA 94086
*Contact:* Personnel Department.
*Description:* Bottler and distributor; headquarters in Purchase, NY.

**Savin Corporation**   (415) 592-2710
981 Industrial Rd.
San Carlos, CA 94070
*Contact:* Joanna French, Personnel
*Description:* Savin copier products.

**Schlage Lock Company**   (415) 467-1100
2401 Bayshore Blvd.
San Francisco, CA 94134
*Contact:* Don Rice, Personnel.
*Description:* Lock manufacturing.

**Shell Oil Company**   (415) 228-6161
PO Box 711
Martinez, CA 94553
*Contact:* William Sharkey, Personnel.
*Description:* Manufacturing facility for petroleum refinement; headquarters is in Houston, TX.

**Sohio Petroleum Company**   (415) 951-8805
100 Pine St.
San Francisco, CA 94111
*Contact:* John Murphy, Personnel.
*Description:* Headquarters for petroleum exploration.

**Standard Brands, Inc.**   (415) 638-3112
921 98th Ave.
Oakland, CA 94603
*Contact:* Bruno Cartisano, Personnel.
*Description:* Consumer products manufacture and sales; headquarters is in New York City, NY, merged with Nabisco.

**Stauffer Chemical Company**   (415) 544-9000
636 California St.
San Francisco, CA 94108
*Contact:* Terry Sutton, Personnel.
*Description:* Western sales and administrative office.

**TRW Systems**   (408) 245-5040
1145 East Arques
Sunnyvale, CA 94086
*Contact:* Ruth Gorski, Personnel.
*Description:* Electronics plant.

**Union Carbide**   (415) 765-1000
1 California St.
San Francisco, CA 94111
*Contact:* Brenda Lowe, Personnel.
*Description:* Manufacturing and sales of plastics and chemicals; headquarters
  is in Danbury, CT.

**Union Oil**   (415) 362-7600
425 1st St.
San Francisco, CA 94105
*Contact:* Personnel.
*Description:* Credit card offices here, also sales office at 1 California St., San
  Francisco, CA 94111; (415) 956-7600. Headquarters is in Los Angeles.

**Xerox**   (415) 570-7811
1 California St.
San Francisco, CA 94111
*Contact:* Shirley Harvey, Personnel.
*Description:* Sales office; other offices include Oakland, Santa Clara, San
  Mateo. Recruits at 2929 Campus Drive, San Mateo, CA 94403;
  headquarters is in Rochester, NY.

# 15

# Wine and Agribusiness

## Wine

Since 1980 sales of wines have surpassed sales of liquor in the United States. This fact is just one indicator of the growth market California wines represent. In the past 10 years the wine market has been growing at about a 6 percent annual rate. Recently this growth rate has slowed, but real growth (on the larger-sales base) continues.

Much of the growth within the wine industry is due to the recent explosion in white wine. Sales increased more than 500 percent in the past decade to a $6 billion domestic market. California wines represent about 70 percent of U.S. production, and California vineyards can take credit for launching white wine popularity in the United States. A significant proportion of California vineyards are in the Bay Area.

If you are considering working in the wine business, there are at least four important points you should know:

1. *Major U.S. and international corporations are investing heavily in the wine business.* Coca-Cola created Taylor California Cellars; Nestles invested in Beringer Vineyards; Heublein bought United Vintners (Inglenook and Colony) and now has been acquired by R. J. Reynolds. National Distillers markets Almaden, Seagrams owns Paul Masson, and Stroh Brewing (through its acquisition of Joseph Schlitz Brewing) owns

Geyser Peak. And still other corporate giants are reputed to be considering vineyard investments, including Carnation, Dart and Kraft, Philip Morris, and Anheuser-Busch.

2. *The wine business is becoming much more consumer marketing-oriented.* The proverbial "little old wine maker" used to determine what the consumer could drink. Now the consumer is determining what the vintner will produce. This change has come about primarily because wine makers were caught unaware by the consumer shift from red wine to white wine. They do not intend to be surprised again. So the big corporations have invested not only in costly wine real estate and production facilities but also in marketing expertise to ensure their businesses by anticipating rather than reacting to consumer tastes.

3. *There are plenty of fascinating marketing challenges facing the wine industry.* Most of the larger wine companies employ packaged goods marketing people and are looking for others with proven ability to handle tough business issues for several reasons.

- Wine companies want to expand the market, and currently only about 5 percent of wine users account for 50 percent of total wine volume.
- Packaging and distribution are changing rapidly. Wine is now sold in kegs, cans, and boxes and is available on planes, in bars, and in supermarkets in more and more states where it once was illegal.
- The advertising cost is high and the advertising challenge complex due to regional brands and highly segmented markets. The newer Coca-Cola brands (e.g., Taylor California Cellars) spend the most in advertising, but Gallo is still the brand share leader.
- Price promoting is pervasive, and consumers are not very brand-loyal.
- Importing of foreign wine is a growing business, and foreign labels often not only undersell California wines but also convey more prestige, whereas California vineyards export only about 1 percent of their production to foreign countries.

These are only a few of the issues to which you might be able to apply your business acumen if you land a job with a wine company.

4. *The wine business is agribusiness, and most of the wine companies are located in rural areas of the Bay Area.* Only United Vintners Inc. and Guild Wineries are located close to or in San Francisco. Most of the companies are in "the wine country," which is about 1–1½ hours north of San Francisco and offers small-town rural living. Other vineyards are found south and east of San Francisco within an hour's drive. So, although the image of wine may be one of glamour, the reality is that the wine business is an agricultural business conducted in rural areas and subject to the vagaries of sunshine, rain, and vineyard harvest.

## WINE RESOURCES

Job searchers may find that contacting the Wine Institute, 165 Post St., San Francisco, CA 94108, (415) 986-0878, in San Francisco is helpful. This organization, among other things, acts as a clearinghouse for resumes.

Good ways to make contacts include:

- Attend the American Marketing Association's annual wine discussion luncheon. Call (415) 495-4036 for information.
- Join the Napa Valley Wine Library Association, where you can rub shoulders with wine presidents and wine makers as well as participate in wine tastings. Call (707) 963-5244.
- Contact the president or general manager of the winery; wineries tend to be small operations, and the head executive will generally respond positively and helpfully to inquiries from enthusiastic job seekers.

For background reading you may wish to ask for these publications at your library:

- *Wine Spectator* (sometimes has employment ads)
- *Directory of the Wine Industry in North America* (especially the annual buyer's guide issue)
- *Wines and Vines*
- *Wine Investor*

As you look through the wine company listings in this chapter, keep in mind that the largest Bay Area wine brands are United Vintners (Inglenook and Colony), Almaden, and Paul Masson. These are the companies most likely to have brand manager or marketing jobs.

## WINE JOB TITLES AND SALARY RANGES

Wine jobs are broadly divided into three functional areas: wine making, marketing and general management, and sales.

## WINE MAKING

These jobs may require a plant science or fermentation BS degree:

- Entry Level: $16,000–$18,000
- With Masters Degree: $17,000–$23,000
- Research and Development Manager: $25,000–$30,000

## MARKETING/GENERAL MANAGER

Jobs are available in product management, public relations, market research and finance. Titles vary widely with the size of the winery.

- Entry Level: $20,000–$30,000
- Product Manager: $35,000–$45,000
- Marketing Director: $50,00–$70,000
- Top Management: $80,000–$120,000

## SALES

- Merchandiser/Display Coordinator: $15,000–$17,000
- Sales Representative: $19,000–$23,000
- Manager: $26,000–$48,000
- Regional or National Sales Manager: $50,000–$75,000

## INSIDERS' ADVICE

Bay Area executives advise that a background in tobacco or alcohol is very useful for wine management because the government's legal restrictions are similar for wine. So the experienced brand manager or market research manager in beer, for example, will have a relatively easy time making the transition to wine and understanding the legal environment.

Another extremely useful background that is often mentioned is one in packaged goods or grocery products, especially involving the grocery distribution channel. This is because more wine is being sold there than ever before and the grocery store is becoming a very important part of wine distribution strategies.

Insiders say knowledge of wines, even as a hobby, may be helpful but is not absolutely necessary.

## WINE DIRECTORY

**Almaden Vineyards, Inc.**   (408) 269-1312
1530 Blossom Hill Rd.
San Jose, CA 95118
*Contact:* John P. McClelland, President.
*Employs:* 750.
*Description:* Subsidiary of National Distillers and third-largest U.S. wine
  company.

**Fromm & Sichel**   (415) 673-6333
655 Beach Street
San Francisco, CA 94117

*Contact:* Wayne Baker, Personnel Manager.
*Employs:* 150.
*Description:* Distributors of Christian Brothers wines, brandies, and
champagnes.

**Guild Wineries & Distillers**   (415) 391-1100
500 Sansome St.
San Francisco, CA 94111
*Contact:* Phyllis Williams, Personnel.
*Employs:* 60 in San Francisco.
*Description:* Grower-owned cooperative.

**Mirassou Vineyards**   (408) 274-3000
3000 Aborn Rd.
San Jose, CA 95135
*Contact:* Director of Sales and Marketing.
*Employs:* 100.
*Description:* Small vineyard producing fine wines.

**Paul Masson**   (408) 257-7800
13150 Saratoga Ave.
Saratoga, CA 95070
*Contact:* Chester Hutchinson, Director, Human Resources
*Employs:* 350.
*Description:* Seagrams subsidiary producing wines and champagnes.

**Sonoma Vineyards**   (707) 433-6511
11455 Old Redwood Highway
Windsor, CA 95492
*Contact:* Kenneth J. Kwit, President.
*Employs:* 140.
*Description:* Production and sales of Sonoma County varietal wines under
Sonoma Vineyards and Windsor labels.

**United Vintners**   (415) 777-6500
601 Fourth St.
San Francisco, CA 94107
*Contact:* Arlene Arty, Human Resources.
*Employs:* 250 (headquarters only).
*Description:* Subsidiary of R.J. Reynolds and second-largest U.S. winery.

**Wine World–Beringer Vineyards**   (707) 963-7115
2000 Main St.
St. Helena, CA 94574
*Contact:* Richard L. Maher, President.
   James Tonjum, Vice-President, Marketing
*Employs:* 100.
*Description:* Subsidiary of Nestles. Markets Beringer and Los Hermanos
brands.

## Agribusiness

Agribusiness includes the production, processing, and distribution of agricultural products.

As the business becomes more technical, companies and associations are looking for higher levels of expertise, especially in technical services, distribution, and research. In these departments employees may develop new products, investigate alternate production and container methods, and recommend improvements in handling and delivery systems. Some of the schools that are mentioned as having fine agribusiness and technical departments are University of California, Davis, and California Polytechnical.

The California Advisory Boards are one important facet of California's agribusiness. These advisory boards are self-help programs for farm producers and handlers. Under the auspices of the California Marketing Act of 1937, these boards are authorized by the State Department of Food and Agriculture to represent the farm membership and to work on their behalf. The boards determine marketing programs for their various products (peaches, milk, raisins, etc.) and manage this implementation through their advertising agencies. They also conduct research programs to combat diseases and develop more efficient production techniques. The director is generally nominated by his peers and appointed by the State Department of Food and Agriculture. The boards are small, but they do hire experts in marketing and scientific research and distribution.

## AGRIBUSINESS PUBLICATIONS

Agribusiness journals which may be helpful include:

- *California Farmer,* 83 Stevenson St., San Francisco, CA 94105; (415) 495-3340
- *California Agriculture,* University of California, Berkeley, CA 94720; (415) 642-2431

Security Pacific Bank's monthly *Summary of Business* and *California Business Magazine* publish overviews of California agribusiness several times a year. To request articles from Security Pacific Bank contact their Research Department, PO Box 7636, San Francisco, CA 94120; (415) 445-4000. *California Business* is available at local libraries and newsstands.

## AGRIBUSINESS JOB TITLES AND SALARIES

Most agribusiness jobs are still nonunion unskilled farm-worker jobs.

However, an increasing number of jobs in farming which are management or business-oriented have come about as many of the small, uneconomical, individual farms in the United States have become absorbed into collectives, cooperatives, partnerships and corporations.

Here is a representative sample of agribusiness jobs in the Bay area with salary ranges.

- Cannery or Plant Supervisor: $12,000–$23,000
- Plant Manager: $20,000–$28,000
- Sales Manager: $17,000–$35,000
- Biologist: $17,000–$26,000
- Researcher: $15,000–$22,000
- Industrial Buyer: $18,000–$27,000
- Purchaser: $17,000–$25,000
- Office Services Manager: $17,000–$22,000
- Community Relations: $17,000–$23,000
- Marketing: $20,000–$32,000
- Board Director: $25,000–$38,000

A full listing of the agricultural boards is available from State Department of Food and Agriculture, 1220 North St., Sacramento, CA 95814; (916) 445-5141. Those located in the Bay Area are listed below.

## AGRIBUSINESS DIRECTORY

**American Crystal Sugar Company**   (415) 933-8880
1500 Newell Avenue #709
Walnut Creek, CA 94596
*Contact:* Personnel
*Description:* Sugar beet cooperative; headquarters in Moorhead, MN.

**California Canners & Growers**   (415) 981-0101
3100 Ferry Bldg.
San Francisco, CA 94111
*Contact:* Dean Johnson, Personnel
*Employs:* 225
*Description:* One of the world's largest grower-owned fruit and vegetable canning and marketing cooperatives. Brands include Sacramento Tomato Juice, and Libby canned fruits.

**C & H Sugar**   (415) 772-3800
1 California St.
San Francisco, CA 94111
*Contact:* Paul Sahlin, Personnel
*Employs:* 130
*Description:* Marketing cooperative that refines raw sugar, owned by member growers and Amfac, Inc.

**Golden Grain Macaroni**    (415) 357-8400
111 139th Ave.
San Leandro, CA 94578
*Contact:* John Sullivan, Personnel Manager
*Employs:* 60
*Description:* Wholesaler of macaroni and Rice-a-Roni.

**Oro Wheat Foods Company**    (415) 854-4666
3000 Sand Hill Rd.
Menlo Park, CA 94025
*Contact:* Bill Blair, Personnel
*Employs:* 10
*Description:* Manufactures bread products; headquartered in Greenwich, CT.

**Pacific Coast Producers**    (408) 295-6335
980 Parkmoor Ave.
San Jose, CA 95126
*Contact:* Nancy Maino, Personnel
*Description:* Processes tomato sauce.

**Parisian Bakeries, Inc.**    (415) 641-1000
1995 Evans Ave.
San Francisco, CA 94124
*Contact:* Lloyd Renner, Personnel
*Description:* Manufactures bread, specializes in sourdough.

**PVO International, Inc.**    (415) 362-0990
World Trade Center
San Francisco, CA 94111
*Contact:* Eugene Geringe, Personnel
*Description:* Manufactures and processes vegetable and animal oils for food
    and chemical products.

**Steak Mate Corporation**    (408) 779-4191
PO Box 818
Morgan Hill, CA 95037
*Contact:* Carol Gardner, Personnel.
*Description:* Subsidiary of Ralston-Purina, specializes in mushroom
    production.

**Tri Valley Growers**    (415) 445-1600
100 California St.
San Francisco, CA 94120
*Contact:* Mariel Green, Personnel
*Employs:* 170
*Description:* Manufacturer and processor of canned fruits and vegetables;
    brands include S&W foods, Obergi Olives and Glorietta foods.

**Union Sugar Company**    (415) 362-4080
100 Pine St.
San Francisco, CA 94111
*Contact:* Dennis Voss, Personnel
*Description:* Produces sugar and molasses.


## BAY AREA ADVISORY BOARDS

**Apricot Advisory Board**    (415) 937-3660
1280 Boulevard Way
Ste. 107
Walnut Creek, CA 94595
*Contact:* Jack Hestilow, Manager.

**California Brandy Advisory Board**    (415) 398-0220
235 Montgomery St.
Rm. 411
San Francisco, CA 94104
*Contact:* James McManus, President.

**California Prune Board**    (415) 986-1452
World Trade Center
Rm. 103
San Francisco, CA 94111
*Contact:* F.W. Davis, Director.

**Pear Association**    (415) 284-5990
3704 Mount Diablo Blvd.
Lafayette, CA 94549
*Contact:* Robert Moser, President.

**Processors Clingstone Peach Advisory Board**    (415) 541-0100
530 Howard St.
San Francisco, CA 94120
*Contact:* Richard Peterson, General Manager.

# 16

# Retailing

Retailers across the country have discovered San Francisco and in some cases—such as Neiman-Marcus department stores, based in Dallas—invested years of time and considerable funds to obtain prime local real estate for their outlets here. Given the relatively small size of San Francisco's population, you may wonder about all the interest. The primary reason is found in the results of a survey published by the Bay Area Chamber of Commerce. Merchants report that sales per square foot in San Francisco have consistently matched or outperformed even those in New York and other big retail shopping locations.

Recently the sluggish economy has adversely affected local retail sales figures. And aggressive retail competition in the form of price promoting has further cut into retail profitability. However, San Francisco has a number of positive features that make the long-term outlook for retailing bright:

- Our retailers service not only our own population but also the many foreign and American visitors to the area.
- The shopping location is very dense and compact. In many other cities you find retail stores scattered over several miles or located amid decaying urban neighborhoods. San Francisco's prime shopping area, on the other hand, is located in a few-block area, and the city's investments in rebuilding Market Street and the Embarcadero have paid off in pleasing shopping and pedestrian environments.

- The Bay Area has a small but thriving fashion merchandising and apparel manufacturing industry. This adds a lot of extra vitality and local imagination to the retail picture here.

## *Firms in the Bay Area*

In terms of apparel or department stores, some of the nicest and most prestigious are located in the San Francisco Bay Area, including I. Magnin, Macy's, Saks, Fifth Avenue, Neiman-Marcus, Brooks Brothers, and Wilkes Bashford. The Bay Area is also home to two of the nation's most successful retailers, Mervyn's and The GAP stores.

Looking beyond apparel retailing, the Bay Area has Safeway, the nation's largest supermarket chain, and Long Drugs, the second-largest drugstore chain in the United States.

## RETAIL RESOURCES

To get some background on retailing, read *Minding the Store* or *Quest for the Best,* by Stanley Marcus of Neiman-Marcus.

Look for these periodicals:

- *Women's Wear Daily*
- *Menswear*
- *Stores*

There are quite a few retail or fashion organizations that may also be helpful to your job search:

American Retail Federation
1616 H Street NW
Washington, DC 20006
(202) 783-7971

California Retailers Association
1127 11th St.
Sacramento, CA 95814
(916) 443-1975

Fashion Institute of Design and Merchandising
790 Market St.
San Francisco, CA 94102
(415) 433-6691

National Retail Merchants Association
100 W. 31st St.
New York, NY 10001
(212) 244-8780

San Francisco Fashion Industries Association
821 Market St.
San Francisco, CA 94105
(415) 974-5105

In the Bay Area there is also an executive recruiter who specializes in retailing who may be of help to experienced merchants. The firm is Colton Bernard, 417 Spruce St., San Francisco, CA 94118; (415) 386-7400. Ask for Harry Bernard.

## RETAIL JOB TITLES AND SALARY RANGES

Retail organizations are generally organized into merchandising, administration, operations, and finance functions. Merchandising is the key career path and leads to top management. After (or during) training, you may start as a *department* or *junior sales manager/analyst,* move to *assistant buyer,* then to *buyer,* and then to *division merchandising manager,* with the goal of perhaps becoming *general merchandise manager* for the organization.

In retailing salaries are dependent on the size and type of the store. Large stores, chains, and some specialty stores tend to pay higher salaries. In some organizations or departments, sales clerks work on commission, and this can dramatically increase their income.

In many retail firms employees are offered a discount, (generally 10–20 percent) on store merchandise bought for themselves or their immediate families. Since this can be a sizable contribution to annual income, salary ranges must be considered within this context.

- Retail Sales Clerk: $15,000–$19,000
- Assistant Buyer: $17,500–$19,000
- Junior Buyer: $19,000–$26,000
- Senior (or experienced) Buyer: $26,000–$40,000
- Merchandise Manager: $35,000–$80,000
- Director Sales Promotion: $29,000–$42,000
- Senior Finance Executive: $37,000–$50,000
- Senior Operations Executive: $38,000–$50,000

## INSIDERS' ADVICE

Whether apparel, food, or pharmaceuticals is your choice for a retail career, Bay Area companies are all fairly consistent in the advice they offer to job hunters:

- If you want a retail career here in the Bay Area, then it is advantageous to get your earliest training in the Bay Area.
- Hiring is done at the store level, though there are exceptions.
- Local merchants prefer to promote and train people already in their own organizations.
- Sales experience is generally more important than the kind of degree you have, especially if you can demonstrate that your selling experience gave you a feel for merchandising and taught you how the business works. In fact, in many retail organizations you do not need a college degree, especially with retail experience.
- Keen analytical and experienced supervisory skills are very important and most sought after.
- Data processing abilities and experience are increasingly important.

## RETAIL DIRECTORY

**John Breuner Co.**    (415) 838-4300
3201 Fostoria Way
San Ramon, CA 94853
*Contact:* Janice Demaris, Personnel
*Description:* Furniture retailer with six stores.

**Bullocks of Northern California**    (415) 324-0950
550 Stanford Shopping Center
Palo Alto, CA 99304
*Contact:* Thurlow Smith, Director of Human Resources
*Description:* Six Bay Area department stores.

**Computerland Stores**    (415) 487-5000
30985 Santana St.
Hayward, CA 94545
*Contact:* Ed Faber, President
*Description:* Retail chain specializing in home and office computers.

**Emporium-Capwell**    (415) 764-3680
835 Market St.
San Francisco, CA 94103
*Contact:* Russ Testa, Manager of Recruiting
*Description:* 20 Bay Area department stores with small yearly training programs.

**The GAP Stores**    (415) 952-4400
900 Cherry Ave.
San Bruno, CA 94006
*Contact:* Craig Smith, Manager, Executive Recruitment

*Employs:* 300 professionals in Bay Area
*Description:* Headquarters of jeans specialty store chain.

**Grodins of California, Inc.**   (415) 278-7000
2225 Grant Ave.
San Lorenzo, CA 94580
*Contact:* Craig Garman, Personnel
*Employs:* 100 professionals
*Description:* Men's specialty clothing stores; 32 stores in Bay Area.

**Gumps**   (415) 982-1616
250 Post St.
San Francisco, CA 94108
*Contact:* Elsa Lane, Personnel Director
*Description:* Division of MacMillan, Inc., specialty retailers.

**Guy's Drug Stores**   (415) 339-1640
6210 Medau Pl.
Oakland, CA 94611
*Contact:* Michael J. Toomey, Merchandising Manager
*Description:* Chain of neighborhood drugstores.

**Liberty House**   (415) 891-2121
1501 Broadway
Oakland, CA 94612
*Contact:* Gera Vaz, Director of Recruitment
*Description:* Moderate– to upper–price fashion department store; eight in Bay
   Area.

**Little Daisy**   (415) 937-3010
3380 Vincent Rd.
Pleasant Hill, CA 94523
*Contact:* Caroline Hanks, Director of Personnel
*Description:* Women's specialty stores; 11 in Bay Area.

**Livingstons Brothers Inc.**   (415) 362-3060
111 O'Farrell St.
San Francisco, CA 94102
*Contact:* Barbara Shacochis, Personnel Director
*Employs:* 100 professionals
*Description:* Women's specialty stores catering to career women; 13 Bay Area
   stores.

**Longs Drug Stores, Inc.**   (415) 937-1170
141 North Civic Dr.
PO Box 5222
Walnut Creek, CA 94596
*Contact:* June Obrochta, Employment Specialist
*Employs:* 50 at headquarters
*Description:* Retail drugstore chain; hires at store level.

**Macy's California**    (415) 393-3319
170 O'Farrell St.
PO Box 7888
San Francisco, CA 94120
*Contact:* Manager of Executive Employment or Philip Schlein, CEO
*Description:* Third-largest retail fashion department store in United States; 22
  stores in northern California and Nevada.

**I. Magnin & Co.**    (415) 362-2100
Geary and Stockton
San Francisco, CA 94108
*Contact:* Nancy Kaye, Director of Human Resources
*Description:* Union Square department store with eight Bay Area branches.

**Joseph Magnin Company**    (415) 772-2500
59 Harrison St.
San Francisco, CA 94105
*Contact:* Erin Spaulding, Recruitment Manager
*Employs:* About 50 professionals
*Description:* Women's fashion retail specialty stores; 10 in Bay Area.

**Mervyn's**    (415) 785- 8800
25001 Industrial Blvd.
Hayward, CA 94545
*Contact:* Jacquie Reynolds-Rush, Vice-President, Executive Development
*Description:* Fastest growing promotion-oriented soft goods department store;
  26 stores in Bay Area.

**Montgomery Ward**    (415) 533-1300
2825 E. 14th St.
Oakland, CA 94616
*Contact:* Marv Tangren, District Personnel Manager
*Description:* Discount department store with 16 stores in Bay Area.

**National Dollar Stores**    (415) 392-1371
929 Market St.
San Francisco, CA 94103
*Contact:* Herbert Chan, Personnel
*Description:* Junior department store; 7 stores in Bay Area.

**Neiman-Marcus**    (415) 362-3900
150 Stockton St.
San Francisco, CA 94108
*Contact:* Ellen Ennis, Director of Personnel
*Description:* High-end department store.

**Nordstroms**    (415) 570-5111
130 Hillsdale Mall
San Mateo, CA 94403

*Contact:* Corporate Personnel Director
*Description:* Fashion specialty apparel store.

**Saks Fifth Avenue**   (415) 986-4300
384 Post St.
San Francisco, CA 94108
*Contact:* Ellen Peters, Personnel Director
*Description:* San Francisco branch of New York organization; two stores in
   Bay Area; all buyers work in New York.

**Sears**   (415) 783-6000
1000 La Playa Dr.
Hayward, CA 94545
*Contact:* Charles Hernandez, Director of Personnel
*Employs:* 150
*Description:* 15 Bay Area stores; Hayward is centralized administrative office
   for Bay Area organization.

**Topps and Trowsers, Inc.**   (415) 777-4222
25 Taylor St.
San Francisco, CA 94102
*Contact:* Michael Raskin, President
*Description:* Young men's clothing chain recently emerged from Chapter 11
   proceedings.

**J.C. Penney Company, Inc.**   (415) 635-1000
Eastmont Mall
Oakland, CA 94612
*Contact:* Personnel Director
*Description:* New York based retail chain, regional credit operation and local
   retail outlet.

**Grand Auto, Inc.**   (415) 568-6500
7200 Edgewater Dr.
Oakland, CA 94621
*Contact:* Deborah Cartright, Personnel
*Description:* Headquarters of chain of 75 tire and auto centers.

**Pacific Stereo**   (415) 428-4000
1313 53rd St.
Emeryville, CA 94608
*Contact:* Joan Lyon, Personnel
*Description:* Chain of stereo outlets; also manufactures private label stereo
   equipment.

# RETAIL APPAREL MANUFACTURERS

The Bay Area has a dynamic and thriving group of apparel manufacturers. Merchants with retail buying experience often have merchandised private label lines for their stores and may therefore be suited for a job in apparel manufacturing. Also apparel merchants frequently leave manufacturing to return to retailing. Because of this close career connection apparel firms are listed in this chapter.

**Fritzi of California**   (415) 986-3800
199 1st St.
San Francisco, CA 94105
*Contact:* Personnel Department.
*Description:* Misses and junior apparel.

**Jessica/Gunne Sax Ltd.**   (415) 495-3030
1400 16th St.
San Francisco, CA 94103
*Contact:* Kathrine Walker, Personnel.
*Description:* Women's apparel, specializes in dresses.

**Koret of North America**   (415) 957-2000
617 Mission St.
San Francisco, CA 94105
*Contact:* Gary Stocker, Personnel.
*Description:* Subsidiary of Levi Strauss & Co. Manufactures mainstream women's and men's and children's apparel.

**Levi Strauss & Co.**   (415) 544-6000
1155 Battery St.
San Francisco, CA 94111
*Contact:* Dick Partida, Personnel Director.
*Description:* Largest apparel company in the world.

**Lilli Ann Corporation**   (415) 863-2720
2701 16th St.
San Francisco, CA 94103
*Contact:* Anthony Montoyo, Personnel.
*Description:* High fashion women's apparel.

**Sawyer of Napa, Inc.**   (707) 253-1000
PO Box 238
Napa, CA 94558
*Contact:* Robert Black, Personnel.
*Description:* Manufactured sheepskin coats worn by 1980 U.S. Winter Olympic Team.

**Sun Garment Manufacturing**   (415) 863-4458
2325 3rd St.
San Francisco, CA 94107
*Contact:* Personnel Manager.
*Description:* Women's apparel.

## FOOD RETAILING

**Alpha Beta Company**   (408) 942-2000
Northern California Region
999 Montague Expressway
Milpitas, CA 95035
*Contact:*  Kent Pembroke, Personnel Director.
*Description:*  Food chain with 82 stores in northern California.

**Cala Foods, Inc.**  (415) 751-9696
3475 California St.
San Francisco, CA 94118
*Contact:*  Edward Cala, Vice President, Labor Relations.
*Description:*  Hires only members of the grocery union.

**Lucky Stores, Inc.**   (415) 639-4200
1701 Marina Blvd.
San Leandro, CA 94577
*Contact:*  Harry Reed, Human Resources.
*Description:*  Headquarters of supermarket chain operating 200 stores in Bay
   Area; 1,000 in U.S.

**Safeway Stores, Inc.**   (415) 891-3000
201 4th St.
Oakland, CA 94660
*Contact:*  Mike Porter, Employee Relations.
*Employs:*  1,000 in Bay Area
*Description:*  Headquarters of largest food retailer in the United States.

# 17

# Law

The United States seems to be developing a glut of lawyers. There are an estimated 575,000 attorneys currently practicing in the nation, with another 100,000 soon to emerge from our law schools.

San Francisco has more lawyers per capita than any other U.S. city. The number that is generally quoted for the Bay Area is one lawyer per 80 citizens, compared to the rough national average of one lawyer per 500 citizens.

San Francisco has a number of the nation's most well-respected and well-known attorneys and law firms. You may have heard of San Francisco's famed personal-injury lawyers Melvin Belli and Bruce Walkup, or the very formal and large (280 attorneys) firm of Pillsbury, Madison & Sutro. This is San Francisco's most famous firm. After the 1906 earthquake the firm performed quite a community service by going to court and proving that most of the city's devastation was due to fire and not the earthquake itself. The resulting claims paid by the insurance companies helped to rebuild the city.

## Law Opportunities in the Bay Area

Bay Area opportunities in law exist in banks, insurance, manufacturing, business, federal, city and state government, as well as in the many Bay Area law firms. A few of the well-known Bay Area law firms

271

include Bronson Bronson & McKinnon, Heller Ehrman White & McAuliffe, and Morrison & Foerster, and Thelen, Marrin, Johnson & Bridges.

Job openings are more numerous for legal secretaries and paralegals than for attorneys. Paralegals are not members of the American Bar Association and so are more limited in legal qualifications and financial remuneration. Paralegals work under the supervision of lawyers and may prepare and interpret legal documents; research and compile information from the law library; draft briefs, wills, deeds, mortgages, and contracts; and conduct client interviews.

Bay Area colleges offer many free or low-fee educational courses leading to careers as paralegals. For information, contact:

San Francisco State University
Extended Education Program
1600 Holloway Ave.
San Francisco, CA 94132
(415) 469-1373

San Francisco Community Colleges
Adult Education Program
33 Gough St.
San Francisco, CA 94103
(415) 239-3070

Job information and job listings are available in the local law newspapers and through the area's attorney's clubs and organizations.


## LAW PUBLICATIONS


### Newspapers

* *The Recorder,* 125 12th St., San Francisco, CA 94103; (415) 621-5400
* *Inner-City Express,* P.O. Box 12067, Oakland, CA 94604; (415) 451-4775


## LAW BOOKS

For more information on issues and trends in the various law specialties, read these books:

* *Administrative Law Review,* 1155 E. 60th St., Chicago, IL 60637; (312) 947-3574

- *American Bar Association Journal,* 1155 E. 60th St., Chicago, IL 60637; (312) 621-9200
- *American Business Law Journal,* American Business Law Association, The Wharton School, University of Pennsylvania, Philadelphia, PA 19104; (215) 243-7691
- *American Lawyer,* 2 Park Ave., New York, NY 10016; (212) 644-1380
- *Business Law,* 1155 E. 60th St., Chicago, IL 60637; (312) 947-3860
- *California Law Review,* University of California, Berkeley, School of Law, Boalt Hall, Berkeley, CA 94720; (415) 642-7562
- *California State Bar Journal,* 1230 W. 3rd St., Los Angeles, CA 90017; (213) 482-8220
- *California Western Law Review,* 550 Cedar St., San Diego, CA 92101; (714) 239-0391

## LAW CLUBS/ORGANIZATIONS

California Young Lawyers Association
c/o State Bar Association
555 Franklin St.
San Francisco, CA 94102
(415) 561-8358

Lawyers Club of San Francisco
870 Market St., Ste. 1115
San Francisco, CA 94102
(415) 433-2133

National Lawyers Guild of San Francisco Bay Area
558 Capp St.
San Francisco, CA 94110
(415) 285-5066

For information on Bar Examinations, contact:

California State Bar
555 Franklin St.
San Francisco, CA 94102
(415) 561-8200

Bar Association of San Francisco
220 Bush St.
San Francisco, CA 94104
(415) 391-3960

Listings of the nation's law firms, including the Bay Area listings, are available at your local library in the *Martindale-Hubbell Law Directory.*

A management recruiter who deals in searches for law firms and corporate legal departments is:

Winship Associates
100 Bush St. Suite 501
San Francisco, CA 94104
(415) 781-8180

## LAW JOB TITLES AND SALARY RANGES

For lawyers who enter a law firm (as opposed to government or business, for example), the entry level attorney is generally called an *associate* (or a *junior attorney*). The junior attorney assists experienced attorneys in their cases, does research, and has very little client contact. During the next two to eight years the progression is made to *senior associate,* and then some of the senior associates are invited to become *partners* of the law firm.

Frequently those who are not offered this opportunity leave the firm to join other law firms or pursue law careers in business.

Variations in salaries occur because of the size of the organization, the prestige of the firm, and the type of practice.

- Legal Secretary: $16,000–$22,000
- Paralegal: $16,000–$26,000
- Associate/Junior Attorney: $22,000–$40,000
- Attorney: $28,000–$45,000
- Senior Associate: $45,000–$80,000
- Partner: $50,000–$150,000

## LAW DIRECTORY

**Baker and McKenzie**   (415) 433-7600
555 California St.
San Francisco, CA 94104
*Description:* General practice; taxation and litigation; international and foreign law.

**Bancroft, Avery and McAlister**   (415) 788-8855
601 Montgomery St.
San Francisco, CA 94111
*Description:* Federal and state taxation and estate planning; business and corporate law; real property, probate and trust law; business litigation.

**Brobeck, Phleger and Harrison**   (415) 442-0900
1 Market Plaza
San Francisco, CA 94105, *and*
2 Palo Alto Sq.   (415) 494-6100
Palo Alto, CA 94306
*Description:* General practice.

**Cooley, Godward, Castro, Huddleson and Tatum**   (415) 981-5252
1 Maritime Plaza
San Francisco, CA 94111, *and*
5 Palo Alto Sq.   (415) 494-7622
Palo Alto, CA 94306
*Description:* General civil and trial practice; corporate banking, insurance and
   probate law.

**Farella, Braun and Martel**   (415) 981-3722
235 Montgomery
San Francisco, CA 94104
*Description:* Business, corporate, banking, bankruptcy, construction, real
   estate, agricultural, securities, taxation, antitrust, fire, casualty, malpractice
   and insurance law, general civil trial and appellate practice.

**Graham and James**   (415) 954-0200
1 Maritime Plaza
San Francisco, CA 94111
*Description:* General practice.

**Heller, Ehrman, White and McAuliffe**   (415) 772-6000
44 Montgomery St.
San Francisco, CA 94104, *and*
2 Palo Alto Sq.   (415) 494-3314
Palo Alto, CA 94306
*Description:* General practice.

**Long and Levit**   (415) 397-2222
4 Embarcadero Center
San Francisco, CA 94111
*Description:* Insurance, subrogation, malpractice, corporate, probate, tax,
   municipal, school and administrative law. General trial and appellate
   practice.

**McCutchen, Doyle, Brown and Enersen**   (415) 393-2000
3 Embarcadero Center
San Francisco, CA 94111, *and*
1 Almaden Blvd.   (408) 947-8400
San Jose, CA 95113
*Description:* General practice.

**Morrison and Foerster**    (415) 777-6000
1 Market Plaza
San Francisco, CA 94105
*Description:* General practice.

**Orrick, Herrington and Sutcliffe**    (415) 392-1122
600 Montgomery St.
San Francisco, CA 94111, *and*
1 Almaden Blvd.    (408) 298-8800
San Jose, CA
*Description:* General practice.

**Pillsbury, Madison and Sutro**    (415) 983-1000
225 Bush St.
San Francisco, CA 94104, *and*
101 Park Center Plaza    (408) 287-2233
San Jose, CA 95113
*Description:* General practice.

**Thelen, Marrin, Johnson and Bridges**    (415) 392-6320
2 Embarcadero Center
San Francisco, CA 94111
*Description:* General practice.

# 18

# Architecture and Interior Design

The Bay Area has attracted a large number of architects because of the natural beauty of the location and because a high degree of creativity in design has been encouraged by Bay Area clients. The Bay Area is still in a growth phase of building and developing. Architects here may work for large architectural firms, the government, major corporations, or in privately owned small practices.

Architects and interior designers are in a service business, and must be responsive to client requests while at the same time protecting the integrity of the recommended design. Thus good communication skills, organizational abilities, salesmanship and flexibility as well as technical competence are required to succeed.

## Architecture Opportunities in the Bay Area

The job openings in the Bay Area for entry-level or middle-level positions in architecture and interior design have always been tight. The best way to increase your chances of being hired is to make contacts in local firms through the professional associations.

American Institute of Architects
790 Market St.
San Francisco, CA 94102
(415) 362-7397

American Society of Interior Designers
300 Broadway
San Francisco, CA 94133
(415) 989-5363

Both of these organizations sponsor monthly meetings and seminars, and provide informal job placement referrals. They also publish membership directories.

## PUBLICATIONS

To familiarize yourself with trends in architecture and interior design you may wish to read the following magazines.

### Architecture

- *Building Design & Construction,* 5 South Wabash Ave., Chicago, IL 60603; (312) 372-6880
- *Western Building Design,* 2801 West 6th St., Los Angeles, CA 90057; (213) 384-1261
- *Progressive Architecture,* 600 Summer St., PO Box 1361, Stamford, CT 06904; (203) 348-7531
- *Architectural Record,* 1221 Avenue of the Americas, New York, NY 10020; (212) 997-2594

### Interior Design

- *Designers West,* 9200 West Sunset Blvd., Los Angeles, CA 90069; (213) 278-4450
- *Interior Design,* 850 3rd Ave., New York City, NY 10022; (212) 593-2100
- *Contract,* 1515 Broadway, New York, NY 10036; (212) 869-1300
- *Architectural Digest,* 5900 Wilshire Blvd., Los Angeles, CA 90036; (213) 937-4740

For executive level jobs in architecture or engineering firms you may wish to contact an executive recruiter, such as Coxe Group, at 3170 Sacramento St., San Francisco, CA 94115. Contact Marjanne Pearson, at (415) 931-1221.

## JOB TITLES AND SALARIES

Most architects begin their careers as *assistant drafters* who prepare drawings and scale models to their supervisors' specifications. Some large offices have *apprentices* who may provide assistance to the junior level drafter. The *chief draftsperson* is responsible for all graphic presentations and reports, and supervises the drafting staff. The *designer* develops the creative design concepts. The *planner* plans the urban design and is responsible for site planning. The *project architect* is responsible for administration of all phases of large complex projects. With more experience an architect advances to *project designer*, then to *project manager* and then perhaps to *design principal* of a firm.

Large architectural firms may have interior design departments, *landscape architects,* and *engineering consultants.* Other interior design jobs are found in retail department stores or small (usually three person) interior design firms.

Bay Area salaries vary according to size of the firm and experience of the manager. These are average annual salaries in the Bay Area.

- Apprentice: $10,000–$12,000
- Assistant Draftsperson: $12,000–$14,000
- Chief Draftsperson: $20,000–$23,000
- Project Architect: $25,000–$27,000
- Project Designer: $25,000–$28,000
- Project Manager: $26,000–$29,000
- Design Principal: $20,000–$100,000
- President: $60,000–$130,000
- Landscape Architect: $20,000–$25,000
- Interior Designer: $17,000–$21,000
- Construction/Engineering: $26,000–$70,000

## INSIDERS' ADVICE

Insiders point out that computer technology is changing the way architects draft and design projects. During the next five years more firms will move to computer aided drafting and design (CAD). Since few architects have knowledge of this technology, educated, experienced people who are familiar with the use of the new equipment will be sought. If you have a knowledge of computers along with training in architecture and good communication skills, you can have an excellent future in this field.

If it is interior design you are interested in, Bay Area experts advise that you get some good experience and visibility by starting as a salesperson at the Galleria or the Design Center (where those in the trade shop for furniture and decorator accessories).

# ARCHITECTURE AND INTERIOR DESIGN DIRECTORY

## Architecture

**Anshen & Allen**    (415) 391-7100
461 Bush St.
San Francisco, CA 94108
*Contact:* Richard Hein, Vice President and Principal
*Employs:* 75.
*Description:* Architecture and interior design firm known for high technology facilities, Bank of California and interior design of American President Lines.

**Barbara Dorn Associates**    (415) 673-5535
2417 Franklin St.
San Francisco, CA 94123
*Contact:* Joszi Meskan, President
*Employs:* 10.
*Description:* Interior design and architecture firm specializing in commercial space, known for "Oz" at St. Francis Hotel and interiors of Sitmar Cruise ships.

**Environmental Planning & Research, Inc.**    (415) 433-4715
649 Front St.
San Francisco, CA 94111
*Contact:* Gina Coffey, Director of Human Resources.
*Employs:* 300.
*Description:* Architecture and interior design firm specializing in commercial stores and offices. This is the headquarters location. Firm has 3 other offices, known for Pacific Lumber Company in San Francisco, Vintage Properties in San Francisco, and interior design of Genstar in San Francisco.

**Gensler & Associates**    (415) 433-3700
550 Kearny St.
San Francisco, CA 94103
*Contact:* Barbara Clock, Personnel Manager.
*Employs:* 160.
*Description:* Architecture and interior design firm specializing in commercial design (especially office space.) This is headquarters location. Firm has 5 U.S. offices; it is known for Hibernia Bank Building, KPIX offices, San Francisco International Airport terminal.

**MBT Associates**    (415) 434-0300
631 Clay St.
San Francisco, CA 94105
*Contact:* Alan Williams, Principal.
*Employs:* 95.

*Description:* 85% architectural and 15% interior design firm, known for IBM in San Jose, Chevron Research in Richmond.

**Robinson, Mills & Williams**    (415) 781-9800
153 Kearny St.
San Francisco, CA 94103
*Contact:* Vicki Shannon, Personnel.
*Employs:* 40.
*Description:* Architecture and interior design firm, known for Fireman's Fund Insurance headquarters in Novato, Gateway Offices in South San Francisco, interior design of Bank of America.

**Skidmore, Owings & Merrill**    (415) 981-1555
1 Maritime Plaza
San Francisco, CA 94111
*Contact:* Jodi Lindberg, Personnel Director.
*Employs:* 300.
*Description:* Specialists in commercial high rise, primarily architectural firm with interior design and engineering departments, known for California 1st Bank Building, Louise M. Davies Symphony Hall, Crocker Bank and The Galleria.

## Interior Design

COMMERCIAL

**Contract Design Associates**    (415) 654-2200
5525 College Ave.
Oakland, CA 94618
*Contact:* Miles Sandstrom.
*Employs:* 9.
*Description:* Full service interior design for commercial space, known for Jade Tree Inn in Carmel, and Oakland Airport.

RESIDENTIAL

**Cole-Wheatman Interior Designers**    (415) 346-8300
1933 Union St.
San Francisco, CA 94123
*Contact:* John K. Wheatman, Owner.
*Employs:* 8.
*Description:* Residential interiors that combine old and new; retail store.

**Gumps**   (415) 982-1616
250 Post St.
San Francisco, CA 94108
*Contact:* Paul Faria, Director.
*Employs:* 10.
*Description:* Retail store and interior design consultants specializing in custom
   designed furniture.

**R. H. Hering Interiors**   (415) 563-4114
3225 Sacramento
San Francisco, CA 94115
*Contact:* Robert Hering, Owner/Manager.
*Employs:* 3.
*Description:* Antique retailer and traditional residential interiors.

**Therien & Co., Inc.**   (415) 956-8850
584 Sutter St.
San Francisco, CA 94108
*Contact:* Collier Gwin, Treasurer
*Employs:* 12.
*Description:* Residential design specializing in 17th/18th century antiques; two
   retail shops featuring European and Oriental antiques.

# 19

# Education

Despite the forecasted decline in student enrollments, there are bright spots in education in the Bay Area. Elementary and secondary school teachers with math, science, and Asian language specialties are needed. Teachers trained in computer usage will also have an advantage. And certain Bay Area communities are forecasting an increase in education jobs. According to a *San Francisco Chronicle* article ("Survey Finds Fewer Bay Area Firms Are Hiring," September 21, 1982) these are in Walnut Creek and Hayward and throughout Santa Clara County.

To teach in California you must be licensed by the state. Currently California has reciprocity agreements with these states:

| | | |
|---|---|---|
| Alabama | Maryland | Pennsylvania |
| Connecticut | Massachusetts | Rhode Island |
| Delaware | Michigan | South Dakota |
| District of Columbia | Nebraska | Utah |
| Florida | New Hampshire | Vermont |
| Hawaii | New Jersey | Virginia |
| Idaho | New York | Washington |
| Indiana | North Carolina | West Virginia |
| Kentucky | Ohio | |
| Maine | Oklahoma | |

For full details on the license procedures, contact:

> Janet Harrigan
> San Francisco Public Schools
> 135 Van Ness Ave.
> San Francisco, CA 94102

## Teaching Opportunities in the Bay Area

If you have not taught in more than 27 months, or if your state does not have a reciprocity agreement with California, it can take up to two years to get a license. In this case you may wish to consider teaching for the San Francisco Catholic Archdiocese (Catholic schools do not require the California license). Contact the archdiocese at (415) 863-5112 or write to 445 Church St., San Francisco, CA 94104.

Other education opportunities to consider are with private day care centers. After all, there is a second, although smaller, baby boom going on in the United States, and working mothers are looking for quality day care for their children. Ambitious teachers may even wish to start a day care center. There appears to be a ready market. For example, at the San Francisco Children's Center (run by the San Francisco Unified School District), there is a waiting list of 5,000 families.

Other opportunities for teachers are as corporate training and development specialists. You may wish to contact the American Society for Training and Development (ASTD), 822 Shepard Way, Redwood City, CA 94062; (415) 366-9965, to make contacts and meet others who have made a successful career in training.

Other opportunities to consider are jobs with educational publishers (see Chapter 8) and careers in technical writing (see Chapter 9 for a list of companies).

### Teaching Resources

These are some helpful books:

- *Aside From Teaching English, What in the World Can You Do?*, by Dorothy Bester.
- *How to Teach School and Make a Living at the Same Time,* by Patrick, Crowe, Sheed, Andrews, and McMeel.

One local career consultant, Ranny Riley, specializes in job changes for teachers. Contact her at:

> Career Design
> 2398 Broadway
> San Francisco, CA 94104
> (415) 929-8150

The Job Forum panel of 40 executives from local firms includes some people in the educational field who will be willing to help you develop additional career options and plan your job search.

Job Forum
Chamber of Commerce
465 California St.
San Francisco, CA 94104
(415) 392-4511

## TEACHING JOB TITLES AND SALARY RANGES

Bay Area teacher salaries increase with additional hours of study toward a master's degree.

- Elementary School Teacher with Bachelor's Degree: $16,000–$26,000
- High School Teacher: $17,000–$28,000
- With 60 hours toward Master's Degree: $19,000–$33,000

## INSIDERS' ADVICE

Knowledgeable insiders advise that one good way to get a teaching job in the Bay Area is through substituting. To become a substitute teacher you must have California teaching credentials (or reciprocity from another approved state). Go to the Board of Education Office at 135 Van Ness (no appointment is needed) and register as a substitute with the credentialist there. Teachers are called in alphabetical order as openings become available. Substituting is considered a good way to get to know the school system, to make contacts with other Bay Area educators, and to find out about any upcoming full time openings.

The Bay Area language institutes and schools were often mentioned as job options for language teachers. There are approximately fifty such schools here. There is an independent language teachers' switchboard which functions as an employment service. Call them at (415) 451-6418.

# 20

# Health Care and Social Services

## Health Care

The Bay Area is in the forefront of health care in the United States. Some of the finest teaching and research hospitals in the nation are located here. There are approximately 40–50 hospitals in the region, along with a diverse collection of medical clinics, health maintenance organizations (HMO's), and health services. There are also a growing number of alternate health care facilities based on holistic medicine, homeopathy, acupuncture, chiropractic, nutrition, and midwifery.

Health services personnel earn higher salaries here in California than in any other region in the country (even New York or Chicago). For example, a nurse earning $13,000–$15,000 in Chicago would likely bring in $17,000–$21,000 in the Bay Area.

Health professionals must be licensed by the Health Department of the State of California. Nurses, for example, must take the state board exam or receive reciprocity approval based on their license in another state. Dental assistants also must be approved by the California Board of Dental Examiners. To become a registered dental assistant you must pass the California Dental Exam.

The large medical centers in the Bay Area include University of California Medical Center, Kaiser Permanente (largest HMO), and

Stanford University Medical Center. And St. Lukes Hospital and University of San Francisco St. Mary's Hospital are known for their particularly strong nursing departments.

Currently the nation's medical and health professions are being affected by the economy and by new legislation regarding government medical funds. In a down economy people tend to defer health care unless it is an emergency. Thus, for example, the number of elective surgery procedures has declined in local hospitals. In addition the new government ruling that requires that Medi-Cal give prior approval before a patient is admitted to a hospital has tended to decrease hospital admissions. And in some fields the Bay Area is oversupplied with health care specialists. For example, there are more dentists and doctors per capita in the Bay Area than in most other regions of the country.

Nevertheless, there are many job opportunities for health care professionals here. The most frequently mentioned specialties that are in demand in the Bay Area include:

- Physical therapists
- Occupational therapists
- Critical care
- Oncology nurses
- Nurse practitioners
- Medical-surgical nurses
- Medical records technicians
- Medical technologists
- Lab technicians
- Blood bank specialists
- Biomedical engineers
- Nuclear medical technologists
- Radiation therapists

Dental assistants and dental technicians are also in demand. There is also always a need for hospital night shift nurses, though the recent move to higher salaries (1¾ of day pay) has increased the ranks.

In California the health profession is more politically organized and politically aware than in many other parts of the country. Many health care professions are unionized or belong to associations that negotiate wages on their behalf. The Hospital and Institutional Union includes LVNs, clinical assistants, and orderlies; and the California Nursing Association represents nurses in collective bargaining for pay.

Feminism has played an important part in the growing political awareness of health care professionals. Hospitals are generally run by male doctors, but it is the female nurses who are actually charged with day-to-day patient care. The nurses want more input into hospital policy making and more emphasis on the importance of nursing care. Currently hospital boards do not even include representatives of nursing services on their Boards of Directors or on policy making boards. One result of this disenfranchisement has been to encourage many health care professionals to shun hospital nursing in favor of home health care.

There is an overall trend to home health care in California, which is caused by the high cost of institutionalized care and the available pool of health care professionals (e.g., visiting nurses, etc.) who prefer the independence this kind of work offers them.

For further insights into the political issues in California health care, contact the California Nursing Association and ask to receive its regular newsletter, called *California Nurse.*

## HEALTH CARE PUBLICATIONS

For more information about the health field you may wish to read these periodicals:

- *Hospital and Health Services Administration,* 840 N. Lake Shore Dr., Chicago, IL 60611; (312) 943-0544. Describes new developments in the health administration field.
- *Modern Health Care,* 740 N. Rush St., Chicago, IL 60611; (312) 649-5342. News magazine for administrative managers in hospitals, nursing homes, and alternative health care facilities.
- *Radiology Digest,* 446 Central Ave., Northfield, IL 60093; (312) 446-4400. Magazine of issues and developments in the radiology field.
- *Hospital and Community Psychiatry,* 1700 18th St. NW, Washington, DC 20009; (202) 797-4926. Magazine for clinical and psychiatric administrators and medical staffs.
- *American Journal of Medicine,* 666 5th Ave., New York, NY 10103; (212) 489-2200. Magazine of new techniques and issues for internists.
- *Health Services Manager,* 135 W. 50th St., New York, NY 10020; (212) 586-8100. Magazine for hospital workers.
- *American Journal of Nursing,* 10 Columbus Circle, New York, NY 10019; (212) 582-8820. Trends and issues in nursing and health care.
- *Journal of Nursing Administration,* 12 Lakeside Park, 607 North Ave., Wakefield, MA 01880; (617) 245-4736. Management techniques and trends in nursing.
- *American Dental Association Journal,* 211 E. Chicago Ave., Chicago, IL 60611; (312) 440-2500. Official publication of the A.D.A.
- *California Dental Association Journal,* Box 91258, Los Angeles, CA 90009; (213) 776-4292. Official publication of the C.D.A.

# HEALTH CARE JOB TITLES AND SALARY RANGES

## Health Care (General)

Health care salaries vary according to whether the job is in private health care or in state or local government health facilities. In general Bay Area vacation and health benefits are generous, and many health care jobs are unionized. The salary ranges below are for a 35-hour work week for the year. Many health care professionals work part-time or in nontraditional shifts, such as four days on and three days off.

- Medical Technologist: $20,000–$25,000
- Nuclear Technologist: $19,000–$24,000
- Occupational Therapist: $19,000–$23,000
- Physical Therapist: $18,000–$22,000
- Surgical Technician: $16,000–$18,000
- Director of Nursing: $31,000–$36,000
- Head Nurse: $22,000–$27,000
- General Duty Nurse: $20,000–$23,000
- Dietitian: $20,000–$23,000
- Licensed Practical Nurse: $15,000–$17,000

## Health Care (Administrative)

Health service administrators provide the business management for health care facilities. They make management decisions regarding budget, personnel, and equipment, and they direct the day-to-day operation of the facility, making sure it functions effectively and efficiently.

In general, Bay Area private hospitals pay better than government hospitals, and most nursing and personal care homes tend to pay less than either private or government hospitals.

The career path usually begins with the position of *assistant administrator* of the facility, or with a specific functional department of a large facility as an assistant in managing a function such as, for example, medical records, nursing, social services, or personnel. The next step could be a promotion to *associate administrator*. Large medical facilities tend to have several associates and smaller hospitals or convalescent homes usually have one. The *associate administrators* run the day-to-day operation of the medical facility. They report to the *chief administrative officer* or *chief executive* of the medical center.

Individuals with backgrounds in psychology, sociology, accounting, natural sciences or public health may find opportunities in this growing field. However, the field is getting increasingly specialized and master's or PhD degrees from health or hospital administration graduate programs are often preferred for job openings.

- Assistant Administrator: $18,000–$26,000 (large hospital); $15,000–$25,000 (small hospital)
- Associate Administrator: $30,000–$50,000 (large hospital); $20,000–$35,000 (small hospital)
- Chief Administrator: $65,000–$100,000 (large hospital); $40,000–$50,000 (small hospital)

## INSIDERS' ADVICE

Health professionals advise newcomers to the area to enter the job market by applying for temporary jobs. This is most easily done through the registries such as Remedy or Allied Nursing Services for RNs, LVNs, attendants, nurse practitioners, etc.; and Dental Fill-ins for dental assistants and hygienists. Of course, the advantage of starting with temporary work is that you can get a good idea of how the various hospitals and clinics function and then select where you want to work on a more regular basis.

## HEALTH CARE DIRECTORY (ASSOCIATIONS AND HOSPITALS)

**Allied Nursing Services**    (415) 391-7850
44 Montgomery St.
San Francisco, CA 94104
*Contact:* Clarence Hunt, Manager.
*Description:* Agency for supplementary nursing positions, can lead to permanent position; places RN's, nursing attendants, critical care, emergency, etc.

**American Physical Therapists Association**    (916) 446-0069
1225 8th St., Suite 335
Sacramento, CA 93815
*Contact:* Lyn Clymer, Golden Gate District manager at her office, Visiting Nurses Association, 937 Pomona Ave., Albany, CA 94706; (415) 658-9211
*Description:* Support association and network.

**American Red Cross**    (415) 776-1500
1550 Sutter St.
San Francisco, CA 94109
*Contact:* Tula Pagonis, Director of Employment.

**Baywood Convalescent Hospital**    (415) 939-5400
550 Patterson Blvd.
Pleasant Hill, CA 94523
*Contact:* Arlene Barnes, Administrator.
*Description:* 166 bed convalescent hospital.

**California Academy for Physicians' Assistants**    (916) 441-6807
1010 11th St., Ste. 200
Sacramento, CA 95814
*Contact:* Elayne Meir, Executive Secretary
*Description:* Professional organization for physicians' assistants; these are mid-level practitioners who perform more medical procedures (e.g., suture, diagnose) than RNs.

**California Dental Association**    (800) 262-1754
6151 Century Blvd., Suite 900
PO Box 91258
Los Angeles, CA 90009
*Contact:* Write or call LA branch to obtain listings for San Francisco chapter which was moving as of this publication date.
*Description:* Lobbying group association.

**California Nurses Association**    (415) 428-1901
5801 Christie Ave.
Emeryville, CA 94608
*Contact:* Sharon Iversen, Executive Director.
*Description:* Collective bargaining association.

**Children's Hospital of San Francisco**    (415) 387-8700
3700 California St.
PO Box 3805
San Francisco, CA 94118
*Contact:* Jane Musser, Personnel.
*Description:* Employs 1,500 in 364 bed hospital.

**Driftwood Convalescent Hospital**    (415) 792-3743
39022 Presido Way
Fremont, CA 94538
*Contact:* Joan Reimers, Administrator.
*Description:* 181 bed convalescent hospital.

**Golden Gate Nurses Association**    (415) 821-7400
2601 Mission St.
San Francisco, CA 94110
*Contact:* Judith Goldberg, Executive Director.
*Description:* Registered nurses association. Offers *Job Book* and newsletter.

**Hospital Council of Northern California**    (415) 871-0633
1000 Cherry Ave.
San Bruno, CA 94066
*Contact:* Dolores Riservato, Office Manager
*Description:* Support association for 129 member hospitals, keeps file of
  resumes for one year and offers referral service to member hospitals.

**Irwin Memorial Blood Bank**    (415) 567-6400
270 Masonic Ave.
San Francisco, CA 94118
*Contact:* Dr. Herbert Perkins, Director of Scientific Services
*Description:* Blood bank employing 300, including doctors, nurses, medical
  technicians, administrative, accounting and personnel.

**Jewish Home for the Aged**    (415) 334-2500
302 Silver Ave.
San Francisco, CA 94112
*Contact:* Sydney Friedman, Administrator.
*Description:* 330 bed home for the elderly.

**Kaiser Permanente Medical Center**    (415) 929-4132
2425 Geary Blvd.
San Francisco, CA 94115
*Contact:* Call the center's Job Hotline for information on openings:
  (415) 929-4170.
*Description:* Large outpatient health clinic and HMO; several Bay Area
  locations.

**Mary's Help Hospital**    (415) 992-6484
1900 Sullivan Ave.
Daly City, CA 94015
*Contact:* Ethel Jackson, Personnel.
  Rex Chase, Executive Director.
*Description:* 350 bed hospital.

**Maxicare Convalescent Hospital**    (707) 644-7401
2200 Tuolumne St.
Vallejo, CA 94590
*Contact:* Cleatus Weller, Administrator
*Description:* 166 bed convalescent hospital.

**Merritt Hospital**    (415) 655-4000
Hawthorne Ave. and Webster
Oakland, CA
*Contact:* Vicki Macklin
*Description:* Largest Oakland hospital.

**Mount Zion Hospital and Medical Center**    (415) 567-6600
1600 Divisadero St.
San Francisco, CA 94115

*Contact:* Florence Duldulao, Personnel
*Description:* 468 bed hospital.

**Northern California Oncology Group**    (415) 497-7512
1801 Page Mill Rd.
Bldg. 3
Palo Alto, CA 94304
*Contact:* Dr. Frank Torti, M.D.
*Description:* Network of oncology nurses and specialists.

**Northern California State Dental Hygienists' Association**
(916) 447-4113
1121 L St.
Sacramento, CA 95814
*Description:* This association has a job bank and local chairpersons are: for San
  Francisco, Maxine Quan at (415) 752-1587; for East Bay, Cindy Vigliotti at
  (415) 537-6712.

**Nurses in Transition**    (415) 282-7999
1078 Hampshire St.
San Francisco, CA 94110
*Contact:* Claudia Deyton
*Description:* Support association for nurses who are starting health–oriented
  businesses themselves, offers individual counseling.

**Pacific Dental Laboratory**    (415) 362-0662
450 Sutter St.
San Francisco, CA 94108
*Contact:* George Goldie, General Manager
*Description:* Dental products and services.

**Raleigh Hills Hospital**    (415) 368-4134
1600 Gordon St.
Redwood City, CA
*Contact:* Sandy McFarland, Personnel.
*Description:* Alcohol treatment facility.

**San Francisco Bay Area Oncology Nursing Society**
(415) 861-8705 M–W (415) 666-4101 T–F
  Group meets in Sutter Boardroom of Mount Zion Hospital every 4th
    Thursday of the month at 5:30.
*Contact:* Jennifer Lillard, President

**Remedy Health Service**    (415) 957-9064
3195 California St.
San Francisco, CA 94115
*Contact:* Lorna Davis
*Description:* Employment agency for RNs.

**Saint Francis Convalescent Pavillion**    (415) 994-3200
99 Escuela Dr.
Daly City, CA 94015
*Contact:* Marjorie Thomas, Administrator
*Description:* 239 bed convalescent hospital.

**San Francisco Department of Public Health**    (415) 558-3042
101 Grove St.
Room 210
San Francisco, CA 94102
*Contact:* Mary Smith, Personnel
*Description:* Employs 4,200, continuously hires RNs, physical therapists, nurse
    practitioners, clinical specialists, microbiologists, chemists, and paramedics.
*Comment:* Part of Civil Service but has own testing and classifications; best
    chance for job is to go to Civil Service Office, 646 Van Ness, San Francisco,
    and fill out a "courtesy card" telling area of interest. You will be called and
    notified of openings.

**San Francisco Home Health Service and Hospice**    (415) 285-5615
225 30th St.
San Francisco, CA 94131
*Contact:* Hadley Dale Hall, Director
*Description:* Home care professional service, home health involves physical and
    occupational therapists, medical social workers, speech therapists,
    nutritionists and home health assistants. Hospice offers senior center and
    nutrition program.

**St. Mary's Hospital and Medical Center**    (415) 668-1000
450 Stanyan St.
San Francisco, CA 94117
*Contact:* Joyce Hegensbach, Personnel.
*Description:* Employs 1,450 in 450 bed hospital.

**Stanford University Medical Center**    (415) 497-1200
300 Pasteur Dr.
Stanford, CA 94305
*Contact:* Don Thomas, Personnel Director
*Description:* 624 bed private hospital.

**Take Care Health Plan**    (415) 321-4121
300 Homer Ave.
Palo Alto, CA 94301
*Contact:* Midge Pierce, Personnel
*Description:* Outpatient health clinic, 600 on staff.

**University of California Hospital**    (415) 666-9000
Parnassus and Third Ave.
San Francisco, CA 94143
*Contact:* Charles H. Francis, Personnel Director.
*Description:* 560 bed hospital.

**Visiting Nurse Association**    (415) 861-8705
401 Dubois
San Francisco, CA 94117
*Contact:* Pat Lotspeich, Coordinator
*Description:* Public health nurses will be sent applications.
*Comment:* Very good prospects for physical therapists.

## Social Services

Social services include individual and family counseling, job training, child care, residential care, family services, mental health, correction, foster care, residential treatment centers, drug and alcohol abuse programs, crisis intervention, geriatrics, and the like.

Because of cutbacks in federal funding (particularly CETA), the hiring prospects in social services are not good. The government sector is the most difficult in which to find a job, and the private sector has not yet been able to pick up the programs being cut back by the government. Social service professionals with advanced degrees and experience are competing for entry level positions.

The National Association of Social Workers (NASW), 7981 Eastern Avenue, Silver Springs, MD 20910; (301) 565-0333; the professional organization for social workers, is in the process of creating a computerized bank of employment opportunities to aid social workers in matching their skills and experience with job opportunities. Their newspaper, the *News,* publishes some job listings now. The California chapter of the NASW is a good way to meet others in social work. The organization also publishes a *Jobs Information Service* for its members. Contact them at 231 Millbrae Avenue, Suite 207, Millbrae, CA 94030; (415) 697-8255.

### SOCIAL SERVICE PUBLICATIONS

Three useful books to read for perspective on expected social work trends are:

- *Perspectives for the Future: Social Work Practice in the '80s,* NASW, 1980; selected papers.
- *Social Work in a Turbulent World,* Miriam Dinerman, Editor, NASW, 1981.
- *Helping: Human Services for the '80s,* by Frank Baker and John Nortman, Times-Mirror Publishing.

Other currently topical books in the social field are:

- *The Business of Psychotherapy,* by Robert Barker, Columbia Press. Examines migration of therapists to private practice.
- *Handbook on Mental Health Administration,* by Michael Austin, Jossey Bass Publishing. Examines all aspects of community mental health programs.
- *Social Work in Hospitals,* by Bascom Ratliff, Elizabeth Timberlake, and David Jentsch, Charles Thomas Publishing. Review of issues and trends in hospital practice.

Some recommended periodicals include:

- *Social Work,* NASW publication, Carol Meyer, Editor.
- *Practice Digest,* NASW publication, Betty Sancier, Editor.
- *Health and Social Work,* NASW publication, Rosalie Kane, Editor.

## JOB TITLES AND SALARY RANGES

The State of California requires that social workers in certain specialties be licensed by the Department of Consumer Affairs, Board of Behavioral Science Examiners, 1020 "N" Street, Sacramento, CA 95814; (916) 445-4933.

The Licensed California Social Worker (LCSW) license is required for psychological counseling. The Marriage, Family and Child Counseling (MFCC) license is needed for marriage and family counseling work. The ACSW is the Academy of Certified Social Workers, which signifies advanced accreditation beyond the LCSW and indicates a level of education and experience that entitles the professional to a clinical practice in psychotherapy.

Salaries in the Bay Area are affected by the oversupply of highly qualified master's and PhD holders who are experienced social service workers *and* the cutbacks in government-supported social spending on both a federal and state level. Salaries in the social work field generally vary according to level of education. Relevant experience can add $3,000-$10,000 to these minimum level annual salaries.

- Social Worker; Bachelor of Social Work: $14,000–$16,000
- Graduate Social Worker; Masters of Social Work: $17,000–$20,000
- Certified Social Worker; Academy of Certified Social Workers: $20,000–$24,000
- PhD level; Doctor of Social Work: $24,000–$28,000
- Administrative Director; Advanced degree and management experience: $26,000–$45,000

Salaries in the different areas of specialization may also vary.

- Medical Social Worker: $17,000–$23,000
- Psychiatric Social Worker: $21,000–$25,000
- Family Services Social Worker: $12,000–$17,000

## INSIDERS' ADVICE

The only truly bright spots in social service in the Bay Area appear to be for those with experience and language skills in Spanish and Asian (especially Korean and Vietnamese), and the Salvadorian languages.

Fund raisers with experience and proven track records are also needed. Trained volunteers are needed at all the private agencies to help cope with the enormous need for social services in the communities now not being adequately served due to cutbacks in Federal funding. These trained volunteers generally have the first chance at paid employment, especially when they have the appropriate credentials.

Insiders advise you to take a so-called "survival job" while you persevere at applying for social work jobs in the area.

A complete listing of social service organizations is available in the San Francisco Business Library, 530 Kearny Street, (415) 558-3946, in the *Social Services Referral Directory,* which lists all local, public, and private organizations in the social service field.

## SOCIAL SERVICE DIRECTORY

**American Red Cross**    (415) 776-1500
150 Sutter St.
San Francisco, CA 94104
*Contact:* James Williams, Manager, Golden Gate Chapter
*Description:* Social and health services.

**Bay Area Community Services, Inc.**    (415) 436-0141
PO Box 12939
Oakland, CA 94604
*Contact:* Personnel Office
*Description:* Community and geriatric social services.

**Belmont Hills Psychiatric Center**    (415) 593-2143
1301 Ralston Ave.
Belmont, CA 94002
*Contact:* Patrick Cecil, Administrator
*Description:* Psychiatric and alcohol treatment.

**The Blind Californians**    (415) 525-9525
648 Kearny
El Cerrito, CA 94530
*Contact:* Don Queen, Personnel
*Description:* Financial and social services for blind handicapped persons.

**Catholic Social Services**    (415) 864-7400
50 Oak St.
San Francisco, CA 94102
*Contact:* Patrick Cannon, Director
*Description:* Non-profit full service social work organization with 150 full time
   staff and programs in refugee care, hearing impaired, adoption, general
   counseling, etc.

**Center for Southeast Asian Refugees Resettlement**    (415) 885-2743
121 Leavenworth
San Francisco, CA 94102
*Contact:* Michael Huynh, Director
*Description:* Full social services for refugee and immigrant families.

**Center for Special Problems**    (415) 558-4801
2107 Van Ness Ave.
San Francisco, CA 94102
*Contact:* Stanford Harris, Director
*Description:* Outpatient service for victims or perpetrators of crime, domestic
   violence, and drug problems.

**Child Health/Disability Prevention Program**    (415) 558-2403
101 Grove St.
San Francisco, CA 94102
*Contact:* Henry B. Bruyn, MD, Director
*Description:* Health service for children.

**Children's Home Society of California**    (415) 922-2803
3000 California St.
San Francisco, CA 94115
*Contact:* James Spradley, Director
*Description:* Children's service agency in San Francisco and Oakland.

**Community Mental Health Services**    (415) 558-4387
555 Polk St.
San Francisco, CA 94102
*Contact:* Alan Leavitt, Director
*Description:* Publicly funded mental health service with 500 on staff including
   psychologists, social workers, and psychiatrists.

**Family Service Agency of San Francisco**    (415) 474-7310
1010 Gough St.
San Francisco, CA 94109
*Contact:* Eleanor Davis, Deputy Director

*Description:* Private agency of 24 programs including counseling, preschool care, infant care, child abuse, crisis intervention, elderly counseling, nursing home care.

**Geriatric Services**   (415) 665-0575
2101 - 20th Ave.
San Francisco, CA 94116
*Contact:* Personnel office
*Description:* Community mental health for the elderly.

**Golden Gate Regional Center**   (415) 546-9222
100 Mission St.
Suite 400
San Francisco, CA 94105
*Contact:* Personnel Office
*Description:* Developmental disability program.

**Goodwill Industries of San Francisco**   (415) 362-0778
980 Howard St.
San Francisco, CA 94103
*Contact:* Personnel Office
*Description:* Charitable and social services.

**Haight-Ashbury Children's Center**   (415) 431-3385
1101 Masonic Ave.
San Francisco, CA 94117
*Contact:* Harriet Ward, Director
*Description:* Day care center for low income families, financed by State Department of Education.

**Oakland Catholic Charities**   (415) 451-8980
433 Jefferson St.
Oakland, CA 94607
*Contact:* Sheryl Kuhn, Director of Case Management
*Description:* Full social services including disabled and geriatric.

**Peralta Alcoholism Facility**   (415) 652-7000
435 Hawthorne Ave.
Oakland, CA 94609
*Contact:* Personnel Office
*Description:* Residential and outpatient service for alcohol and drug dependency.

**Quest Systems, Inc.**   (415) 570-5217
1181 Chess Dr.
Foster City, CA 94404
*Contact:* William Giguiere, Director
*Description:* Outpatient alcohol and drug treatment.

**San Francisco Department of Public Health/California Children's Services**   (415) 558-3406
101 Grove St.
San Francisco, CA 94102
*Contact:* Lorraine Smookler, MD, Program Director
*Description:* Financial assistance for medical care of handicapped children.

**United Way**   (415) 772-4300
410 Bush St.
San Francisco, CA 94105
*Contact:* Loretta Menchacha, Personnel
*Description:* Raises and distributes funds for community services.

**Walnut Creek Hospital**   (415) 933-7990
175 La Casa Via
Walnut Creek, CA 94598
*Contact:* Kenneth Pierce, Administrator
*Description:* Community psychiatric center.

**YMCA**   (415) 885-0460
220 Golden Gate Ave.
San Francisco, CA 94102
*Contact:* Personnel Office
*Description:* Community social services.

# 21

# Government

Before 1980 government was the largest employer in San Francisco. Currently services and manufacturing employ more people. Government employment is declining due to reductions in federal funds and the impact of the "Proposition 13" tax law. Employment in city government, for example, has decreased by more than 1,300 jobs since Proposition 13 was passed in 1978. Still the city and county of San Francisco employ about 85,000 people and remain among the biggest employers in the area. In total, government contributes 287,000 jobs to the Bay Area.

## Government Jobs in the Bay Area

To apply for government jobs in San Francisco, contact:
Civil Service Office
City and County of San Francisco
646 Van Ness Ave.
San Francisco, CA
(415) 558-5477
Or contact the Civil Service offices of the other Bay Area counties.

To get a government job you need to determine when and where the Civil Service examination for your field of interest will be held. There are 1,800 different Civil Service job classifications in the city (for example, managerial assistant 1840, administrative analyst 1823, accountant 1650). Exams are given to determine your qualifications for a position, and the top three scorers on each exam are the candidates whose names will be sent to hiring managers first. Based on the test scores, lists of qualified candidates are developed. The list is active for two or four years (depending on the job category). To be hired as a full-time, permanent employee, you must be on the list or have special experience and education that qualifies you as an exempt employee. Exams are given only "as needed," so your first step should be to find out what the job categories are and then how soon the next test is. Request the Civil Service pamphlet *How to Get a City Job* and talk to the counselors at the Civil Service office.

The city's exempt positions include mayor's staff, the judiciary, and the city hospital staff.

To apply for jobs with state government, contact:

Personnel Board of the State of California
455 Golden Gate Ave.
Rm. 2202
San Francisco, CA 94102
(415) 557-0576

*After* you apply, you will be told the date and location of examinations. The San Francisco office will provide only two listings of job classifications. For more information, write to:

Personnel Board of State of California
801 Capital Mall
Sacramento, CA 95814

To apply for jobs with the federal government, contact:

Federal Employment Office
450 Golden Gate Ave.
San Francisco, CA 94102
(415) 556-6667

## GOVERNMENT JOB TITLES AND SALARY RANGES

Here are a few examples of the salary ranges in the Bay Area for government jobs:

- Accountant: $16,000–$30,000
- Computer Programmer: $18,000–$25,000
- Administrative Assistant: $11,000–$38,000
- County Clerk: $19,000–$50,000
- Research Assistant: $10,000–$23,000
- Meter Collector: $9,000–$21,000
- City Attorney: $32,000–$35,000
- Public Relations Officer: $13,000–$31,000
- Police Officer/Firefighter: $20,000–$25,000
- Probation Officer: $22,000–$24,000
- Librarian: $19,000–$25,000

# Part III: Additional Resources and Special Advice

# 22

# Bay Area Resources, Associations, and Career Counseling

There are a surprising number of resources that Bay Area job seekers can turn to for guidance, advice, and helpful tips. Usually individual job seekers have to find these generous people and associations on their own. This book takes care of that problem for you.

Because contacts are the best way to get the job you want, here is a list of many of the Bay Area resources you can use to get additional information and to make contacts in your target field. Other associations and publications are listed in each industry chapter in this book.

Before you approach these organizations, plan to take the time to think about what kind of work you want to find. These resources, generous and helpful though they are, cannot decide for you what you should do. Only you can decide and make your life turn out the way you want.

**Academy of TV Arts and Sciences**
24 California St.
San Francisco, CA 94108
(415) 392-8002
*Contact:* Jack Armstrong,
    Administrator.

**Advocates for Women**
414 Mason St.
San Francisco, CA 94102
(415) 391-4870
*Contact:* Barbara Woodward,
    President/Project Director.
Also Berkeley and Hayward locations.
    Counseling, resource library, job
    listings, workshops.

**Alumnae Resources**
965 Mission St.
San Francisco, CA 94103
(415) 546-7220
*Contact:* Susan Kaplan, Director
Specializes in helping women with
liberal arts degrees. Network of
400 Bay Area women. Job list
newsletter.

**American Advertising Federation**
251 Post St.
San Francisco, CA 94120
(415) 421-6867
*Contact:* Janet Kennedy, Acting
Director

**American Association for
Advancement of Science**
California Academy of Science
Golden Gate Park
San Francisco, CA 94118
(415) 221-5100
*Contact:* Dr. Alan Leviton, Executive
Director

**American Association of University
Professors**
582 Market St.
San Francisco, CA 94103
(415) 989-5430
*Contact:* Peter M. Arun

**American Association of University
Women**
312 Market St., Suite 506
San Francisco, CA 94108
(415) 391-4050
Membership association. Job
listings.

**American Electronic Association**
2680 Hanover St.
Palo Alto, CA 94306
(415) 857-9300
*Contact:* Ed Ferrey, Director

**American Institute of Banking**
650 California St.
San Francisco, CA 94108
(415) 392-5286
*Contact:* Henry Shine, Director

**American Insurance Association**
465 California St.
San Francisco, CA 94104
(415) 957-0711
*Contact:* W. Victor Slevin, President

**American Society for Training and
Development**
822 Shepard Way
Redwood City, CA 94062
(415) 366-9965
*Contact:* Judy Yoakim, Membership
Professional membership society.

**American Society for Women
Accountants**
2 Embarcadero
San Francisco, CA 94111
(415) 981-7720
*Contact:* Georgia Donner, President

**American Society of Travel Agents**
291 Geary St.
San Francisco, CA 94102
(415) 391-5159
*Contact:* Blanche Berger, Exec.
Secretary

**American Statistical Association**
85 2nd St.
San Francisco, CA 94105
(415) 542-3755
*Contact:* H. M. Ardley, President

**American Women in Radio and
Television**
c/o Marlene Holderbaum,
Membership Committee
KTVU
Jack London Sq.
Oakland, CA 94607
(415) 834-1212

Local Golden Gate chapter of national organization. Seminars, career programs, job bank for members.

**Architects and Design Professional Organization for Women**
PO Box 26570
San Francisco, CA 94126

**Artists Guild**
499 Alabama, #217
San Francisco, CA 94110
(415) 359-3749
*Contact:* Marsh Nelson, President

**Association for Women in Mathematics**
Mills College
Oakland, CA 94013
(415) 430-2255
*Contact:* Lenore Blum, President

**Bay Area Educational Television Association**
1011 Bryant St.
San Francisco, CA 94108
(415) 864-2000
*Contact:* Anthony Tiano, President

**Bay Area Executive Womens Forum**
4095 17th St.
San Francisco, CA
(415) 546-7390
*Contact:* Karen Torrey, President

**Bay Area Professional Womens Network**
55 Sutter St.
San Francisco, CA 94104
(415) 391-9197
*Contact:* Kathie Phillips, Membership Director

**Berkeley Womens Center**
2908 Ellsworth Ave.
Berkeley, CA 94705
(415) 548-4343

*Contact:* Meryl Lieberman, Director Information and referral, writers' workshop.

**Business and Professional Womens Club Inc.**
California Federal Office
609 Sutter St., Ste. 202
San Francisco, CA 94103
(415) 776-0625
*Contact:* Joan Simmons, Director
Three groups in San Francisco. Membership by invitation.

**California Bankers Association**
650 California St.
San Francisco, CA 94104
(415) 433-1894
*Contact:* Henry Shine, Executive Vice-President

**California Hotel & Motel Association**
520 Capital Mall #706
Sacramento, CA 95814
(916) 444-5780
*Contact:* Edwin Sloan, Executive Vice-President

**California Medical Assistants' Association**
731 Market St.
San Francisco, CA 94103
(415) 777-2200, ext. 224
*Contact:* Ms. Dale W. Lee

**California Nurses Association**
1855 Folsom St.
San Francisco, CA 94110
(415) 864-4141
*Contact:* Susan Harris, President

**California Society of Certified Public Accountants**
1000 Welsh Rd.
Palo Alto, CA 94304
(415) 321-9545
*Contact:* James Kurtz, Executive Director

**California Teachers Association**
1705 Murchison Dr.
Burlingame, CA 94010
(415) 697-1400
*Contact:* Ralph Flynn, Executive
   Director

**California Women in Government**
c/o California Commission on Status
   of Women
Sacramento, CA 95814
(916) 445-3173
*Contact:* Lee Norrick, Executive
   Director
State agency.

**Career Design**
2398 Broadway
San Francisco, CA 94104
(415) 929-8150
*Contact:* Rannie Riley, President
Career and life counseling; fee
   charged.

**Career Development Institute**
690 Market St.
San Francisco, CA 94104
(415) 982-2636
*Contact:* Phil Tecau
Career counseling; fee charged.

**Careers for Women**
1 Hallidie Plaza
San Francisco, CA 94102
(415) 391-7613
*Contact:* Peggy Keon
Career counseling, fee charged.
   Contact for class schedule.

**Catholic Social Services**
50 Oak St.
San Francisco, CA 94102
(415) 864-7405
*Contact:* Patrick Cannon, Director
Career and family counseling.

**College of Marin Women's Center**
Kentfield, CA 94904
(415) 485-9641
*Contact:* Dana Prichard, Manager
Career counseling.

**Coro Foundation**
1370 Mission St.
San Francisco, CA 94103
(415) 864-4601
*Contact:* Martha Bredon, Executive
   Director
Institute for training and research in
   public affairs; no charge.

**EDD (Employment Development
   Division State of CA)**
745 Franklin St.
San Francisco, CA 94102
(415) 557-8651
*Contact:* Chet Crawley, Job
   Workshop Director
State employment agency; job search
   library.

**Equal Rights Advocates**
1370 Mission St.
San Francisco, CA 94103
(415) 621-0505
*Contact:* Nancy Davis, Executive
   Director
Employment issues; legal service; fee.

**Experience Unlimited**
1225 Fourth Ave.
Oakland, CA 94606
(415) 464-1259
*Contact:* Herman Leopold, State
   Coordinator
Volunteer self-help group of
   professional men and women job
   seekers.

**The Foundation Center**
312 Sutter St.
San Francisco, CA 94108
(415) 397-0902
*Contact:* Caroline McGilvray,
   Director
Information on philanthropic
   foundations; library services.

**The Fund Raising School**
Box 3237
San Rafael, CA 94912
(415) 457-3520

*Contact:* Henry Rosso, Director
Instructions in techniques.

**Golden Gate Nurses Association**
2601 Mission St.
San Francisco, CA 94105
(415) 821-7400
*Contact:* Judith Goldberg, Executive
Director
Association for RN's; job bank and
newsletter.

**International Association of Business
Communicators**
870 Market St.
San Francisco, CA 94102
(415) 433-3400
*Contact:* John Bailey, Executive
Director
Monthly meetings; newsletter.

**Insurance Services Office**
550 California St.
San Francisco, CA 94104
(415) 781-8828
*Contact:* Steve Spellman, Director

**Jewish Community Center**
3200 California St.
San Francisco, CA 94118
(415) 346-6040
*Contact:* Jerry Ringerman
Classes and support.

**Jewish Vocational and Career
Counselling**
870 Market St.
San Francisco, CA 94102
(415) 391-3595
*Contact:* Lawrence Lucks, Director
Testing and career counseling; fee
charged.

**Job Forum**
Chamber of Commerce Board Room
465 California St.
San Francisco, CA 94104
(415) 392-4511
*Contact:* William Cobaugh, Director
Open job forum Wednesdays
7:00 P.M.; career guidance; no fee.

**KNBR (NBC)**
1700 Montgomery St.
San Francisco, CA 94111
(415) 951-7000
*Contact:* Jane Morrison
Intern program. Posts job listings for
all area TV and radio stations.

**The Lawyers Club**
870 Market St.
San Francisco, CA 95105
(415) 433-2133
*Contact:* Marti Lochridge

**Licensed Vocational Nurses Guild**
161 7 Webster St.
Oakland, CA
(415) 452-4033
*Contact:* Marie Eckles, President

**Media Alliance**
Fort Mason Center
Bldg. D
San Francisco, CA 94123
(441) 441-2557
*Contact:* Daniel Ben-Horn
Job bank; newsletter.

**National Association of Bank Women**
558 Sacramento St.
San Francisco, CA 94108
(415) 434-1093
*Contact:* Rose Cohan, West Coast
Director

**New Career Channels**
PO Box 1726
San Francisco, CA 94101
Research information center;
quarterly newsletters and resume
referrals.

**New Ways to Work**
149 9th St.
San Francisco, CA 94103
(415) 552-1000
*Contact:* Jean Leonard, President
Open information meetings; reference
library; job sharing.

**Options for Women Over 40**
3543 18th St.
San Francisco, CA 94120
(415) 431-6944
*Contact:* Pat Durham, Coordinator

**Pacific Area Travel Association**
228 Grant Ave.
San Francisco, CA 94108
(415) 986-4646
*Contact:* Joyce Gardner

**Production Womens Club of San Francisco**
622 Green St.
San Francisco, CA 94133
(415) 621-2464
*Contact:* Sue Bevilacqua
Graphic arts; weekly meetings.

**Public Interest Clearing House**
198 McAllister St.
San Francisco, CA 94102
(415) 557-4014
*Contact:* Mary Viviano, Executive Director
Information training center; public interest.

**Public Relations Society of America**
1 Market Plaza
c/o Southern Pacific
San Francisco, CA 94105
(415) 541-1661
*Contact:* Henry Ortiz, President

**Queens Bench**
1255 Post St.
San Francisco, CA 94109
(415) 673-3850
*Contact:* Judy Hawthorne
Professional organization for lawyers.

**Resource Center For Women**
445 Sherman Ave.
Palo Alto, CA 94306
(415) 324-1710
*Contact:* Judy Ousterhout, Director
Career counseling; job listings.

**Sales and Marketing Executives Association**
300 Montgomery St., Ste. 1104
San Francisco, CA 94104
(415) 392-5577
*Contact:* Margaret Morris, Director

**San Francisco Advertising Club**
681 Market St.
San Francisco, CA 94105
(415) 986-3878
*Contact:* Paula Byrens, Executive Director

**San Francisco Commission on the Status of Women**
170 Fell St.
San Francisco, CA 94102
(415) 558-3653
*Contact:* Dorothy Hutchens, Acting Chairman

**San Francisco Community College**
31 Gough St.
San Francisco, CA 94103
(415) 239-3000
*Contact:* Maxwell Gilette or Jack Harrington, Counselors
Career counseling; vocational testing.

**San Francisco Fashion Industries**
821 Market St.
San Francisco, CA 94105
(415) 974-5105
*Contact:* Leonard Joseph, Executive Director

**San Francisco Insurance Women's Association, Inc.**
c/o Richard Goldman & Co.
1 Maritime Plaza
San Francisco, CA 94111
(415) 981-1141
*Contact:* Helen Castro, President

**San Francisco Life Insurance Brokers**
22 Battery St.
San Francisco, CA 94104
(415) 392-1625
*Contact:* M. Lowe

**San Francisco Press Club**
555 Post St.
San Francisco, CA 94102
(415) 775-7800
*Contact:* Dave McElhatton, President

**San Francisco Real Estate Board**
246 Van Ness Ave.
San Francisco, CA 94102
(415) 431-8500
*Contact:* James C. Fabris, Vice-
President

**San Francisco Society of
Communicating Arts**
445 Bryant St.
San Francisco, CA 94105
(415) 777-5287
*Contact:* Program Manager

**San Francisco Women in Advertising**
861 Market St.
San Francisco, CA
(415) 957-1264
*Contact:* Trish Preble, President

**Small Business Administration**
211 Main St.
San Francisco, CA 94105
(415) 974-0649
*Contact:* Lawrence J. Wodarski
Federal government agency;
counseling; training.

**Society for Technical Communication**
315 Montgomery
Floor 14
San Francisco, CA 94104
(415) 953-7381
*Contact:* Paula Dierkop

**Sonoma State University**
Rohert Park, CA 94928
(707) 664-2441
*Contact:* Dr. Jak Richards
Reentry program.

**The State Bar of California**
555 Franklin St.
San Francisco, CA 94102
(415) 561-8200
*Contact:* Mary Wales, Secretary

**Theatre Association of California**
988 Market St.
San Francisco, CA 94103
(415) 776-4846
*Contact:* William Kartozian,
Chairman

**Visiting Nurse Association of San
Francisco**
401 Duboce Ave.
San Francisco, CA 94117
(415) 861-8705
*Contact:* Louise Heyneman,
Executive Director

**Western Association of Insurance
Brokers**
235 Montgomery St.
San Francisco, CA 94104
(415) 392-5383

**Wine Institute**
165 Post St.
San Francisco, CA 94102
(415) 986-0878
*Contact:* John De Luca, President

**Women Entrepreneurs**
3061 Fillmore St.
San Francisco, CA 94123
(415) 929-0129
*Contact:* Nancy Scott-Ince, President

**Women in Communications, Inc.**
4861 Geranium Pl.
Oakland, CA 94619
(415) 531-8241
*Contact:* Sally Jockey

**Women in Design**
PO Box 2607
San Francisco, CA 94126
(415) 397-1748
*Contact:* Rosalee Black, Susany
Shawl

**Women's Building**
3543 18th St.
San Francisco, CA
(415) 863-5255
*Contact:* Janice Tookey, Director

**Women's Career Resource Center**
42 Miller
Mill Valley, CA 94941
(415) 383-0520
*Contact:* Mary Harper

**Women's Center**
Bldg. T-9
University of California
Berkeley, CA
(415) 642-4786
*Contact:* Margaret Wilkerson,
  Director
Job listings and counseling.

**Women's Council of Realtors**
301 Grove St.
San Francisco, CA 94102
(415) 431-8500
*Contact:* Doris Gelini

**Women's Forum West**
1777 Union St.
San Francisco, CA 94123
(415) 885-3493
*Contact:* Ann Carol Brown

**Women's Insurance Network**
485 29th St.
San Francisco, CA 94131
(415) 459-5284

**Women's Referral Service**
PO Box 3093
Van Nuys, CA 91407
(415) 221-1751
*Contact:* Nancy Sardella

**Women's Resource Center**
31 Gough St.
San Francisco, CA 94103
(415) 239-3005
*Contact:* Karin Marty

**Women's Way Resource Center**
710 C St.
San Rafael, CA 94901
(415) 453-4490
*Contact:* Ann Kennedy, Bonnie
  Hough; Co-directors
Quarterly newsletter; job counseling.

# 23

# Job Search Opportunities for Women

While, in general, the simple job search method outlined in Chapter 5 of this book should provide both men and women with a solid, successful job-hunt plan, I do have a bit of advice primarily relevant to women job-seekers. My purpose is threefold: 1) to encourage women to investigate nontraditional careers that offer good job prospects in the Bay Area; 2) to provide some job-searching advice that is relevant primarily to women; and 3) to point out some of the excellent Bay Area resources designed especially to support women during a career search.

## *Nontraditional Work*

Among the job areas heading the list of nontraditional careers for women are fields such as sales, management consulting, finance, and high technology. You should actively consider these fields because the opportunities are there and the salaries are excellent.

There is a broad range of sales jobs, and not all the jobs involve the stereotypical selling techniques you might imagine. For example, consider media sales where you may work representing a magazine or television or radio station. Or consider sales for one of the newer technical companies in the Silicon Valley, or for big firms such as Xerox and

IBM that provide excellent sales training, pay well, and offer independence and flexible work schedules. Commercial real estate is another sales area to think seriously about.

Management consulting is still a man's field; however, there are opportunities for women, especially those women with an MBA or with at least four years of experience in advertising or marketing. The salaries are excellent, and the opportunity to consult for a client firm and then move into management there may arise. Many women have also set out on their own and started their own consultancies. This is a rather lonely job unless you have some "ready-made" clients to start off. However, for those who make it, the rewards are many in both money and independence.

Finance jobs, especially investments and brokerage, are another good area to look into. Traditionally, brokers have been men, but the field is open to women and Bay Area women brokers say it's worth it. You might consider calling one of the brokerage houses and asking to speak to a woman broker to get her perspective and more advice.

The U.S. Commissioner on Civil Rights recently declared the Silicon Valley "wide open" to all who obtain the proper training.[*] The truth is, it is wide open to nontechnically trained people as well. Computer science, microelectronics, and biotechnology are growing industries and therefore require not only technicians but technical writers, communications experts, marketing managers, personnel managers, art directors, training personnel, and so forth. But, to prepare yourself for hunting in this field, you have to understand the fundamentals of the industries. Do not wander down to Silicon Valley before getting at least a bit educated. For example, you could visit a local computer store or the computer department at Sears to learn some basic information about home and office computers.

For more information on a wide range of additional job opportunities for women, write to Catalyst, 14 East 60th Street, New York, NY 10022. This source offers a range of inexpensive, well-written pamphlets on 60 career options.

It is important to realistically investigate and consider the culture—the overall atmosphere or pervasive philosophy—of the corporation you are about to enter. In general, companies that innovate in one area will be more open to advances (such as the promotion of women to higher corporate levels) in other areas. For example, you might look for corporations that experiment in quality circles (such as Hewlett-Packard, Xerox, and R.J. Reynolds) or in flex-time (Levi Strauss & Company offers this) or in jobsharing. Of course, there is no proof as reliable as

---

[*] "Silicon Valley Civil Rights Hearing," *San Francisco Chronicle,* Tuesday, September 21, 1982.

the actual positions of the women in a company. So if you are in the latter stages of the interviewing process, be sure to find out about the number of women with seniority at each firm. Some ways to get this kind of information are to attend association meetings in your chosen field, or to contact headhunters and ask people for their impression of the firm's record with women.

## Women's Resources

There are many women's organizations, associations, and clubs which will be extremely helpful to you in your search. I have listed most of these in the relevant subject chapters and in Chapter 22. Below are some additional (or especially helpful) organizations and books.

## ORGANIZATIONS

**Alumnae Resources**
965 Mission St.
Suite 514
San Francisco, CA 94103
(415) 546-7220
Specializes in helping women with degrees in the liberal arts, and provides a network of 400 women in the Bay Area who will give job seekers advice; provides job list newsletter.

**The Women's Bureau**
U.S. Department of Labor
Room 11411 Federal Building
450 Golden Gate Avenue
San Francisco, CA 94102
(415) 556-2377
Bureau's objective is to improve the economic status of women; it offers advice and provides excellent pamphlets in a variety of career fields.

**The Women's Center**
Building T–9
University of California
Berkeley, CA 94720
(415) 642-4786
Center provides workshops, library and lecture series; it welcomes older women and is open to the public.

**The Resource Center for Women**
445 Sherman Ave.
Palo Alto, CA 94304
(415) 324-1710
Counseling and seminars are offered; job listing service has over 1,000 jobs per month.

## BOOKS

- *Late Bloomer,* by Lois Rich-McCoy.
- *Women's Guide to Re-Entry Employment,* by Mary Zimmerman.
- *What Every Woman Needs to Know to Find a Job in Today's Tough Market,* by Lucia Movat.
- *1001 Job Ideas for Today's Woman,* by R. Lembeck.
- *How to Go to Work When Your Husband Is Against It, Your Children Aren't Old Enough And There's Nothing You Can Do Anyhow,* by F. Schwartz, M. Schifter, and S.S. Gillotti.
- *Equal to the Task: How Working Women Are Managing in Corporate America,* by Susan Easton, Joan Mills, and Diane Winokur.

# 24

# If All Else Fails

When you have tried virtually everything and you still don't have that job, what do you do?

I asked 35 top Bay Area management and employment professionals this question: "If all else fails, what else can a job hunter do?" Their answers provide a helpful array of additional job-hunting techniques to try and a reemphasis and redefinition of some of the fundamentals.

The number one suggestion of the experts is "Go back to the basics." Again and again they stress that job searchers may know they should research a company and try to develop contacts and know they should take the time to define their own strengths in order to better sell themselves, *but most don't do it.*

So, if you haven't yet found the job you want, please take it from the experts and go back to fundamentals.

- Clarify and restate your objectives.
- Talk to more people or go back to your original contacts and ask for more advice.
- Do more research on the field or company.
- Analyze how much time and effort you have invested in each phase of the job search.

After you have identified your job objective and the benefits of hiring you, most of your time and effort should be spent first on contacts with people (70 percent) and second on more research. (Remember that spring cleaning or getting the car fixed should be left until after you

317

have a job.) Analyze where the emphasis in your job search effort has been. A shift in emphasis may bring the results you want.

A vice-president from Boyden Associates (executive recruitment) offers this suggestion: "Plan your job campaign as if you are on assignment to write a magazine article about your target job and career field. If you were a writer with this assignment, what would you do? You would probably interview as many people as possible for ideas and information, and you'd likely do library research." This approach may be helpful especially if you feel stuck and have developed a sense of futility. Pretending or playing a role can allow you to be creative again and thus develop opportunities.

Another related suggestion is to select a couple of role models and try to find out how they got their jobs, step by step. You can find potential role models by asking everyone you know, "Who has a job similar to the one I'm looking for at your firm?" Then try to arrange an introduction and question them on every step of their past job searches and current job skills. This may help you generate more leads or slightly shift the focus or presentation of yourself to better advantage.

Chet Crowley of the Employment Development Department's Job Search Workshop arranges for workshop participants to role play a future interview session. This can be tremendously helpful, and you can do a role play like this with helpful friends or family members. Acting out the interview situation may immediately show you (or your helpful friends) where you need to strengthen or revise your style.

An associate at Korn Ferry (executive recruiter) recommends that you offer to be a consultant at your target firm. She says, "Identify a problem and offer to work (for free) at solving it for them." A good way to do this might be to write an offer letter to the president or hiring manager at your target firm.

Other Bay Area experts offer the related suggestion "volunteer to work for free for a month." (This seems to be the latest hot idea for a nontraditional way of job searching.) It may get you in the door of your target company and get you the attention you are looking for. Of course, this suggestion doesn't pay the rent, so you may have to take what Chet Crowley calls a survival job while you are job hunting (but make sure you still have time to focus on the search) or offer to work as a temporary on a project rather than for free.

Another route to consider if all else fails is to hire a professional career consultant to help you. Florence Lewis (author of a Bay Area guide to career counselors called *Help Wanted*) points out that "career counseling is tax deductible (for the year you get the job)".

Here are some of the career counselors frequently mentioned to me during my research.

## Santa Clara County

*TEOI (Techno Economic Opportunity Institute)*
625 Hamilton Ave.
Palo Alto, CA 94301
(415) 321-8364
Specializes in technology jobs.

## Marin County

*Viki Zenoff—Career and Leisure Alternatives Specialist*
919 W. California St.
Mill Valley, CA 94941
(415) 383-6537
Specializes in techniques from Bolle's *What Color Is Your Parachute?*

## East Bay

*The National Career Development Project*
PO Box 379
Walnut Creek, CA 94596
(415) 935-1865
Self-assessment courses headed by Richard Bolles.

## San Francisco

*Career Design*
Ranny Riley, President
2398 Broadway
San Francisco, CA 94115
(415) 929-8150
Specializes in redirecting work lives.

*Bernard Haldane Associates*
Hearst Bldg., Ste. 430, 5 3rd St.
San Francisco, CA 94103
(415) 391-8350
Specializes in packaging you for the marketplace.

*Dru Scott Associates, Inc.*
106 Point Lobos
San Francisco, CA 94121
(415) 387-0461
Specializes in affirmative action for women.

*Stanley, Barber, Southard, Brown and Associates*
Career Management
100 California St.
Ste. 1090
San Francisco, CA 94111
(415) 986-1435
Specializes in professional jobs and offers psychological consultation.

Most people know that executive recruiters can be extremely helpful, but you may not know how to make contact effectively with them. Chuck Strotz of Harreus and Strotz suggests that you discuss good headhunters with friends or contacts in your target field and ask them to give you a written or telephone introduction to a headhunter they know or have worked with before. This will increase the chance that your job search will be given full consideration and that you'll be given helpful advice about what to try next.

A top Bay Area management consultant points out that associates and senior associates at the medium and large executive recruiting firms are trying to build up contacts and clientele. So it may be mutually beneficial for you to meet them. By all means learn who they are and invite a recruiter to coffee. You will be making a good contact and gathering information at the same time.

According to most Bay Area executives I spoke with, making contacts is the key to getting a job here. The first half of this book described ways to make contacts:

- Go to clubs or organization meetings in your field.
- Go over to the target firm and introduce yourself.
- Canvass your family and friends for people they know whom you could meet.

Here are some other ways to try to make contacts if all else fails:

- Become a political fundraiser or local party supporter.
- Volunteer for the United Way or other charitable groups.
- Go to workshops on business skills. Two good ones to consider in San Francisco are Effective Communicating [contact Bert Decker at (415) 775-6111] and Communispond [contact Robert Denny at (714) 851-9200, Los Angeles telephone number for West Coast office.]

In these courses you can accomplish two things at once. You can dramatically improve your presentation of yourself (great for interviews) while meeting other businesspeople, most of whom are sponsored in the course by their companies.

Above all, do not keep being out of work a secret. The contacts you meet can't help you effectively if they don't know you could use the help.

The hiring managers interviewed for this book also provide some interesting clues for how to increase your job options. Over and over again they told me about lack of enthusiasm and lack of commitment or follow-through on the part of interviewees. You can translate these negatives into positives and apply them to your search strategy by thinking creatively about this question: "How can I show by my actions (not just my words) that I am enthusiastic about this job?"

Here are some suggestions:

- Take the initiative to prepare samples of your past work and offer to send them or drop them off with the hiring manager to review.
- Provide a stamped postcard (as a response card) when writing and asking for an interview. Suggest a specific time and date and then make things easy for the manager with the handy postcard to respond. If they don't send it back, you can still call them to follow up. This method will make it likely that they will think of you as someone who makes things easy for them and is very interested in the job.
- Research a course you could take in the field and tell the hiring manager you are planning to take it to increase your knowledge.
- Most of all, don't be afraid to seem enthusiastic. This will distinguish you from other people who are busy being reserved and sophisticated.

Many job search experts also encourage you to contact the president or general manager of target firms. They may take an interest in you or may pass your resume along to another manager, who will then be sure to respond to you.

The best way to contact the chief executive is to write a strong letter introducing yourself and then follow up with a phone call. The best times to call are early in the morning and early in the evening. (7:00 A.M. to 9:00 A.M. or 5:30 P.M. on). At these times the executive will probably answer the phone, and you can request some advice and show your interest in the firm.

Another creative way to generate ideas was suggested by a senior banking executive. He recommends that job hunters read John Naisbitt's book *Megatrends*. This book describes the changes taking place in our society as we move toward an information society and away from an industrial society. In reading this book you will be stimulated to think creatively about trends in the workplace. This will prepare you to present to prospective employers the benefits of hiring you in a thoughtful and impressive way.

If all your efforts to land the job you want fail (and sometimes they do), use your analytical and research skills to identify why. You may find that you have to revise your objectives and begin a new search.

I hope the ideas offered here will be a stimulus to your own thinking and help you to develop more options and strategies worth considering.

The Bay Area has much to offer. I hope you find a satisfying career here.

Any comments, suggestions or additional information will be most welcome.

Janet Beach
150 Lombard Street, Suite 907
San Francisco, CA 94111

# Appendix:

## Top 100 Bay Area Companies

This top 100 Bay Area companies listing is a profit ranking of the top 100 industrials, utilities, banks, and savings and loans. The information is based on the *San Francisco Examiner Chronicle*, "The Bay Area 100" (June 20, 1982), and *California Business,* "California's Top 500" (May 1982).

1. **Standard Oil Co. of California**
   225 Bush St.
   San Francisco, CA 94104
   (415) 894-7700
   *President:* John Grey

   Petroleum exploration, refining, transportation, and marketing
   *Employees:* 43,000
   *Net Worth:* $12.7 billion
   *Assets:* $23.7 billion

2. **Safeway Stores Inc.**
   201 4th St.
   Oakland, CA 94660
   (415) 891-3000
   *President:* D.L. Lynch

   Largest food retailer in U.S.
   *Employees:* 45,000
   *Net Worth:* $1.1 billion
   *Assets:* $3.7 billion

3. **Lucky Stores Inc.**
   6300 Clark Ave.
   Dublin, CA 94566
   (415) 828-6000
   *President:* S. Donley Ritchey

   Food, drug, auto, and department stores
   *Employees:* 66,000
   *Net Worth:* $481.1 million
   *Assets:* $1.5 billion

4. **Transamerica Corp.**
   600 Montgomery St.
   San Francisco, CA 94111
   (415) 983-4000
   *President:* J.R. Harvey

   Insurance, leasing, transportation, and financial services
   *Employees:* 26,000
   *Net Worth:* $1.6 billion
   *Assets:* $9.0 billion

5. **Foremost-McKesson Inc.**
   1 Post St.
   San Francisco, CA 94104
   (415) 983-8300
   *President:* Thomas Drohan

   Drug, toiletry, liquor, and chemical products
   *Employees:* 17,000
   *Net Worth:* $454 million
   *Assets:* $1.3 billion

6. **Hewlett-Packard Co.**
   3000 Hanover St.
   Palo Alto, CA 94304
   (415) 857-1501
   *President:* John A. Young

   Computers, medical and electronic instruments
   *Employees:* 65,000
   *Net Worth:* $1.9 billion
   *Assets:* $2.7 billion

7. **Southern Pacific Co.**
   1 Market Plaza
   San Francisco, CA 94105
   (415) 541-1000
   *President:* A.C. Furth

   Railroad, telecommunications, pipelines
   *Employees:* 56,000
   *Net Worth:* $2.3 billion
   *Assets:* $5.5 billion

8. **Kaiser Aluminum & Chemical Corp.**
   300 Lakeside Dr.
   Oakland, CA 94643
   (415) 271-3300
   *President:* A.S. Hutchcrafter, Jr.

   Aluminum, agricultural and industrial chemicals
   *Employees:* 26,250
   *Net Worth:* $1.5 billion
   *Assets:* $3.8 billion

9. **Crown Zellerbach Corp**
   1 Bush St.
   San Francisco, CA 94104
   (415) 951-5000
   *President/Chairman:* William Creson

   Paper, lumber, and other forest products
   *Employees:* 25,000
   *Net Worth:* $1.2 billion
   *Assets:* $2.6 billion

10. **Levi Strauss & Co.**
    1155 Battery St.
    San Francisco, CA 94111
    (415) 544-6000
    *CEO:* Robert T. Grohman

    Jeans, casual apparel, and sportswear
    *Employees:* 44,000
    *Net Worth:* $949.1 million
    *Assets:* $1.6 billion

11. **Genstar Ltd.**
    4 Embarcadero Center
    San Francisco, CA 94111
    (415) 986-7200
    *President:* A.A. MacNaughton

    Cement and building materials
    *Employees:* 20,000
    *Net Worth:* $808.2 million
    *Assets:* $2.4 billion

12. **Natomas Co.**
    601 California St.
    San Francisco, CA 94108
    (415) 981-5700
    *President:* Dorman Commons

    Oil, gas, and geothermal energy
    production
    *Employees:* 4,500
    *Net Worth:* $1.1 billion
    *Assets:* $2.6 billion

13. **Consolidated Freightways**
    3240 Hillview Ave.
    Palo Alto, CA 94303
    (415) 494-2900
    *President:* Raymond O'Brien

    Trucking and freight forwarding
    *Employees:* 17,000
    *Net Worth:* $464.8 million
    *Assets:* $828.3 million

14. **National Semiconductor Corp.**
    2900 Semiconductor Dr.
    Santa Clara, CA 95051
    (408) 221-5000
    *President:* C.E. Sporck

    Semiconductor components
    *Employees:* 35,000
    *Net Worth:* $333.4 million
    *Assets:* $753.7 million

15. **Kaiser Steel Corp.**
    300 Lakeside Dr.
    Oakland, CA 94693
    (415) 271-2711
    *President/Chairman:* Stephen
    Girard

    Steel production
    *Employees:* 9,000
    *Net Worth:* $262.3 million
    *Assets:* $975.9 million

16. **Longs Drug Stores Inc.**
    141 N. Civic Dr.
    Walnut Creek, CA 94596
    (415) 937-1170
    *President:* R.M. Long

    Self-service drugstore chain
    *Employees:* 7,700
    *Net Worth:* $178 million
    *Assets:* $273.2 million

17. **Di Giorgia Corp.**
    1 Maritime Plaza
    San Francisco, CA 94111
    (415) 362-8972
    *President:* Peter Scott

    Food processing and prepackaged
    foods (TreeSweet brand)
    *Employees:* 5,800
    *Net Worth:* $117.5 million
    *Assets:* $310.6 million

18. **Potlatch Corp.**
    1 Maritime Plaza
    San Francisco, CA 94119
    (415) 981-5980
    *President:* R.M. Steele

    Wood and paper products, railroads,
    real estate
    *Employees:* 9,320
    *Net Worth:* $544.3 million
    *Assets:* $1.2 billion

19. **SAGA Corp.**
    1 SAGA Lane
    Menlo Park, CA 94025
    (415) 854-5150
    *President:* Charles Lynch

    Institutional food management and
    restaurant franchises (Straw Hat
    Pizza, Black Angus, Velvet Turtle)
    *Employees:* 40,000
    *Net Worth:* $74.3 million
    *Assets:* $203.3 million

20. **Intel Corp.**
    3065 Bowers Ave.
    Santa Clara, CA 95051
    (408) 987-8080
    *President:* A.S. Grove

    Semiconductor components
    *Employees:* 17,000
    *Net Worth:* $487.8 million
    *Assets:* $871.5 million

21. **Arcata Corp.**
    2750 Sand Hill Rd.
    Menlo Park, CA 94025
    (415) 854-5222
    *President:* J. Frank Leach

    Forest and paper products, printing,
    containers
    *Employees:* 11,000
    *Net Worth:* $288.6 million
    *Assets:* $716.2 million

22. **The Clorox Co.**
    1221 Broadway
    Oakland, CA 94623
    (415) 271-7000
    *President/Chairman:* C.R.
      Weaver

    Household and food packaged goods
    *Employees:* 5,200
    *Net Worth:* $416.0 million
    *Assets:* $250.3 million

23. **Syntex Corp.**
    3401 Hillview Ave.
    Palo Alto, CA 94304
    (415) 855-5050
    *President:* Albert Bowers

    Pharmaceuticals, health and beauty
    products, chemicals
    *Employees:* 10,000
    *Net Worth:* $467.5 million
    *Assets:* $771.2 million

24. **Varian Associates**
    611 Hansen Way
    Palo Alto, CA 94303
    (415) 493-4000
    *President:* Thomas Sege

    Electronics manufacturer
    *Employees:* 12,800
    *Net Worth:* $192 million
    *Assets:* $495.1 million

25. **Raychem Corp.**
    300 Constitution Dr.
    Menlo Park, CA 94025
    (415) 361-3333
    *President/Chairman:* Paul
      Cook

    High-technology plastic components
    and systems
    *Employees:* 8,000
    *Net Worth:* $252.7 million
    *Assets:* $446.3 million

26. **Shaklee Corp.**
    444 Market St.
    San Francisco, CA 94111
    (415) 954-3000
    *Chairman/President:* J. Gary
      Shansby

    Personal care, household and
    nutritional products
    *Employees:* 1,200
    *Net Worth:* $105.6 million
    *Assets:* $191.7 million

27. **Amdahl Corp.**
    1250 E. Arques Ave.
    Sunnyvale, CA 94086
    (408) 746-6000
    *President:* John Lewis

    Large-scale computers
    *Employees:* 7,000
    *Net Worth:* $266.2 million
    *Assets:* $457.1 million

28. **Liquid Air Corp.**
    1 Embarcadero Center
    San Francisco, CA 94111
    (415) 765-4500
    *President:* P.A. Salbaing

    Industrial gases
    *Employees:* 4,000
    *Net Worth:* $235 million
    *Assets:* $484.3 million

29. **The GAP Stores Inc.**
    900 Cherry Ave.
    San Bruno, CA 94066
    (415) 952-4400
    *President:* Donald Fisher

    Chain of jeans and sportswear stores
    *Employees:* 8,500
    *Net Worth:* $67.8 million
    *Assets:* $145.7 million

30. **World Airways Inc.**
    1100 Airport Dr.
    Oakland, CA 94614
    (415) 577-2000
    *President/Chairman:* Edward
       Daly

    Airline transportation and cargo
    *Employees:* 2,100
    *Net Worth:* $67.6 million
    *Assets:* $499.0 million

31. **Apple Computer Inc**
    20525 Mariani Ave.
    Cupertino, CA 95014
    (408) 996-1010
    *President:* Mike Markkula

    Personal Computers
    *Employees:* 2,600
    *Net Worth:* $177.4 million
    *Assets:* $255.0 million

32. **Advanced Micro Devices Inc.**
    901 Thompson Pl.
    Sunnyvale, CA 94086
    (408) 732-2400
    *Chairman/President:* W.J.
       Sanders

    Semiconductors
    *Employees:* 10,000
    *Net Worth:* $118.6 million
    *Assets:* $224.7 million

33. **Pacific Lumber Co.**
    500 Washington Street
    San Francisco, CA 94111
    (415) 421-3000
    *President:* G.G. Elam

    Lumber, machinery, farming, real
    estate
    *Employees:* 4,000
    *Net Worth:* $209.9 million
    *Assets:* $288.4 million

34. **Rolm Corp.**
    4900 Old Ironsides Rd.
    Santa Clara, CA 95050
    (408) 988-2900
    *President:* M. Oshman

    Computer-controlled telephone
    exchange systems and related
    products
    *Employees:* 5,000
    *Net Worth:* $121.8 million
    *Assets:* $206.9 million

35. **Tymshare Inc.**
    20705 Valley Green Dr.
    Cupertino, CA 95014
    (408) 446-6000
    *Chairman/President:* T.J.
       O'Rourke

    Data processing services using its own
    computer hardware and software
    systems and data communications
    network
    *Employees:* 4,000
    *Net Worth:* $90.1 million
    *Assets:* $251.1 million

36. **American Building Maintenance Industries**
333 Fell St.
San Francisco, CA 94102
(415) 864-5150
*President:* S.J. Rosenberg

Consulting, contract cleaning, air conditioning and insulation, and other services for commercial and industrial properties
*Employees:* 22,000
*Net Worth:* $46.8 million
*Assets:* $73.7 million

37. **United Artists Communications Inc.**
172 Golden Gate Ave.
San Francisco, CA 94102
(415) 928-3200
*Chairman/President:* R. Naify

Operates a chain of motion picture theaters
*Employees:* 5,300
*Net Worth:* $63.0 million
*Assets:* $203.1 million

38. **Kaiser Cement Corp.**
300 Lakeside Dr.
Oakland, CA 94612
(415) 271-2000
*Chairman/President:* W.E. Ousterman

Makes cements, aggregates, and concrete
*Employees:* 1,700
*Net Worth:* $223.8 million
*Assets:* $496.8 million

39. **Cooper Laboratories Inc.**
3145 Porter Dr
Palo Alto, CA 94304
(415) 856-5000
*President:* A.K. Nilsson

Makes and sells toothbrushes and other dental, ophthalmic, and dermatological products
*Employees:* 4,600
*Net Worth:* $119.7 million
*Assets:* $328.2 million

40. **Homestake Mining Co.**
650 California St.
San Francisco, CA 94108
(415) 981-8150
*Chairman/President:* Harry Conger

Operates gold, silver, lead, zinc, uranium, and copper mines and conducts timber and lumber operations
*Employees:* 2,700
*Net Worth:* $294.3 million
*Assets:* $351.9 million

41. **United States Leasing International Inc.**
633 Battery St.
San Francisco, CA 94111
(415) 445-7400
*President:* D.E. Mundell

Buys and leases out various types of machinery and equipment
*Employees:* 1,400
*Net Worth:* $135.9 million
*Assets:* $713.5 million

42. **Four-Phase Systems Inc.**
10700 N. De Anza Blvd.
Cupertino, CA 95014
(408) 255-0900
*Chairman/President:* Lee L. Boysel

Maker of computer systems
*Employees:* 4,500
*Net Worth:* $121.0 million
*Assets:* $215.5 million

43. **Tandem Computers Inc.**
19333 Vallco Parkway
Cupertino, CA 95014
(408) 725-6000
*President:* James Treybig

Makes multiple-processor computer
systems
*Employees:* 2,000
*Net Worth:* $204.8 million
*Assets:* $256.0 million

44. **Itel Corporation**
1 Embarcadero Center
San Francisco, CA 94111
*President:* Herbert Kunzel

(In bankruptcy proceedings) leases
cargo containers and freightcars,
provides related financial services
*Net Worth:* $259.3 million
*Assets:* $1.3 billion

45. **The Harper Group**
545 Sansome St.
San Francisco, CA 94111
(415) 983-9600
*Chairman/President:* John
Robinson

International freight forwarding and
customs house brokerage
*Employees:* 1,600
*Net Worth:* $39.0 million
*Assets:* $107.3 million

46. **Western Pacific Railroad Co.**
526 Mission St.
San Francisco, CA 94105
(415) 982-2100
*President:* Robert C. Marquis

(Currently in merger proceedings
with the Union Pacific and Missouri
Pacific railroads) operates a railroad
*Employees:* 2,600
*Net Worth:* $33.0 million
*Assets:* $202.2 million

47. **Buttes Gas & Oil Co.**
1221 Broadway
Oakland, CA 94612
(415) 839-1600
*President:* John Boreta

Explores and produces oil and natural
gas domestically and internationally
and does contract drilling
*Employees:* 1,100
*Net Worth:* $37.3 million
*Assets:* $294.5 million

48. **Hexcel Corp.**
650 California St.
San Francisco, CA 94108
(415) 956-3333
*Chairman/President:* H.M.
Merrill

Makes aluminum and paper
honeycomb, fiberglass materials,
orthopedic specialty items,
preimpregnated fabrics, bonded
panels, epoxy compounds, flame
retardants, solvents, and
biodegradable and specialty cleaners
*Employees:* 2,200
*Net Worth:* $49.1 million
*Assets:* $105.3 million

49. **American Microsystems Inc.**
3800 Homestead Rd.
Santa Clara, CA 95051
(408) 246-0330
*President:* Dr. Robert M. Penn

Semiconductors and microprocessor
test and development systems
*Employees:* 3,600
*Net Worth:* $68.5 million
*Assets:* $100.7 million

50. **Spectra-Physics, Inc.**
3333 N. 1st St.
San Jose, CA 95134
(408) 946-6080
*Chairman/President:* Samuel
   Colella

Lasers and laser systems
*Employees:* 2,104
*Net Worth:* $64.4 million
*Assets:* $77.5 million

51. **Victoria Station, Inc.**
Wood Island
Larkspur, CA 94939
(415) 461-4550
*Chairman/President:* Terrance
   Collins

Chain of Victoria Station and other
restaurants
*Employees:* 5,000
*Net Worth:* $36.3 million
*Assets:* $96.6 million

52. **Watkins-Johnson Co. Inc.**
3333 Hillview Ave.
Palo Alto, CA 94304
(415) 493-4141
*President:* H. R. Johnson

Electronic systems and components
*Employees:* 2,540
*Net Worth:* $71.1 million
*Assets:* $116.1 million

53. **Grand Auto, Inc.**
7200 Edgewater Dr.
Oakland, CA 94621
(415) 568-6500
*Chairman/President:* Irving
   Krantzman

Retail automotive stores
*Employees:* 1,700
*Net Worth:* $18.5 million
*Assets:* $55.5 million

54. **Measurex Corporation**
1 Results Way
Cupertino, CA 95014
(408) 255-1500
*President:* D. A. Bossen

Sensor-based computer process
control systems
*Employees:* 2,200
*Net Worth:* $76.6 million
*Assets:* $122.2 million

55. **Consolidated Fibres, Inc.**
50 California St.
San Francisco, CA 94111
(415) 788-5300
*President:* G. F. Ryles

Recyclable waste paper and wood
pulp
*Employees:* 687
*Net Worth:* $17.4 million
*Assets:* $38.6 million

56. **Distribuco, Inc.**
25954 Eden Landing Rd.
Hayward, CA 94545
(415) 887-8400
*President:* William
   McGaughey

Distributor of food to restaurants and
institutions
*Employees:* 250
*Net Worth:* $4.5 million
*Assets:* $16.8 million

57. **Dysan Corporation**
5201 Patrick Henry Dr.
Santa Clara, CA 95050
(408) 727-4109
*Chairman/President:* C.
   Norman Dion

Data storage discs for computer
*Employees:* 2,300
*Net Worth:* $56.2 million
*Assets:* $128.8 million

58. **Plantronics, Inc.**
    1762 Technology Dr.
    San Jose, CA 95110
    (408) 998-8388
    *Chairman/President:* Neil
      Hynes

    Telecommunications and electronic
    testing equipment
    *Employees:* 2,000
    *Net Worth:* $67.3 million
    *Assets:* $97.5 million

59. **Community Psychiatric Centers**
    517 Washington St.
    San Francisco, CA 94111
    (415) 397-6151
    *President:* J. W. Conte

    Psychiatric hospitals; outpatient
    hemodialysis centers
    *Employees:* 1,500
    *Net Worth:* $58.7 million
    *Assets:* $120.1 million

60. **Tab Products Company**
    2690 Hanover St.
    Palo Alto, CA 94304
    (415) 493-5790
    *Chairman/President:* H. W.
      LeClaire

    Office filing systems; shelving
    *Employees:* 1,150
    *Net Worth:* $23.6 million
    *Assets:* $43.7 million

61. **Brae Corporation**
    4 Embarcadero Center
    San Francisco, CA 94111
    (415) 951-1500
    *President:* William Texido

    Transportation equipment and related
    management services
    *Employees:* 500
    *Net Worth:* $38.8 million
    *Assets:* $215.1 million

62. **Avantek, Inc.**
    3175 Bowers Ave.
    Santa Clara, CA 95051
    (408) 727-0700
    *Chairman:* L. R. Thielen
    *President:* James Dobbie

    Semiconductor components and
    telecommunications equipment
    *Employees:* 1,500
    *Net Worth:* $64.7 million
    *Assets:* $76.5 million

63. **Triad Systems Corporation**
    1252 Orleans Dr.
    Sunnyvale, CA 94086
    (408) 734-9720
    *Chairman/President:* W. W.
      Stevens

    Computer systems for the automotive
    parts distribution industry
    *Employees:* 1,000
    *Net Worth:* $28.1 million
    *Assets:* $64.9 million

64. **URS Corporation**
    155 Bovet Rd.
    San Mateo, CA 94402
    (415) 574-5000
    *Chairman/President:* Arthur
      Stromberg

    Energy, health care, pollution
    abatement
    *Employees:* 1,500
    *Net Worth:* $25.8 million
    *Assets:* $74.9 million

65. **Applied Materials, Inc.**
    3050 Bowers Ave.
    Santa Clara, CA 95051
    *President:* J. Morgan

    Equipment for semiconductor
    manufacturers
    *Employees:* 1,150
    *Net Worth:* $30.1 million
    *Assets:* $68.3 million

66. **Monolithic Memories, Inc.**
    1165 E. Arques Ave.
    Sunnyvale, CA 94096
    (408) 739-3535
    *President:* Irwin Federman

    Programmable, integrated
    semiconductor memory
    *Employees:* 1,100
    *Net Worth:* $50.3 million
    *Assets:* $75.96 million

67. **Impell Corporation**
    220 Montgomery St.
    San Francisco, CA 94104
    (415) 421-2288
    *Chairman/President:* Robert
        Feibusch

    Engineering services for nuclear
    power
    *Employees:* 1,100
    *Net Worth:* $32.1 million
    *Assets:* $44.6 million

68. **Quadrex**
    1700 Dell Ave.
    Campbell, CA 95008
    (408) 866-4510
    *President:* Sherman Naymark

    Technical consultants to the nuclear
    power industry
    *Employees:* 950
    *Net Worth:* $31.2 million
    *Assets:* $44.5 million

69. **Xidex Corporation**
    305 Soquel Way
    Sunnyvale, CA 94086
    (408) 739-4170
    *Chairman/President:*
        L. L. Colbert, Jr.

    Microfilm, microprinting products
    *Employees:* 575
    *Net Worth:* $33 million
    *Assets:* $79.7 million

70. **Falstaff Brewing Corporation**
    21 Tamal Vista Blvd.
    Corte Madera, CA 94925
    (415) 924-3691
    *Chairman/President:*
        P. Kalmanovitz

    Beer manufacturer
    *Employees:* 449
    *Net Worth:* $48.9 million
    *Assets:* $59.3 million

71. **Coherent, Inc.**
    3210 Porter Dr.
    Palo Alto, CA 94304
    (415) 494-2111
    *Chairman/President:*
        J. L. Hobart

    Electro-optical products
    *Employees:* 800
    *Net Worth:* $31 million
    *Assets:* $65 million

72. **Finnigan Corporation**
    355 River Oaks Pkwy.
    Sunnyvale, CA 94086
    (408) 946-4848
    *Chairman/President:*
        T. Z. Chu

    Spectrometer systems
    *Employees:* 500
    *Net Worth:* $21.4 million
    *Assets:* $57.8 million

73. **System Industries**
1855 Barber Ln.
Milpitas, CA 95035
(408) 942-1212
*President:* Harold Shattuck

Disc storage systems
*Employees:* 453
*Net Worth:* $26.4 million
*Assets:* $39.4 million

74. **Siliconix, Inc.**
2201 Laurelwood Rd.
Santa Clara, CA 95054
(408) 988-8000
*Chairman/President:* R. E. Lee

Specialty semiconductor components
*Employees:* 900
*Net Worth:* $32.1 million
*Assets:* $56.8 million

75. **Fritizi of California**
      **Manufacturing Corporation**
199 First St.
San Francisco, CA 94105
(415) 986-3800
*Chairman/President:* E. A.
      Benesch

Women's and girls' sportswear
*Employees:* 475
*Net Worth:* $11.5 million
*Assets:* $25.8 million

76. **California Microwave**
990 Almanor Ave.
Sunnyvale, CA 94086
(408) 732-4000
*President:* David Leeson

Satellite, telecommunications and
avionics equipment
*Employees:* 1,000
*Net Worth:* $23.1 million
*Assets:* $37.2 million

77. **Verbatim Corporation**
323 Soquel Way
Sunnyvale, CA 94086
(408) 245-4400
*President:* Malcolm Northup

Magnetic data storage devices and
electronic communications equipment
*Employees:* 1,400
*Net Worth:* $30.4 million
*Assets:* $49.7 million

78. **Grubb & Ellis Company**
1333 Broadway
Oakland, CA 94612
(415) 839-9600
*Chairman/President:* H. A.
      Ellis, Jr.

Real estate broker, manager, and
developer
*Employees:* 1,300
*Net Worth:* $15 million
*Assets:* $43 million

79. **Bio-Rad Laboratories, Inc.**
2200 Wright Ave.
Richmond, CA 94804
(415) 234-4130
*President:* David Schwartz

Specialty chemical products and
measuring instruments
*Employees:* 726
*Net Worth:* $15.4 million
*Assets:* $41.6 million

80. **Anderson Jacobson, Inc.**
521 Charcot Ave.
San Jose, CA 95131
(408) 263-8520
*Chairman/President:*
      Raymond E. Jacobson

Designs and manufactures data
communications equipment
*Employees:* 870
*Net Worth:* $29.8 million
*Assets:* $40.8 million

81. **Technical Equities Corporation**
    1922 The Alameda
    San Jose, CA 95126
    (408) 246-7502
    *President:*  Paul C. Knauff

    Diversified industries
    *Employees:* 1,120
    *Net Worth:* $13.3 million
    *Assets:* $45.1 million

82. **Sonoma Vineyards**
    11455 Old Redwood Hwy.
    Healdsburg, CA 95448
    (707) 433-6511
    *Chairman/President:*  Kenneth
      J. Kwit

    Premium wines
    *Employees:* 650
    *Net Worth:* $10.7 million
    *Assets:* $50.9 million

83. **Up-Right Inc.**
    2600 10th St
    Berkeley, CA 94710
    (415) 843-0770
    *President:*  T. S. Ockels

    Portable and mobile work platforms
    *Employees:* 740
    *Net Worth:* $20.6 million
    *Assets:* $38.8 million

84. **Dreyer's Grand Ice Cream**
    5929 College Ave.
    Oakland, CA 94618
    (415) 655-8187
    *President:*  Rick Cronk

    Quality ice cream
    *Employees:* 150
    *Net Worth:* $6.9 million
    *Assets:* $14.4 million

85. **Calny Inc.**
    1650 Borel Pl.
    San Mateo, CA 94402
    (415) 574-2455
    *President:*  Marvinn Bonine

    Fast food and family restaurant
    operator
    *Employees:* 1,880
    *Net Worth:* $2.4 million
    *Assets:* $8.3 million

## *Utilities*

1. **Pacific Telephone & Telegraph
    Company**
    140 New Montgomery St.
    San Francisco, CA 94105
    (415) 542-9000
    *President:*  Theodore Saenger

    Local and long-distance telephone
    service
    *Employees:* 112,000
    *Net Worth:* $4.7 billion
    *Assets:* $16.6 billion

2. **PG&E**
    77 Beale St.
    San Francisco, CA 94106
    (415) 781-4211
    *President:*  Barton Schackelford

    Electricity and natural gas
    *Employees:* 27,000
    *Net Worth:* $3.9 billion
    *Assets:* $12.4 billion

3. **Pacific Gas Transmission Company**
   245 Market St.
   San Francisco, CA 94105
   (415) 781-0474
   *President:* Harry Prudhomme

   Natural gas pipelines
   *Employees:* 185
   *Net Worth:* $142.8 million
   *Assets:* $454.6 million

4. **CP National Corporation**
   1355 Willow Way
   Concord, CA 94520
   (415) 680-7700
   *Chairman/President:* Ben Agee

   Electricity, gas, water and telephone service
   *Employees:* 1,326
   *Net Worth:* $64.5 million
   *Assets:* $268.6 million

5. **California Water Service**
   1720 N. 1st St.
   San Jose, CA 95112
   (408) 298-1414
   *President:* C. H. Stump

   Water
   *Employees:* 500
   *Net Worth:* $65.2 million
   *Assets:* $204.2 million

## *Banks*

1. **BankAmerica Corporation**
   555 California St.
   San Francisco, CA 94104
   (415) 622-3456
   *President:* Samuel Armacost

   Holding company for the nation's largest bank by assets
   *Employees:* 84,000
   *Net Worth:* $4.1 billion
   *Assets:* $121.6 billion

2. **Wells Fargo & Company**
   420 Montgomery St.
   San Francisco, CA 94163
   (415) 396-0123
   *President:* Carl Reichardt

   Holding company for Wells Fargo Bank, the nation's 11th largest
   *Employees:* 17,400
   *Net Worth:* $1 billion
   *Assets:* $23.2 billion

3. **Crocker National Corporation**
   1 Montgomery St.
   San Francisco, CA 94104
   (415) 477-0456
   *President:* J. Hallam Dawson

   Holding company for the nation's 12th largest bank
   *Employees:* 15,000
   *Net Worth:* $1 billion
   *Assets:* $22.5 billion

4. **California First Bank**
   350 California St.
   San Francisco, CA 94104
   (415) 445-0200
   *President:* Yasushi Sumya

   Bank has more than 100 branches throughout California
   *Employees:* 3,700
   *Net Worth:* $184.4 million
   *Assets:* $4.1 billion

5. **Bancal Tri-State Corporation**
   400 California St.
   San Francisco, CA 94104
   (415) 765-0400
   *Chairman/President:*  C. E.
   Schmidt

Holding company for the oldest
incorporated bank in the West
*Employees:* 3,000
*Net Worth:* $189.4 million
*Assets:* $3.9 billion

## Savings and Loans

1. **Golden West Financial
   Corporation**
   1970 Broadway
   Oakland, CA 94612
   (415) 645-9420
   *President:*  Marion Sandler

Holding company for World S&L,
eighth largest in the nation
*Employees:* 1,384
*Net Worth:* $177.2 million
*Assets:* $5.5 billion

2. **Fidelity Financial Corporation**
   1430 Franklin St.
   Oakland, CA 94612
   (415) 465-0628
   *President:*  A. C. Meyer, Jr.

Holding company for Fidelity S&L,
the nation's 21st largest
*Net Worth:* $32.8 million
*Assets:* $2.9 billion

3. **Northern California Savings &
   Loan Association, Inc.**
   300 Hamilton Ave.
   Palo Alto, CA 94301
   (415) 326-2790
   *President:*  Firmin Gryp

Nation's 40th largest S&L
*Employees:* 800
*Net Worth:* $107.3 million
*Assets:* $1.9 billion

4. **Homestead Financial
   Corporation**
   1777 Murchison Dr.
   Burlingame, CA 94010
   (415) 692-1432
   *Chairman/President:*
   Lawrence Weissberg

Holding company for Homestead
S&L, which has 28 offices in
California
*Employees:* 340
*Net Worth:* $25.4 million
*Assets:* $570.6 million

5. **Pacific Coast Holdings, Inc.**
   650 California St.
   San Francisco, CA 94108
   (415) 433-3960
   *Chairman/President:*  Clyde
   Charlton

Holding company for Bell Savings
and Loan Association
*Employees:* 205
*Net Worth:* $14.2 million
*Assets:* $337.5 million

# Index

## *Additional Listings*

### AD AGENCY DIRECTORY
### San Francisco

**Allen & Dorward**
747 Front St.
San Francisco, CA 94111
*Contact:* Bob Hoffman, Senior Vice-President.
*Employs:* 80.
*Billings:* $35 million.
*Possible Entry Level Position:* Media estimator, account coordinator, summer
  intern.
*Some Major Clients:* Beninger vineyards, Castle & Cooke, KGO-TV, Matson
  Navigation.

### UTILITIES DIRECTORY
### Telecommunications

**GTE-Sprint**
1818 Gilbreth
Burlingame, CA 94010
*Contact:* Eric Shepcaro, Personnel.
*Employs:* 4,000.
*Description:* Long distance telephone service that competes with "Ma Bell."

### LAW DIRECTORY (PUBLISHERS)

**Matthew Bender & Co., Inc.** (415) 433-0565
450 Sansome St.
San Francisco, CA 94126
*Contact:* Ken Levy, Director of Personnel.
*Employs:* 200.
*Description:* Subsidiary of Times Mirror Corporation. This well-known legal
  publisher has recently added an electronic publishing group to its staff.
*Positions in Bay Area:* Attorney authors, technical writers, technical editors, editors.

### HEALTH CARE DIRECTORY (ASSOCIATIONS AND
### HOSPITALS)

**American Hospital Supply** (415) 487-7070
31353 Huntwood Ave.
Hayward, CA 94544
*Contact:* William A. Donan, Vice-President, Northwest.
*Description:* Distribution center for largest hospital supply company in the U.S.